BELIEVING AND ACCEPTING

PHILOSOPHICAL STUDIES SERIES

VOLUME 83

The titles published in this series are listed at the end of this volume.

BELIEVING AND ACCEPTING

Edited by

PASCAL ENGEL
Université de Paris IV,
Sorbonne, France

SPRINGER-SCIENCE+BUSINESS MEDIA, B.V.

A C.I.P. Catalogue record for this book is available from the Library of Congress.

ISBN 978-94-010-5782-0   ISBN 978-94-011-4042-3 (eBook)
DOI 10.1007/978-94-011-4042-3

TABLE OF CONTENTS

INTRODUCTION:
THE VARIETIES OF BELIEF AND ACCEPTANCE

Pascal Engel
University of Caen, CREA and
Institut Universitaire de France

1. BELIEVING

The notion of belief is ubiquitous in contemporary philosophy: it occurs in epistemology, when one discusses questions about the rationality of belief and the difference between belief and knowledge, in the philosophy of mind when one raises questions about the nature of mental states and contents and about our various ways of ascribing them to people through a "folk psychology", and in the philosophy of language, when one deals with "the semantics of propositional attitudes" and with the logic of "belief sentences" of the form "X believes that p". The ramifications of these questions and their interconnections are numerous, and here, as elsewhere in philosophy, it is not obvious that one field of inquiry or one angle of approach dominates the others and deserves to be taken as primary or basic. Questions about what beliefs really are, metaphysically, cannot be easily divorced from epistemological questions about what differentiates belief from knowledge, nor from questions about the meanings of the sentences through which we attribute beliefs to other people or to ourselves, and the latter cannot be separated from the former. A good example of these interconnections is provided by "Moore's paradox": "It rains, but I do not believe that it rains" (or "It does not rain, but I believe that it rains"). According to Wittgenstein[1], Moore made a point, through such sentences, about "the *logic* of

assertion", namely that it makes no sense, in ordinary talk, to say that
p, and to say, in the same breath, that one does not believe that p. This
simple "logical" point, however, does not pertain only to the "logic" of
assertion and belief talk. For, if Wittgenstein is right to say that "I
believe that p " is not a *description* by the speaker of one of her mental
states, but the *expression* of it, it is difficult to evade the question of
what *constitutes* a genuine description of a mental state, in contrast to
a mere expression of it. If there is a real contrast between such forms
as "I believe that p " and "He believes that p " (for "p, but he does not
believe that p " does not give rise to a paradox), then any theory of
belief which gives a uniform account of the meaning of "believes"
when used in the first person and in the third person is bound to be
false. For instance the functionalist account of belief according to
which "believes" means in both cases "is a state apt to cause behaviour"
is threatened by this contrast.[2] Hence this simple "logical" point is not
innocuous with respect to what belief actually *is*. It is not innocuous
either with respect to the difference between belief and knowledge, for
a related simple "logical" point is that, unlike in the case of belief, a
genuine contradiction emerges when ones says, "I know that it rains,
but it does not rain": for knowledge implies the truth of the proposition
known, which is thus incompatible with the assertion of its falsity. The
Moorean sentences invite us to reflect on this difference, which is, at
bottom, an epistemological one. It also invites us to reflect on the
difference between ascribing a belief content to oneself and ascribing
a belief content to others: when I ascribe a belief to myself, I know
what I believe, whereas there is, one the face of it, no such knowledge
when I ascribe a belief to someone else. This raises the question
whether there is a single notion of belief content apt to be used in both
cases. Moore's paradox is a good way of thinking about the
interconnections between the psychology, the epistemology, and the
semantics of belief. But it is not the only way.

Another way, and a good point of departure for dealing with the
issues raised in this collection of essays, is to start from an intuitive
conception of belief, as a mental state which has the following set of
features. [3]

(1) Beliefs are involuntary, and not normally subject to direct voluntary control. For instance I cannot believe at will that my trousers are on fire, or that the Dalaï Lama is a living God, even if you pay me a large amount of money for believing such things.

(2) Beliefs are normally shaped by evidence for what is believed, unless they are, in some sense, irrational. In general a belief is rational if it is proportioned to the degree of evidence that one has for its truth. In this sense, one often says that "beliefs aim at truth".This is why it is, on the face of it, irrational to believe against the evidence that one has. A subject whose beliefs are not shaped by a concern for their truth, but by what she wants to be the case, is more or less a wishful thinker or a self-deceiver.

(3) Beliefs are context independent, in the sense that at one time a subject believes something or does not believe it; she does not believe it relative to one context and not relative to another. For instance if I believe that Paris is a polluted city, I cannot believe that on Monday and not on Tuesday; that would be a change of belief, or a change of mind, but not a case of believing one thing in one context and another thing in another context. If I believe something, the belief is more or less permanent across various contexts.[4]

(4) An individual's beliefs are subject to an ideal of coherence. Other things being equal, one should be able to agglomerate one's beliefs into a larger, coherent, set of beliefs. This is what one generally means when one says that beliefs have a "normative" or "rational" character: we try, in general to have *correct* or, in that sense, rational beliefs, and this feature is revealed by our ordinary beliefs ascriptions: on the whole we tend to ascribe to people beliefs which it is normal or rational to have.

The overall familiar picture of belief which emerges from these four features is that belief is a passive state of mind, rather than an active one. Whether one conceives of beliefs as inner feelings (in the Humean way), or as dispositions to act in various ways (in the Peircean or the Rylean way), beliefs are states which we can't help having, and which belong to the passive side of our natures. The fact that beliefs are, in general, shaped by evidence, means that they have, in Searle's useful phrase, the "world to mind direction of fit", rather than, like desires and wants, the "mind to world direction of fit"; in other words they are cognitive attitudes, aimed at being true or false to the facts, and not conative attitudes, aimed at changing the way the world is in order, to try to make it fit to our wants. An action is contextual in a sense in which a belief is not: according to the context, I may decide to act in such or such a way, and in another context in another way, but I cannot decide to believe in such or such a way depending on the context. The rationality and the coherence of my beliefs are pressed on me by the way the world is, or by general rules of rationality which come, at least in part, from logic. I cannot change at will the rules which provide inductive support for my beliefs, nor the logical rules which make them coherent.

One may object here to this familiar picture of beliefs as passive states that there do seem to be some beliefs which we may decide to have, sometimes against contrary evidence. For instance may not a wife decide to believe that her husband is faithful to her, in spite of all the lipstick she regularly finds on his collars? May not the Pascalian who does not believe in God decide to believe in God when he is shown the immense advantages of the eternal bliss provided by that belief? To such cases the defender of the familiar picture usually responds that in so far as these are cases of belief, these are either cases of *irrational* —or in some sense abnormal—beliefs, produced, as in the wife's example, through some form of irrational belief-forming process, whereas the above features are supposed to apply to what we call in general *rational* beliefs, or cases of rational *actions* , not of rational beliefs. In the latter sort of case, it may be rational for me to believe in God, but the very fact that I find the belief useful or beneficial in some way is not enough to create in me the corresponding state, which remains as passive and as shaped by evidence as it can be in the first place. This is why Pascal, after giving his famous wager argument for belief in God, advises us to go to church, to take the holy water, and to get the habits which regularly go with such a belief: *This will dull you ("Cela vous abêtira")* . Getting oneself to get an habit does not count as stopping to have a belief as a matter of habit or of passive disposition; quite the contrary. Getting the habit to have an habit may be voluntary, but the habit itself is not. Similarly I may induce myself to have a belief by, say, taking a certain drug, or by being subjected to hypnosis, but the very fact that I need to acquire the belief through some sort of *causal* process does show that beliefs are in general caused by some processes, even when the processes are, to a certain extent, under our control. In other words, I may have some *reasons* to acquire certain beliefs, just in the same way as I may have some reasons to take an action, but the fact that I have these reasons does not imply that my beliefs are shaped by my reasons to have them.

Still, and even if one grants this point, one may want to argue that it is not obvious that having a belief is a purely passive and involuntary state; the fact that I believe, for instance, that Pomerol is expensive, may be a dispositional state which leads me to certain actions, such as, say, refraining to order a bottle of Pomerol in a restaurant when I do not want to pay an excessive price, or, alternatively, hastening to order this wine when my desire to drink good wine overrides my brief awareness of the state of my finances. The belief that Pomerol is expensive may even be what some philosophers call a "tacit belief", a belief which is not conscious until it is directly present to my mind, or which does not occur to me unless it "crosses" my mind. But I may nevertheless hold the belief to be true, give my assent to it, approve of it, or even defend it against somebody who would urge the contrary. Is not my *assenting to* the content of a belief, or my *judging that* a proposition is true a voluntary act? The Stoïcs called such an assent *sunkatathesis*, and they considered it to be voluntary and under our control. Descartes held that belief[5] is a matter of the will when the will assents to the ideas that are given to it by the understanding. Whether one conceives of beliefs as inner acts of assent, or as tied in some way to assertions, an assent is a mental act, and an assertion is a speech act. So in that respect at least, belief seems to involve some voluntary element. In this sense, I may feel responsible for my beliefs, I may want to hold them and to defend them, which I would not do if they were purely passive and involuntary. Does not that account, partly, for the fact that our beliefs are, in general, subject to an ideal of integration and coherence? Our beliefs are not rational simply because they happen to be so; they are rational because we want them to be so, and irrational sometimes because we do not want them to be so. Not all of our reasons for believing are evidential in nature.

2. ACCEPTING

At this point, the partisan of the orthodox conception of belief as a passive state may want to reconcile the two conflicting intuitions—that, on the one hand beliefs are not under direct voluntary control, and that, on the other hand, they can be, to some extent, under our control—by arguing that there are in fact two distinct kinds of mental states which one conflates under the ordinary term "belief". One would be the notion of belief as a passive, largely dispositional state, which may or may not be conscious. This would be the sense in which I may believe, for instance, that oysters are tasty without ever thinking about it. Belief in this sense would be, as Peirce and Ramsey have argued, mainly a habit of action, or a disposition to act or to speak in certain ways, which can be revealed, as the "Bayesian" picture has it, through our being prepared to make certain bets, and which could be assigned various degrees or "subjective probabilities" through such bets. The other notion of "belief" would correspond to the senses in which we say that we give assent to certain of our beliefs, and hold them as true, while rejecting others. This other notion would be more appropriate to the circumstances where we give *adhesion* to the contents of our beliefs, and *maintain* them, or to the circumstances where we *refuse* to believe certain things, while we *agree* to believe other things. "Belief" in this second sense would be at least partly voluntary, and under our control. These two kinds of belief-attitudes are often, in ordinary talk, put under the same name—belief. But one may suggest that these are different mental states. They differ in particular because the first is, in the philosopher's phrase, a propositional attitude, which may be an attitude towards a proposition, a sentence, a representation, or a state of affairs—depending on the kind of theory that philosophers may hold about this propositional attitude—whereas the second is an *attitude towards an attitude*, namely a ("second-order") attitude towards one's beliefs in the first sense ("first-order" beliefs).

There are many ways of drawing this contrast, and here the terminologies vary. For instance, in a classic paper Ronald de Sousa draws a distinction between *belief proper* , which he assimilates more or less to a dispositional state, susceptible to vary in degrees approximately in the Bayesian sense, and *assent,* as a reflexive, voluntary act.[6] Daniel Dennett makes a similar distinction, between *belief,* which he takes to be largely dispositional, and *opinion* , which is for him a "linguistically infected" state, in which we are when we reflect upon our beliefs and shape their contents with words.[7] Dennett is fond of quoting E.M. Foster's famous remark: "How can I tell what I think until I see what I say?". There are, according to him, beliefs which we have and the content of which is not determined by particular words or sentences which we utter, silently or overtly; but many of our beliefs take shape, so to say, through the words we use to express them; the latter are rather called *opinions*. Animals, maybe, have beliefs in the first sense; man, being a talking animal, has not only beliefs, but also opinions. Other writers prefer to draw a similar contrast by distinguishing belief from *judgment*.[8] This is not to say that these distinctions are equivalent. In order to see whether they are, one needs to say a lot more about the relationship between thinking a particular thought and affirming it, or between thinking, in Plato's phrase, as "an inner dialogue" of the mind with itself, and speaking out loud what one thinks. And one needs to say a lot more about the possession of beliefs, be they purely mental episodes or "linguistically infected" ones on the one hand, and the act of *holding a belief as true* , and of maintaining it, as a matter of cognitive or of practical policy on the other hand.

This is what the writers in this volume attempt to do. They all consider the possibility of dividing the general class of believing attitudes into at least two subclasses: one would be the class of *beliefs* proper, and the other would be the class of *acceptances*. The notion of acceptance has been used widely in the past in the context of discussions about what is called "rational acceptance" of hypotheses in epistemology and in the philosophy of science, without much concern for the implications of these issues for the philosophy of mind.[9] But recent discussions have focused on a somewhat broader set of issues. In the recent literature, the distinction between belief and acceptance has been proposed by a number of writers: Keith Lehrer[10], Bas Van Fraassen[11], Robert Stalnaker [12], John Perry [13], Michael Bratman [14], and Jonathan Cohen , who develops it in his *Essay on Belief and Acceptance*.[15] These writers do not draw the belief/acceptance distinction in the same way, and there are in fact several non equivalent versions of it. But we may start from Cohen's version, because it serves as a basis for a number of the essays of this collection.

3. COHEN ON BELIEF AND ACCEPTANCE

Jonathan Cohen reserves the term "belief" to designate a purely passive psychological state, which is for him neither fully dispositional nor fully "occurrent": a belief is "a disposition normally to feel that a proposition is true".[16] Because belief is a disposition, it is not identified to the conscious and reflective thinking of a thought which would be always present in the mind's eye. Because it is a disposition to *feel* that a proposition is true, it must a least be in principle or potentially conscious. Acceptance, on the contrary, is an active attitude, which is neither a feeling nor a disposition, and which involves some mental action taken by a subject:

> "To accept that p is to have or to adopt a policy of deeming, or postulating that p—i.e of including that proposition or rule among one's premises for deciding what to do or think in a particular context, whether or not one feels it true that p."[17]

Acceptance, according to Cohen, shares with belief a number of features.[18] Like belief it is, or at least involves, an attitude towards a certain proposition or content. Like belief it involves a form of epistemic commitment in the sense (4) above that it implies an ideal of coherence and integration, and so has an inferential role in the mind of a subject: acceptances, like beliefs, can be used for inferring other acceptances from previous ones. But it is otherwise a completely different attitude. Unlike belief, acceptance is active and "occurs at will, whether by an immediate decision or through a gradually formed intention".[19] It is not a feeling. So it does not share with belief feature (1) above. Unlike belief, which is not necessarily verbal or linguistic, acceptance is for Cohen closely linked to language, at least potentially.[20] The main contrast is that one can accept a proposition without believing it, against evidence one has for believing it to be true. So it does not share with belief feature (2). Acceptance thus does not entail belief. Cohen gives the example of an attorney, who believes that his client is guilty, but accepts that he is not guilty, for it is duty to accept this, in spite of the evidence that he has. Two sorts of cases are to be distinguished here. There are, in the first place, as in the attorney example, cases where one can accept a proposition *against* one's evidence for believing it to be true. And there are, in the second place, cases where one accepts a proposition although one has *insufficient* evidence for its truth, i.e although one believes it to a certain degree, which is insufficient to be carried over into full assent. For instance a doctor may have some evidence, though not enough evidence, to believe that the symptoms observed on a patient indicate that he has tuberculosis, but he may nevertheless accept that it is a case of tuberculosis, because it is safer to accept this for the sake of saving the patient's life. In this respect, acceptance is more a matter of *supposing,* of *assuming,* or of *hypothesizing* that *p* is true, for prudential or practical reasons, rather than a matter of believing in proportion to evidence that one has. In other words, acceptance is more the outcome of a practical, pragmatic decision than the outcome of a cognitive, epistemic reason.[21] This does not mean, however, that there are not cases of acceptances for epistemic reasons. For instance, a scientist may, in the context of his inquiry, accept, or take it for granted, that a given theory is true, although the theory is insufficiently confirmed. He may do this because, like in the other, prudential, cases, he has *further* reasons, other than those provided by his beliefs, which may or may not be purely epistemic, to hold certain propositions as true. So acceptance does not share feature (3) with belief: although I cannot believe something in one context and not in another context, I can accept that *p* in one context, and fail to accept that *p* in another context. Stalnaker and Bratman, like Cohen, have insisted on this contextual and pragmatic character of acceptance which distinguishes it from belief. For instance Stalnaker says that:

> "To accept a proposition is to treat it as a true proposition in one way or another— to ignore, for the moment, the possibility that it is false. One may do this for different reasons, more or less tentatively, more or less self consciously, with more or less justification, and with more or less feeling of commitment.... A person may accept a proposition for the moment without the expectation that he will continue to accept it for very long. If a person expects a particular one of his *beliefs* to be overturned, he has already begun to loose it, but an assumption he makes may be quite explicit temporarily, and he may presume that something is true even when expecting to be contradicted.[22]

And Bratman has emphasized the role of acceptance in the framing of *plans* for making decisions, in the course of practical reasoning or of inquiry.[23] The reasons for accepting a proposition need not be simply personal of subjective; they may be social. For instance a person may believe certain things, but nevertheless fail to accept them, or accept others, because of his desire to be cooperative or otherwise socially attuned to the attitudes of the group or collectivity to which he belongs.

Cohen, in his book, labours many other aspects of the contrast between belief and acceptance, and he draws many conclusions from it for various issues. In particular he applies the distinction to the problem of the explanation of action and of purposive behaviour, by claiming that philosophers have overlooked a crucial aspect of this kind of explanations, which involve not only desires and beliefs as reasons for actions, as it is presupposed by the current model of practical reasoning, but also more reflective attitudes, such as goals and acceptances. He is thus led to make a sharp distinction between the purposes of animals, infants and machines, which may involve beliefs as passive states, but not active ones such as acceptances. He also applies his distinction to Moore's paradox, by claiming that no such paradox arises when the "paradoxical" sentences "p, but I do not believe that p" are understood as involving, in the first member, an attitude of acceptance rather than an attitude of belief. He draws various consequences for the difference between belief and knowledge, and for an account of knowledge in terms of rational acceptance rather than in terms of rational belief. Finally, he applies the distinction to the problem of self-deception, by pointing out that the self-deceiver who is usually described as believing, for good reasons, that p, but also as believing that *not p*, because of a desire that *not p* be true, need not be a victim of contradiction or of irrationality, if one understands his states of mind as an instance of *believing* that p on the one side, while *accepting* that *not p* on the other.

The overall picture which emerges from Cohen's account of the belief/acceptance distinction seems both to vindicate the familiar Humean conception according to which belief belongs to the passive side of the mind, and the Cartesian picture according to which we are free to accept or to reject our beliefs, and to promote them willfully, through various policies and strategies of acceptance. The picture, however, is more Cartesian than Humean, since a thinker can always, on this view, decide to accept the contents of his thoughts, or refuse to hold them as true, in order to reach a better rational state, or alternatively because he opts, in some sense, for less than full rationality. In that sense we can be responsible for our acceptances, although we are not responsible for our beliefs. The important conceptual clarification thus achieved leaves us, nevertheless, with a number of questions. First, is the distinction between belief and acceptance so clear cut? In particular is it the case that acts of acceptance are fully under the control of the will, whereas attitudes of belief are purely passive? Cohen says that acceptance is not, unlike belief, a matter of degree: one believes a given proposition to a certain degree, which may be identified with the subjective probability associated to this belief, but one does not accept a proposition to a certain degree—either one accepts it or not. This is because acceptance is conceived by him more as the production of an intention, and therefore as a kind of action; and intention, unlike belief, seems to be an all or nothing matter: there are no "partial" intentions, whereas there can be partial beliefs. But not all writers on acceptance agree with this. Stalnaker, for instance, says that acceptance "may be more active or more passive"[24], and he grants that acceptances may be not only reflective and conscious suppositions, but also "tacit presuppositions". In that respect the question arises whether acceptance is so unlike belief and independent from it as it seems to be. As Cohen himself admits, many of the things that we accept are things which we also believe, so the cases of acceptance without belief may form only a limiting case of the various kinds of acceptance. Another problem concerns the nature of the representations which are the objects respectively of belief and acceptance, and their relationship to language. For Cohen, as we saw, beliefs may not be, though acceptances are, necessarily linked to language. This does not imply, for him, that acceptance is always tied to an assertion or to a speech act. It may be a mental act, or the inner analogue of the assertion to a proposition. But if there are such inner acts of assent, to what extent do they differ from beliefs, if beliefs are mental feelings of approval of a proposition (or dispositions to have such feelings)? One must be careful here to distinguish various levels. On a broadly functionalist picture, one may hypothesize that, at one level, the mind receives, from various environmental inputs, different pieces of information, which, as the outcomes of various processes, produce certain representations, that we may call beliefs. At this level, beliefs are lower-order mental outputs, which are the products of causal processes. But the mind—the human mind at least—has the capacity of representing these lower-level representations, of forming *meta-representations*, i.e second-order representations, or beliefs *about* beliefs. For some philosophers and psychologists, this capacity of forming metarepresentation *is* the capacity to form beliefs, for beliefs are, essentially, second-order representations. And for many philosophers and psychologists, the capacity to have beliefs in this sense is essentially tied to language and to the possibility of embedding representations into other representations. For instance Davidson claims that one cannot have beliefs unless one has the concept of belief, that is the capacity to have beliefs about one's beliefs, and for this reason he excludes animals from the creatures who have genuine beliefs.[25] And many developmental psychologists claim that children acquire beliefs only through their capacity of forming beliefs about their beliefs and about beliefs in other, through a "theory of mind".[26] It may be tempting here to assimilate acceptance to a belief about a belief, and to draw the dividing line at the point where belief, as a first-order attitude, can be separated from belief about belief, as a second-order attitude. To a certain extent, this what Lehrer suggests, when he claims that "acceptance is a metamental operation"[27], and it is also reminiscent of De Sousa's distinction between belief and *assent*, or of Dennett's distinction between belief and *opinion*. This is in part largely a matter of terminology, but one should not confuse the notion of acceptance as a metarepresentational psychological state with Cohen's pragmatic and contextual notion of acceptance as a mental act or policy. For the latter, but not the former, is the product of an intention or of an act of the will. The fact that the mind is able to represent itself through metarepresentations is one thing, which may well be the outcome of a purely causal and passive process, and the fact that a subject is able to adopt or to reject the metarepresentations which he forms, to take various stances towards them, to submit them to various inferences, and to use them for various purposes in the course of epistemic or practical policies, is quite another thing. These remarks seem to reinforce Cohen's distinction between the passive and the active side of cognition, but on reflection they do not. For if belief, as metarepresentation, is essentially tied to language, what ground is there for claiming that acceptance, unlike belief, is necessarily language-linked? And if beliefs can be, like acceptances, subject to various inferences, what ground is there for putting on the one side the rational deliberations of a conscious agent, and on the other side the purely passive states of information that he is caused to have? We are led to the image of a continuum, rather than of a sharp dividing line between belief and acceptance.

These questions are raised and explored in various ways by the authors of the following essays. David Clarke questions Cohen's and others' thesis that acceptance does not entail belief, and that one can accept things that one does not believe to be true. He does not deny that there is an important distinction to be made between believing and accepting, but he claims that the cases of pragmatic or contextual acceptance of a given proposition which are adduced by Cohen, Stalnaker and Bratman are not genuine cases of acceptance without belief, but are either cases of belief in a different proposition from that which is used in the report of an "acceptance" state, or are not cases of accepting or believing at all, but cases of simply taking a certain action. Thus, according to Clarke, the attorney who believes that his client is guilty does not accept, without believing it, that his client is innocent; he just makes a decision, and performs a certain action. We should take seriously the fact that acceptance is a matter of doing something rather than having a cognitive attitude, and in so far as it involves a cognitive attitude, it is not independent from belief, and presupposes it. According to Clarke, the connection between acceptance and belief can be traced back to two uses of belief reports, one descriptive of the mental content attributed, the other evaluative, only the latter being correct. It is because one presupposes that belief reports have a purely descriptive use that one is led to divorce acceptance from belief. But their evaluative use is recognized, their connection is reinstored. In his response to Clarke, Cohen points out that the distinction between two kinds of attitude reports cannot show that acceptance presupposes belief, for the same distinction can be applied to beliefs, which are voluntary, as well as to acceptances, which are not. He also objects to Clarke that although, in judicial contexts, a lawyer or a juror may take a decision or a reach a verdict, which are indeed acts of a particular ind, this does not imply that the lawyer or the juror do not accept, in the sense of having an attitude towards a certain proposition, a certain premiss from which they reach their decision or verdict. Here obviously much hinges upon how we describe the relevant situations, and the course of the practical reasonings which lead so such judicial decisions. The problem, in particular, is whether, if one defines, as Stalnaker does, acceptance as acting "in certain respects *as if* one believed" something[28], and if one says that the attorney merely *simulates* his having the belief that his client is innocent, such a simulation of belief is distinct from, and can be present in the absence of, the corresponding belief. And in this case, it seems that it can, although it is not evident in other cases.

4. MOORE'S PARADOX

In his account of belief reports, Clarke touches the topic of Moore's paradox, which, as we noted above, can be interpreted in the light of the belief/ acceptance distinction. This topic is examined in more detail in Laurence Goldstein's and Robert Stalnaker's contributions. Goldstein objects to Cohen's diagnostic, according to which the reading of the paradoxical sentence can be split into two distinct attitudes, one of acceptance, the other of belief, which are therefore not logical contradictories. He defends Wittgenstein's solution, which involves, as we saw, a distinction between the description and the expression of a belief content: when one, in the first person, ascribes to oneself a given proposition, one does not describe the state of one's mind. This slack between self-ascription and self description, added to the familiar slack between the actual content of a belief and its content as reported in linguistic ascriptions, is, according to Goldstein, what accounts for the apparent oddity of the Moorean sentences. Robert Stalnaker objects that Moore's paradox is neither a logical contradiction, nor an oddity about the way we use words or express ourselves linguistically; it is rather a problem about belief itself: the very fact that it seems impossible, for the same subject, to ascribe to himself a given belief and to deny than he has it, seems to show, under the hypothesis that a self ascription cannot be a self description, that it is impossible for a subject to describe his own state of mind.[29] As Stalnaker says, we would be led, ironically, to the idea that the mind is opaque to itself, precisely *because* it is so transparent to itself, when it attributes various contents to itself. This raises some fascinating and difficult issues, which overlap only partly those raised by the belief / acceptance distinction. For if Wittgenstein and his commentators are right to claim that Moore's paradox involves an essential distinction between first-person (present tense) third (or second) person (or first person past-tense), the kind of authority which go with the former but not with the latter needs to be explained. And the fact that the distinction can be made for *beliefs* , suggests that the kind of Cartesian transparence of the mind to itself which is held to belong mainly to acts of assents or to acts of acceptance of various contents exists also for beliefs as well. Therefore here too the distinction cannot be as sharp as it seems to be.

5. THE VOLUNTARINESS OF BELIEF

Michael Losonsky faces squarely the main issue raised by the ordinary characterization of belief: is belief a matter of the will? Those who answer positively are called "volitionalists" or "voluntarists". The issue is complex, because it involves at least three different strands, and as a result there are various kinds of voluntarism and of anti-voluntarism . One concerns the question whether the mental act of assenting to the content of a belief is the product of an act of the will. Another concerns the question, alluded to above, whether one can decide at will to believe that p, just as one decides to take a walk or to raise one's arm. Here most writers seem to agree on the following point: one cannot *directly* decide to believe something as the outcome of a particular act of the will. But there is no widespread agreement on the question whether one can *indirectly* induce oneself to believe something, and whether it can count as "believing at will". We have seen that there are familiar arguments against this claim, when "indirectly" means deciding to acquire an habit, or inducing oneself to acquire a belief through some sort of causal process (e.g drug, neurochirurgy, and so on). But the answer seems to be different when "indirectly" a form of *commitment* towards beliefs that one has already acquired, or towards beliefs that one would like to acquire. If "belief" is understood in this sense of *rational commitment* towards one's beliefs it seems to be apt to be an active, rather than a passive, kind of attitude. It is in this sense that W.K. Clifford claimed that "It is wrong, always, and for anyone, to believe anything upon insufficient evidence", and that Williams James opposed to him that there can be a "will to believe", sometimes against evidence.[30] Both Clifford and James were dealing with the attitude than one must have towards one's beliefs, and were disagreeing upon the proper rational course to take, but they were not dealing with the processes of belief formation. The dispute can be reduced to a merely verbal one, if Cohen's distinction between belief and acceptance is respected. Clifford and James disagreed about two kinds of acceptance policies: one according to which one *should* believe only what one has evidence for, the other according to which one should sometimes believe against evidence. But this conflict between different *norms* of rational acceptance does not seem to affect the matter of belief proper: it is one thing to acquire beliefs through various causal routes (through perception, learning, inference, and so on) and quite another to adopt a policy or a strategy of maintaining or rejecting these beliefs. And the latter *is* a matter of the will, to the extent that one chooses a certain regulative ideal in the course of inquiry. Losonsky does not quite agree. First, he grants the anti-voluntarist point that a belief cannot directly be produced by an act of the will, if the latter is to be understood in the sense of a particular event which would be the cause of the belief. But, using Dretske's distinction between a "triggering cause" of an action and a "structuring cause" of an action, he claims that some beliefs can be the outcome of a motivational structure which prepares, so to say, the ground for the belief. So he subscribes to the view that belief formation can be indirectly the product of the will. Second, Losonsky points out that the primary function of beliefs is, in Ramsey's celebrated phrase, to provide us with "maps by which we steer", representations of the world which we use in our actions. But he claims that there is another function of beliefs, which is to serve not only as maps, but also as "insignias" which have a social function and which tie them to goals which are external to us. When beliefs serve as "insignias", we do not simply use them to represent the world to ourselves and to act in various ways: we use them to get a certain conception of ourselves as subjects, and of ourselves as believers in relation to other believers. Many social and religious beliefs are like this. In so far as we do not only believe things, but believe things we think that we *should* believe if we are to be the kind of *persons* that we would like to be, belief can indeed be "a matter of the will".

Jean Pierre Dupuy agrees with Losonsky that the Cohenian division between belief and acceptance cannot be so sharp that it does not allow intermediate degrees. He points out that the thesis that acceptance is to the product of an intention is just as firm that the thesis that there can be separate mental events identified as "intentions", and distinct from other motivational states, such as desires and reasons for actions, a familiar theme since Anscombe's (1957) and Davidson's (1963) discussion of practical reason, which he illustrates here with Kavka's celebrated "toxin puzzle", which seems to show that intentions can be as involuntary as beliefs are claimed to be. He further objects to Cohen's diagnostic on the self-deception paradox, which makes it a product of both an non voluntary attitude—belief—and of a voluntary one—acceptance. Taking the case of a particular religious belief—the Calvinist faith in predestination—he claims that the Calvinist is not necessarily irrational when he believes that, although God has already decided whether he is placed among the elect, he is free to make the opposite choice. Choosing to believe that one is among the elect, in this case, is not merely the choice of a world which has certain already fixed features; it *reveals* such a world, without *causing it*. Thus the Calvinist can find himself in a state of belief which is at the same time the product of his will and independent from it.

6. BELIEFS AND DEGREES OF BELIEFS

A number of other writers have recently defended the voluntariness of belief in spite of the fact that belief is thought primarily as a passive state of the mind. At one point of his analysis, Losonsky encounters Van Fraassen's (1984) recent defense of voluntarism. Van Fraassen argues that beliefs, even when they are understood in the Bayesian sense as gradations of subjective probabilities, are voluntary, because the "Bayesian" believer should respect a certain principle of self confidence in his future beliefs, to the effect that, when an individual has a present subjective degree of belief n in a proposition p, if he also believes that in the future he will give a certain degree r to p, then his present degree n in p should equal r. As Van Fraassen notes, a person who would not conform to this principle would be in a situation similar to that of the person who utters the Moorean sentence (in a degree-theoretic version): " p (to degree n), but I do not believe that p (to degree n)".[31] This "principle of reflection", as Van Fraassen calls it, if it is really a constraint on rational belief, is a form of metaprinciple, according to which a person should not only have certain commitments towards her own beliefs, but also "stand behind" her commitments. In Cohen's terminology, it seems to be a constraint on *acceptance*, rather than a constraint on *beliefs*. But given that, as we saw, Cohen claims that acceptances are not susceptible of degrees, and that the principle of reflection is formulated for beliefs in degree-theoretic terms, the concept of acceptance does not seem to fit the Bayesian scheme.[32] Here again, we are confronted with the following question: are acceptance and belief really two distinct attitudes, the one voluntary and the other not, or is there only one single attitude, belief, we may be more or less voluntary ?

The answer to this question depends in part upon whether the classical Bayesian conception of beliefs as degrees of probability is correct. Richard Jeffrey is a leading proponent of this conception. According to Bayesianism, one can determine whether an agent has a given degree of belief in a proposition p by looking at the odds that the agent is prepared to put upon bets about the truth of p. In this sense belief goes with the actions that the agent is disposed to take, given his preferences. But in order to determine whether an action is rational, one does not need to ascribe to the agent any *full* belief or any assent to a proposition, but only *partial* beliefs, or degrees of beliefs (and similarly for desires). So Bayesianism seems to leave no room to acts of acceptance, conceived as acts of assent, except as limiting cases of partial belief (beliefs to degree 0 or 1). To this many object that the Bayesian picture ill suits the phenomenology of ordinary decision making and of reasoning: we do not seem to assign any precise degrees to the propositions that we believe, and when we premiss a given proposition for an inference, we seem to believe it fully, i.e to accept it. Moreover, the probability calculations required if belief had to be assigned precise degrees would soon be enormously complicated.[33] To this objection, Jeffrey answers that probabilistic judgment does not need to assign precise, but only indeterminate probabilities to propositions. He also shows how the Bayesian scheme can overcome the familiar Duhemian problem of holism in the confirmation of hypotheses by data, and account for ordinary inferences such as *modus ponens.* Bayesianism, in Jeffrey's version, involves what he calls "radical probabilism", the anti-Cartesian view that judgmental probabilities are not based on certainties, and that judgment is a matter of subjective probability "all the way down, to the roots".[34] He points out that it is consistent in general with a pragmatist view, both in the sense in which pragmatism involves a form of fallibilism, according to which are never certain of the grounds of our beliefs, and an action-oriented view of belief. The problem is whether such a pragmatic attitude is necessarily incompatible with the emphasis led upon acceptance rather than beliefs. For acceptance need not be tied only to a Cartesian view according to which inquiry proceeds from proposition that we fully believe and deem certain. In particular the contextualist view of acceptance emphasizes the fact that we accept some propositions but at some point cease to take them for granted. So the question arises whether Bayesians, in so far as they are pragmatists and fallibilists about inquiry and rational belief, need to proceed only in terms of partial beliefs, and whether their scheme cannot accommodate also acceptances rather than beliefs.[35]

A related question is examined here by Jacques Dubucs. The rules of the probability calculus are supposed to be operative for a Bayesian believer, if he is supposed to be rational: if he did not obey these rules, a "Dutch book" could always be made against him. But this seems to impose an unnecessarily strong requirement on the coherence of his beliefs, given that actual subjects do not seem always to conform themselves to the Bayesians standards of rationality.[36] Notoriously, a similar problem arises for deductive beliefs: although a subject ought to believe all the logical consequences of his beliefs, he actually does not, and cannot, for this would imply a form of logical omniscience. Cohen attempts here to evade this difficulty by distinguishing objective closure under the rules of deduction from subjective closure, the latter applying to acceptances, and the former to beliefs. Subjective closure would be, on this view a matter of what deductions can be made for a given subject, from his point of view. But this is still unsatisfactory. Dubucs objets that the distinction between objective and subjective closure can also arise for acceptance, and that one needs a less psychologistic criterion of "subjective"closure to make the relevant distinction. Building from the notion of effective proof invoked by constructivists logicians, he proposes another notion of deducibility ("$_c$deducibility") which would have the effect of restricting the number of allowable inferences to the *feasible* ones. He further applies the same strategy to solve Kyburg's notorious "lottery paradox": in a fair lottery of n tickets there is only one winning one, you should believe of any ticket that it does not win, since you believe, for any single ticket, that there is only a very low probability that it wins ($(n-1)/n$) although you believe that one ticket wins. The paradox illustrates the difficulties of moving from beliefs which have a given degree of subjective probability to full beliefs. But the paradox can be reproduced in terms of acceptance. Dubucs proposes to reduce the acceptance worthiness of a proposition, in such a situation, to only a limited set of propositions, and to license the application of our logical rules to certain cases, in order to block their generalisation. The strategy of acceptance in a context will, therefore, call for at least local revisions of logic.

Peter Railton examines the relationship between our attitudes of belief and our attitudes of acceptance within the domain of scientific inquiry. If one grants that belief in general "aims at truth" and that there is an internal or constitutive connection between belief and truth as its target, does it follow that we should, in any scientific inquiry, look after the truth? Railton rejects both a strong realist conception according to which scientific inquiry aims at describing an independent objective world and a strong relativist conception according to which objectivity is but a construction out of social forces and factors at work in science. He proposes a model of scientific objectivity where subjective factors—cases where we are tempted to accept our theories as true even though we do not have strong evidence for them—and objective factors—where we take our theories as true because we believe them to be true and have strong evidence for them, can coexist and equilibrate each other. The sort of moral obligation to seek the truth that Clifford defended in his ethics of belief as well as the strong self confidence in one's aim, or the commitment to one's theories that James and other voluntarists philosophers recommend, are equally inadequate. Scientific objectivity is compatible with both over-confidence and scepticism, with both attitudes of acceptance and attitudes of belief.

7. MIND, METAMIND AND SIMULATION

The question which occupies most of the contributors—is there a class of attitudes distinct from beliefs and what is the ground for such a distinction?—is examined by the last three authors under a somewhat different angle. They all notice that if there are such psychological states as acceptances, these must at least belong to the category of second-order beliefs, beliefs about beliefs, or reflective beliefs, and so must presuppose some metarepresentational capacity of the mind. Starting from a broadly representational and cognitivist conception of the mind, they ask what is the nature of this capacity and explore the ways by which it is related to language.

Keith Lehrer was among the first, in the contemporary philosophical literature, to advocate the need of a distinction between belief and acceptance.[37] His distinction rests upon a more fundamental one between *first order* mental states, which carry some information to which a thinker has access, and *second-order* mental states, which use this information in reasoning. First-order beliefs, according to Lehrer, belong to the ground floor of mind, whereas second-order beliefs belong to what he calls "metamind". But what exactly is the difference? In his previous writings, Lehrer drew the distinction in terms of the kind of speech act that express acceptances ("I accept that *p* "), in contrast with belief as a dispositional state. This seemed to imply that acceptances are voluntary acts, whereas beliefs are not voluntary. Lehrer also took inspiration from Fodor's distinction between input systems, which are modular, and the central system, which is non modular, states of belief and reception of information being "informationally encapsulated" and automatic, while states of acceptance being the output of the central system. (This was actually an adaptation of Fodor's scheme, since Fodor calls "beliefs" the output of he central system, not the outputs of the modular sensory systems). But Lehrer now rejects these too simple divisions. His present view is that beliefs, as well as acceptances, are both *functional states* (hence the distinction is not between states which are functional and states which are not), but of a different kind. Beliefs provide us with information and inference, and are functionally related to states of information, to desires, and to other beliefs. Acceptances are a matter of reflecting upon one's beliefs, and are functionally related to (first-order) beliefs, to preferences, and to other acceptances. Their proper role is a *reasoning role*, which implies that inferences are not only performed, but evaluated. An important difference between the two states is the following. Beliefs, like acceptances, can be a matter of degree, and that degree can be represented by subjective probabilities. Both are based on evidence, and upon the conditionalization of evidence, according to the Bayesian rule of conditionalisation. But belief, unlike acceptance does not rest upon an *evaluation* of the evidence. So the probability of an hypothesis is not stabilized when it is merely believed to be true. Acceptance, on the contrary, stabilizes the probability of an hypothesis over conditionalizatin on rational evidence. A believer does not consider the synchronic aspect of his probabilities; an accepter does. This is what makes a subject who accepts a certain proposition a rational being, capable of reasoning, whereas a subject who believes a proposition may be rational in drawing certain inferences, and irrational in drawing others (as famous experiments in the psychology of reasoning testify). An accepter, so to say, can be in two minds: he can feel a conflict between what his mind produces, and what his metamind evaluates. As Lehrer indicates, this may provide useful insights in analyses of the problem of irrationality, as well as of the problem of practical reasoning, for a similar distinction as the belief/ acceptance distinction can be made between desires, as first-order mental states, and preferences, as second-order ones.

Andrew Woodfield argues that, for there to be the acceptance of a proposition, it is not sufficient that there be, as Cohen suggests, a sort of mental analogue to the assertion of a linguistic sentence; there must be some actual linguistic input which is *proposed* to the would-be accepter, and internalized by her. Woodfield suggests various ways of how this could be possible, given a plausible, broadly functionalist conception of cognitive architecture, according to which the "language-processor" is both independent from the "central-processor" and closely linked to it. Such an account, however, does not imply that the meaning and contents of acceptance-attitudes are determined only by what goes on within the confines of an individual's mind. Given that acceptance (or the kinds of metarepresentational beliefs which fall broadly under this category) is directed towards contents apt to be used in communication in a *public* language, such contents are likely to be in part external to the mind of a particular speaker, in the sense required by the "externalist" or "social" accounts of content.

Dan Sperber explores further the nature of the metarepresentational ability involved. Like Woodfield, he sees as distinctive of the human mind that it can process not only first-order beliefs or representations, but also second-order, or, in his terminology, "reflective" ones. The latter embed a given representation into a metarepresentation, which can have a variety of forms: one can metarepresent a given content by *reporting* what is said under an occasion, *supposing* it to be true, *doubting* that it is true, and so on, through various "validating contexts". He further hypothesizes that every such embedded representation can be "disembedded" or "disquoted" from its validating context, and dropped into the "belief box", where it joins the other non reflective, primary, representations. If *all* metarepresentational contents could be so disquoted, there would not be any reflective belief, and thus the metarepresentational capacity would not give rise to a distinct set of attitudes. Sperber argues to the contrary that reflective beliefs can acquire a life of their own. In particular, they differ from what he calls "intuitive beliefs", which are the outputs of perceptual and inferential processes, and which are understood in terms of the elementary conceptual repertoire formed by perceptions and inferences. The distinction turns upon the fact that reflective beliefs, unlike intuitive ones, can be had without understanding the conditions under which they are true, or through only a *partial* understanding of their truth conditions. For instance I may believe (reflectively) that, say, "space is isotropic", by reading a geometry book, without having a clear idea of what it means. Sperber suggests that we can acquire such beliefs just by thinking about them, in the reflective mode. He also suggests that many beliefs which are studied by anthropologists — social and religious beliefs—occur through such a mechanism. Sperber's "reflective beliefs" differ from acceptances in the pragmatic contextualist sense considered above, in so far as acceptances are supposed to be (more or less, as we saw) voluntary ad intentional. Reflective beliefs involve a causal and passive element, since they depend, in an essential way, upon a particular feature of the human mind, the metarepresentational capacity. Sperber does not consider the interactions between the "belief box" and other "boxes" such as the "desire" box, and so he does not consider the possibility that reflective beliefs could be, in some sense, under our intentional control. This does not, however, prevent us from asking the following question: to what extent can our reflective belief be more or less intentional? For instance reflective beliefs acquired on the basis of some authority, such as religious beliefs proposed by priests, or scientific beliefs proposed by authoritative scientists, tend to be acquired through some sort of trust, i.e through a desire to follow these authorities. Is this necessarily irrational? The answer seems to depend upon whether we are prepared to say that only "intuitive" beliefs—i.e beliefs we fully understand—can be rational, and upon whether we can postulate a further (even higher-order) "reflective" capacity: the capacity that we have to accept or to reject the outputs of our metarepresentational cognitive architecture, and to form a more general view of the coherence of our reflective beliefs, that is to impose standards of rationality to them.

François Récanati elaborates Sperber's notion of reflective beliefs which are only "quasi-believed", that is which are believed with only an partial grasp of their content. He points out two difficulties in Sperber's framework. One is that quasi or reflective belief is still a belief, i.e that it can be put back in the belief-box by being disquoted; so to what extent is it a genuinely different kind of attitude? Another difficulty is that, on Sperber's view, a reflective belief is indeterminate in his content. According to Récanati, it need not be, or rather it may be only *epistemically* indeterminate, while being *semantically* determinate, i.e although it expresses a definite proposition, the believer does not know which. Récanati postulates that there is a *further* kind of attitude, distinct both from belief and quasi-belief:

"acceptance". He distinguishes two varieties of it: acceptance *with belief* (roughly when we accept what we believe) and acceptance *without belief,* where we accept propositions which we do not fully understand, or where we accept propositions which we do not believe but understand, which he calls *assumptions.* The latter are approximatively equivalent to what we have called above, following Cohen, pragmatic acceptances. Here Récanati takes seriously Stalnaker's suggestion that such acceptances are cases of "as if belief" or of *pretending to believe* things which we actually do not believe, or *simulations* of belief. This is not the same as quasi-believing, for to pretend that one believes that p it seems that one understands p, and that one can believe that p. And here we find again the issue which was raised in Clarke's paper: are simulations of belief or "assumptions" *independent* from beliefs? The issue is complex, not only for the reasons adduced above about Clarke's paper, but also because a number of writers have argued recently that the process of attributing beliefs to others goes through some sort of process of simulating in them the beliefs that we would have in we were in their place.[38] But such a simulative process, because it would be a species of analogical projection, would fall more on the side of what Récanati calls "quasi-belief", since a projected content is not necessarily a content which is fully understood or grasped. So if, as Récanati suggests, quasi-beliefs *are* beliefs of a certain kind (though different from "primary" belief processed through regular processes of perception and inference), it would follow that the simulation -process, under this hypothesis, is a genuine process of belief formation and attribution, and thus "depends" upon belief in some sense. But acceptances or "assumptions", in Récanati's sense, are not genuine beliefs, although they can be considered as an extension of the belief faculty. Récanati provides a detailed study of their mechanism of formation, in particular through communication, through the framework of Barwise and Perry's "situation semantics". The picture which emerges is a complex one, which allows, as we have already suggested, much more continuity between beliefs in the proper sense and "acceptances" than it was originally proposed under the Cohenian analysis.

I have suggested, at the beginning of this introduction, that there are many interconnections between the traditionally debated topics of belief attribution and belief content, of the rationality or irrationality of belief formation, and of the epistemology of belief. The essays in this collection not only attest the varieties of these connexions; they provide new pathways for understanding the link between what we may conceive as two complementary, rather than separate, sides of human cognition: the capacity that human subjects have not only to process beliefs, but also to use these beliefs for further epistemic or practical goals.[39]

NOTES

[1] cf. Moore (1944) in Moore 1993, ch.12. Wittgenstein 1953, part II, X

[2] As Jane Heal (1994, p.12-14) remarks.

[3] Bratman 1993. see also the classic discussion by Williams (1973)

[4] This means that the *attitude* of believing that *p* is non contextual. Of course it does not mean that a number of belief *contents*, in particular those which are indexical, are not context dependent. For instance my belief that *this book* is read obviously depends on which book I am referring to in which context. And it does not mean that belief *reports*, as expressed in language are not, to a large extent, contextual.

[5] The term "belief" here is not exactly the proper translation of Descartes 's and other XVIIth century philosophers *assensio* or "assentiment" in these contexts.

[6] De Sousa 1971

[7] Dennett 1978, ch. 16 ("How to Change your Mind")

[8] Vickers 1968

[9] See for example the essays in Swain 1970, and Kaplan 1980.

[10] Lehrer 1979, 1990, 1990a

[11] Van Fraassen 1981, 1985

[12] Stalnaker 1984, ch. 5

[13] Perry 1980

[14] Bratman 1993

[15] Cohen 1992. Cohen first proposed his account of the distinction in his 1989

[16] Cohen 1992, p.4, p.7

[17] Cohen 1992, p.4

[18] See the useful map of the distinction given by Andrew Woodfield in his essay in the present volume.

[19] Cohen 1992, p. 22

[20] Cohen 1992, p.12

[21] In this sense acceptance is closer to what Kant, who himself gives the doctor example (Kant, *Kritik der Reinen Vernunft, "Transcendental methodology"*,) terms "pragmatic belief". See Ulman-Margalit and Margalit 1992

[22] Stalnaker 1984, ch. 5

[23] Bratman 1993. For the role of acceptance in epistemic inquiry, see also Harman 1986.

[24] Stalnaker 1984, p.80.

[25] Davidson 1982

[26] See e.g the essays in Wellman 1993, Davies and Stone 1995

[27] Lehrer 1990, p.11

[28] Stalnaker 1984, p.80. (My emphasis)

[29] The same point if made by Heal 1992, p.6

[30] Clifford 1876, James 1901

[31] Van Fraassen 1995. Or it would be a version of Moore's paradox where someone says: " *p*, but I will believe that *not p*". See also Bovens 1995.

[32] See Cohen 1992, p.113-115

[33] See for instance Harman 1986.

[34] Jeffrey 1992, p.11

[35] see in particular Lance 1995, and the papers in the same issue of *Philosophical Studies*, on "Belief and probability". Isaac Levi (1967) is a also writer who has long emphasized the need to make room for such a notion of acceptance in inquiry.

[36] *Locus classicus* : Kahnemann & Tversky 1982.

[37] See the references in note 10 above.

[38] See in particular the papers collected in Davies and Stone 1995 (note 26 above) and the references to the literature thereof.

[39] Most of the present essays come from a conference that I organized in the Université de Caen in 1995. It could not have existed without the Institut Universitaire de France. I thank also the University de Caen, the CNRS (Délagation de Basse-Normandie), the UFR des Sciences de l'Homme. Among the participants, I thank Alain Boyer, Richard Bradley, Fabrice Clément, Jérôme Dokic, Bengt Hansson, David Miller, Daniel Schulthess, Maurice Salles, and Elie Zahar. To Keith Lehrer, who could not attend the conference, I owe a special debt: not only he made the publication of this volume possible, but he also contributed by a fine essay.

REFERENCES

Bratman, M.(1993) "Belief and Acceptance in a Context", *Mind*

Clifford, W.K. (1879) "The Ethics of Belief", in his *Lectures and Essays*,London

Cohen, L.J. (1989) "Belief and Acceptance", *Mind* (1992) *An Essay on Belief and Acceptance*, Oxford, Oxford University Press

Davidson, D. (1982) "Rational Animals", *Dialectica*,

Davies, M. and Stone T. eds (1995) *Mental Simulation*

de Sousa , R. de (1971) "How to Give a Piece of Your Mind, or: The Logic of Belief an Assent", *Philosophical Review* , XXXV, 52-79

Dennett, D. (1978) "How to Change your Mind", in his *Brainstorms*, Bradford Books, Cambridge Mass

Engel, P.(1998) "Believing, Accepting, and Holding-True", *Philosophical Explorations* , 2

Harman, G. (1986) *Change in View*, MIT Press, Cambridge Mass.

Heal, J. (1994) "Moore's Paradox: a Wittgensteinian Solution", *Mind*

James, W. (1901) *The Will to Believe and Other Essays*, Longman and Green, New York

Jeffrey, R. (1992) *Probability and the Art of Judgment*, Cambridge, Cambridge University Press.

Kahneman D., Slovic, P. & Tversky, A.eds (1982) *Judgment under Uncertainty, Heuristics and Biases*, Cambridge, Cambridge University Press

Kaplan, M. (1980) "A Theory of Rational Acceptance",*Journal of Philosophy*

Lance, M. (1995) " Subjective Probability and Acceptance", Philosophical Studies

Leher, K. (1979) "The Gettier Problem and the Analysis of Knowledge", in G.S. Pappas, ed. *Justification and Knoweldge*, Dordrecht, Reidel (1990) *Theory of Knowledge*, Westview, Boulder, Co (1990a) *Metamind*, Oxford, Clarendon Press

Levi, I. (1980) *The Enterprise of Knowledge*, Harvard, Harvard University Press

Moore, G.E. (1944) "Moore's Paradox", in G.E. Moore, *Selected Writings*, ed. T. Baldwin, Routledge, London, 1993 ch.12.

Perry, J. (1980) "Belief and Acceptance", in P. Frech, T. Uehling and S. Weinsein eds, *Midwest Studies in Philosophy*, 5, 533-542

Stalnaker, R. (1984) *Inquiry* , The MIT Press, Cambridge Mass.

Swain, M. (ed.) (1970) *Induction, Acceptance and Rational Belief*, Reidel, Dordrecht

Ullman-Margalit, E. and A. Margalit (1992), "Holding-True and Holding as True", *Synthese*

Van Fraassen, B. C. (1981) *The Scientific Image*, Oxford, Oxford University Press (1984) "Belief and the Will", *The Journal of Philosophy* (1985) *Laws and Symmetries*, Oxford, Oxford University Press (1995) "Belief and the Problem of Ulysses and the Syrens", *Philosophical Studies*

Vickers, J. (1968) "Judgment and Belief", in K. Lambert, ed. *The Logical Way of Doing Things*, Yale University Press

Wellman, H. (1993) *Children's theory of mind* , Blackwell, Oxford

Williams (1973) "Deciding to believe", in his *Problems of the Self*, Cambridge, Cambridge University Press

Wittgenstein, L. (1953) *Philosophical Investigations*, Blackwell, Oxford

THE POSSIBILITY OF ACCEPTANCE WITHOUT BELIEF

D. S. Clarke
Southern Illinois University at Carbondale

My topic is the problem of determining whether it is possible for a person to accept a proposition without believing it, to accept, for example, that a table in a room is four feet long but not believe this to be true, or to accept but not believe that the universe originated with a big bang. I don't think it is possible to have acceptance without belief, but this is in opposition to some writers who think it is, and we must look at their reasoning. It should be noted that the argument before us is restricted to propositional belief and does not extend to the relationship between acceptance and non-propositional believing in (or having faith in, placing trust in) something or someone. Coming to believe in something seems to be a species of acceptance, and as such some of the contrasts to acceptance outlined below fail to apply.

Before tackling our problem head on I want to lay some grounds for a solution by first considering the data we appeal to in making our various claims about acceptance and belief, and then reviewing in some contrasts that seem to suggest our being able to separate the two.

I. BASES FOR PHILOSOPHIC CLAIMS
ABOUT BELIEF AND ACCEPTANCE

In philosophy questions about substantive matters are invariably intertwined with questions about how we arrive at answers. If we had the introspective powers thought to exist in the Nineteenth Century, we could simply peer inside ourselves and read off from the psychological data the relations between belief as a mental state and acceptance as act. But we don't have such powers, for if we did we wouldn't have the disputes facing us. We must therefore approach our problem more indirectly. For belief, language seems to be our most trustworthy guide, as "belief" is a term used in ordinary language, and its uses would seem to guide philosophic conclusions. The question "What is a belief?" seems to be a question of how belief ascriptions are used in ordinary language, whether they are used to describe dispositions, states of affairs, relations, or whatever, and the conditions for proper use. As a result, questions about what is believed, the content of a belief, are questions about the "that" clauses of ascriptions of the form "S believes that p". Some may dispute this, but if they do, it seems incumbent upon them to provide some other grounds for philosophic claims.

While for belief language seems to be our guide, when we turn to acceptance a different situation confront us. The term "acceptance" as used by philosophers seems to be a term of art derived the Nineteenth Century term "judgment", and with no clear derivation from ordinary language. The term "accept" does occur in everyday speech, as when we say "He accepts the fact that he must go to prison", but here it suggests regret or resignation of a kind not present for the generalized philosophic sense of the verb. Without language as a guide and without powers of introspection, we seem to lack a clear basis for conclusions about the act of acceptance. Moreover, we lack a basis for claims we might want to make about the propositional content of an acceptance, about exactly what a person is accepting as true.

One solution is to relate acceptance to performative uses of "assert" and "assent" and the speech acts of assertion and assent, as we do have available to us Austin's descriptions of conditions for the performance of these public speech acts. Acceptance can then be regarded as a kind of internalized assertion or assent to sentence tokens that may or may not be given public expression. Thus, my acceptance of the proposition that the table is four feet long may be regarded as an internalized assent to a mental token of "The table is four feet long". In this form we can draw an analogy between this internalized assent and the public speech act of assent performed when saying "Yes, I agree" in response to another's remark.

With this relationship between acceptance as a mental act and assent and assertions as speech acts established, it is easy to understand the paradox noted by G. E. Moore arising from someone saying "The table is four feet long, but I don't believe it is this long".[1] The role of a first person sentence of the form "I believe that p" is normally to qualify an assertion, to express hesitation about p' s truth. In this respect it contrasts with a sentence such as "I know that p", which, as Austin noted, has the illocutionary force of a guarantee. One who asserts "The table is four feet long" and then denies its qualification with a "I believe that" prefix has violated the conventions of illocutionary force indicators. He or she would have used a sentence with assertive force and then withheld its weaker qualification. If to assert is to accept, then in such a case there can be no acceptance without belief.

Moore's Paradox arises from a first person use of "believe", but it is not obvious that its conclusion can be extended to third person uses. Suppose a person X asserts "The table is four feet long" or on hearing this sentence uttered by another says "Yes, I agree". Is it possible for someone else to use a third person belief ascription to say "X doesn't believe the table is four feet long"? Here standard analyses of speech acts seem to require a negative answer. It is widely accepted that the conditions for the successful performance of speech acts of assertion and assent include belief on the part of the speaker. One lacking this belief may have uttered the words of a sentence or uttered the words "Yes, I agree", but what Searle calls a "sincerity condition" (or Gricean "conversational implicature") would not have been fulfilled, and hence the speech act of assent has not been performed. With acceptance being regarded as a kind of general assent or assertion that may be internalized, this reasoning now results in denying there can be acceptance without belief. We may claim someone accepts a certain proposition p, but if it becomes obvious he or she doesn't believe p, then we would withdraw our original claim. Acceptance presupposes belief, just as does assent and assertion.

Though this conclusion seems to me to be correct, the speech act solution to our problem overlooks some difficulties. One of them is that it fails to account for the fact that we speak of acceptance within a community in a way that resists any obvious analysis into speech acts. The community of chemists can be said to accept, for example, that the boiling point of methanol is 64.5 degrees Centigrade. But only individual chemists can be described as performing the speech acts of asserting (assenting to) this proposition or as engaged in internal assertion or assent. At least in such cases, then, acceptance seems to separate off from speech acts.[2]

This doesn't seem to deny us means of determining acceptance, however, for there are other tests for community-wide acceptance that we do seem able to apply. One of them is meaning transference from predicate to subject, which occurs after acceptance of a sentence leads to a change in criteria for identifying an instance of the subject. At some previous stage, chemists observed that the boiling point of methanol is 64.5 degrees. After accepting this as true, this boiling point became one of the criteria for identifying a liquid as methanol and distinguishing it from other forms of alcohol. Such transferences thus provide us with a way of determining acceptance: A sentence of the form S is P can be established as having been accepted as true if P has become one of the criteria for identifying an instance of S. Another test of acceptance seems provided by the transition of a proposition from the status of a tentative hypothesis to part of the background assumptions used in the testing of other hypotheses, either in the form of auxiliary assumptions used to derive observable consequences or in the interpretation of experimental evidence. Einstein's general theory of relativity was once a tentative hypothesis. The fact that it is assumed in the testing of cosmological theories and thus made the transition to the status of what we call "background knowledge" is an indication of its acceptance within the scientific community.

We thus have two different criteria for community acceptance: predicate to subject transference and transition to background assumptions. They seem to provide us a basis for determining acceptance of a proposition that can be applied independently of speech acts of assent and assertion by observing scientific practice and determining whether in fact the transference and transition have taken place. The question before us, then, can be reformulated as the question whether acceptance, either as indicated by assent or practice, must be accompanied by belief.

II. CONTRASTS BETWEEN BELIEF AND ACCEPTANCE

Reasons for thinking that we can separate off belief from acceptance arise from a number of contrasts we seem to be able to draw between belief and acceptance. Most of them are presented by Pascal Engel in his Introduction to this volume, and so I can summarize them very briefly. Some seem more secure than others. My aim is principally to make initially plausible the separation under consideration.

Persistence.

Perhaps the most obvious of the contrasts is with respect to persistence. Beliefs have duration, and usually lack clear boundaries of origination or end. In this sense they can be said to be *global* in nature, applicable in a variety of situations at different times and places. Acts of acceptance, in contrast, are *localized* occurrences to which we can assign definite times and places. Some writers have distinguished "occurrent" from "dispositional" beliefs as a way of making the contrast just outlined. So far as I can see, they introduce only a terminological variant for the acceptance of a proposition.

Degrees.

Another obvious contrast is with respect to degrees. We can believe more or less strongly in a proposition, and some have proposed ways of measuring degrees of belief. Acceptance, on the other hand, seems all-or-nothing, for we are faced with the choice of either accepting a proposition, rejecting it as false, or refusing to accept or reject it on the basis of there being insufficient evidence. This all-or-nothing character of acceptance is obscured by the fact that often it is directed towards probabilities. On the basis of weather reports I accept now that there is a 80% chance of rain tomorrow, that is, accept the probability of rain to be .8; tomorrow I may accept that there is a 30% chance for the day following. It is not that I accept the first more strongly than the second, but rather I assign a higher probability to the rain occurring tomorrow than to it occurring the day after. In both cases acceptance is definite, though if the statistical evidence is insufficient, I may want to withhold acceptance of any probability proposition about rain.[3]

Control.

The fact that acceptance can be withheld and is in this sense voluntary introduces another contrast that has been formulated in admirably clear fashion by Jonathan Cohen in his *Essay on Belief and Acceptance*.[4] To accept a proposition as true is, in effect, a decision not to inquire further about it, usually by not seeking out further evidence that might bear on its truth or falsity.[5] In contrast, as Bernard Williams notes, many beliefs seem never to have been acquired as the result of a decision.[6] I believe the earth is roughly spherical, but I never decided to believe this. I was taught this, and the belief was thereby inculcated. Also, I believe the table before me is brown, but I don't choose to believe this. The belief is there whenever I open my eyes.

Context Dependence and Purposes.

The final contrast I want to sketch is the most difficult to clearly formulate, but is also the one most directly relevant to our central problem. We may recall that the persistence contrast was between the local character of acceptance, its occurrence at a certain time and place, and the global character of belief, its relative persistence and independence from a particular context. This contrast leads naturally to another between the dependence of acceptance on interests and purposes that an agent may have relative to given contexts and the independence of belief from these varying context-dependent purposes. As Descartes noted, acceptance (or what he called "judgment") is often forced by the exigencies of action, with accepted propositions becoming the premises of the practical inferences used in making decisions forced on us by circumstances. I must decide tomorrow morning whether to carry my umbrella. To accept there will be a 80% chance of rain will lead, let us suppose, to my carrying it, while acceptance of an 30% chance will lead to my leaving it behind. Also, whatever I accept will be also be a decision to forego further search for relevant evidence. With little cost to me if I'm mistaken, I would probably readily accept what a single news report tells me about the probability of rain. With more at stake, say in deciding whether to invest my life savings in a mutual fund on the basis of reports of past earnings, I might consult several sources before making a decision.

If beliefs are indeed global in application, then it would seem they are held independently of such varying practical considerations. Of course, I can believe here and now that the table in front of me is brown, but whether I hold this belief as such seems not dependent on what I now want or my interest in this information. For science this independence seems even more obvious. The beliefs within the scientific community that the universe is expanding and that it originated with a big bang seem divorced from all human purposes and conceivable applications. They are purely cognitive in nature, without any admixture of those practical considerations that infect acts of acceptance embedded within practical inference contexts.

So much for this quick survey of some contrasts. We should recognize how their formulation seems more based on informal intuitions than on the kinds of standards discussed in Part I. In discussing beliefs, for example, considerations about how we use belief ascriptions have faded from consideration. We will return to uses of ascriptions briefly in the next part and more explicitly at the end, and in this way attempt to improve understanding of the contrasts. But at least these contrasts just reviewed provide some initial plausibility to the separation of acceptance and belief. Indeed, the control contrast does provide a basis for claiming there can be belief without acceptance. Since many beliefs are acquired through inculcation or are the effect of causes beyond our control, we have them without ever having accepted their propositional content. I am happy to concede this claim of belief without acceptance to be true, and shall not be discussing it further. The last of the contrasts, the context dependence contrast, has also suggested to some philosophers the more controversial and, I think, false claim that there can be acceptance without belief. We now turn to the reasoning they have used to reach this conclusion.

III. THE PRAGMATIC SEPARATION OF BELIEF
FROM ACCEPTANCE

The most straightforward and plausible arguments I can find for separating belief from acceptance have been formulated by Robert Stalnaker and Jonathan Cohen. Stalnaker's reasoning appeals to the variation of informational content with interests, while Cohen appeals to a kind of cognitive/practical contrast between belief and acceptance. I consider these arguments in turn.

Acceptance and Information.

We measure the informational content of a sentence by what linguists call the "field" of its predicate and the number of incompatible alternatives within this field the predicate excludes. To take an obvious example, in the sentence "This book is red" the field for "red" is color, and the adjective excludes other color adjectives such as "purple", "yellow", "blue", and "green" . For the sentence "This book is magenta", on the other hand, the field for "magenta" would be shades of color, and this field has many more potential values. Since "magenta" excludes the shades of red described by "pink", "scarlet", etc., any sentence in which it occurs as predicate will evidently convey more information than one containing "red". Which field we choose, whether simple colors or their shades, will depend on how exactly we need to discriminate one from another. Simple colors will do probably for describing books; shades will be needed for wall paints.

Stalnaker uses such considerations to argue that there may be situations in which for certain purposes we accept as true an utterance of a sentence with low informational content, but don't believe it true relative to higher standards of exactness.[7] As an example, suppose I measure a table with a ruler accurate to a sixteenth of an inch and determine its length to be three feet and 11 and 7/16 inches. This description of length I believe true as based on the measurement. Faced with the problem of buying a covering cloth for the table, I might accept as true a description of the table as being 4 feet long, as such a description is sufficiently exact for this purpose. I might then both assert and assent to this description, and use it as a basis for my purchase. But though I accept the imprecise description as true, I wouldn't believe it true. On some other occasion, say when replacing a plank on the table's top, I would instead accept the description with an accuracy to the nearest sixteenth of an inch. The field I choose for acceptance (or the "grid" I impose, to use Wittgenstein's metaphor), whether inches or sixteenths of inches, will vary with purposes that may change from one situation to another, but global belief will be in the most accurate description available to me. Thus, there can be acceptance without belief.

The plausibility of this reasoning is derived, I think, from the vagueness of the concepts of acceptance and belief used in its formulation. When we relate them to language use this plausibility tends to disappear. To say "The table is four feet long, but I believe it is 3 feet, 11 and 7/16 inches" is an instance of Moore's Paradox, and should be rejected as declining to follow a strong assertion with a weakened one. But can this same solution be applied to a third person belief ascription? It does seem that if X were to say to us "The table is four feet long", we would choose his form of language with its degree of exactness and describe his belief by "X believes the table to be four feet long". We would not describe it by "X believes the table to be 3 feet 11 and 7/16 inches long", even if aware of a prior measurement. In reporting the belief we are thus guided by the same purposes he had in making his assertion. In this respect the belief ascriptions we make of others are just as dependent on purposes as are the assertions on which they are based. As noted in Part I, it seems our philosophic conclusions about belief must be guided by our use of "believe" in making ascriptions. This use, both in the first and third person, certainly does not support Stalnaker's separation of belief from acceptance.

Moreover, what is our basis for describing the content of our subject's acceptance? We have described him as accepting for the purposes of buying the table cloth that the table is four feet long. But it seems more plausible to describe him as accepting this length within some implied interval of accuracy, say four feet plus or minus one inch. For the purpose of replacing a plank for the table the description of three feet, 11 and 7/16 inches would be accepted within an interval of one sixteenth of an inch. What varies from context to context, it would seem, is acceptance of an implied degree of accuracy, the interval of an acknowledged possible error. Similar considerations would seem to hold for descriptions of color. A person may be aware of the shade of red of a book, but choose to describe it with "red" and not "magenta". What that person would be accepting is the proposition that the book is red relative to the accuracy and information content of the color field. If these considerations are correct, there is belief consistent with acceptance, for the person is accepting four feet plus or minus an inch as a length and believing the description in terms of sixteenth inches to be true and accepting that the book is red relative to the color field and believing it to be magenta. In science such intervals of possible error and degrees of exactness are made explicit. The fact that they are left implicit in daily speech should not justify ignoring them in our descriptions of what a person accepts.

Acceptance, Fallibility, and Scientific Practice.

When we turn to Professor Cohen's reasons for thinking acceptance does not require belief we find different types of arguments, though a similar appeal to a pragmatic contrast between acceptance and belief. Acceptance of a propositionp within science, Cohen says, is determined by the empirical adequacy of p and its consistency with other parts of the corpus of science. When accepted p becomes a premiss used in making predictions and explanations and takes on the role for accepted propositions outlined at the beginning of this paper. It also becomes the basis for further inquiries and programs of research, as occurred for Einstein's general relativity theory. But such acceptance as a basis for scientific practice is quite consistent, Cohen thinks, with absence of belief on the part of individual scientists. As an active participant in the science of physics, an individual scientist may accept Einstein's theory, and use this as an assumption in formulating and testing other hypotheses. But given the fallibility of all scientific theories, the possibility that at some later date they may be falsified, the individual physicist may withhold belief from the theory, accepting it but not believing it. Indeed, Cohen thinks this fallibility always justifies withholding belief, as belief may interfere with the objectivity necessary at some later stage to replace the theory with another. "Perhaps there is not *much* harm," he says, if in the end, as well as accepting that p, the scientist also believes that p. But in principle he would do better to school himself into practising a greater intellectual detachment. There is a danger that possession of a belief that p might make him less ready to change his mind about accepting that p if new evidence crops up or a better theory becomes available.[8] For Cohen acceptance is tied to the day-to-day practice of science, while belief is to be reserved for the disinterested theoretical pursuit of truth. There is no need for the one to sully the other. Cohen's reasoning illustrates the problem of extending a familiar everyday concept such as belief, which is typically applied to individuals, to the cooperative domain of science with its specialization of activities. There is a sense in which the personal beliefs of individual scientists are irrelevant to their practice of proposing and testing hypotheses, and the use of the results of these tests for later proposals and tests. Who cares whether Einstein as an individual actually believed in the truth of his gravitational theory? It is important only that he proposed a theory that eventually gained community acceptance. But since it is community acceptance that Cohen seems to be appealing to, the practice of transforming a hypothesis into a premiss used in other inferences, it must be paired with community belief. We do, after all, speak of belief within a community of inquirers, for example, the belief of physicists in the general relativity theory or the belief of biologists in the Watson-Crick helical model of DNA. If acceptance within science is to be understood as a communal practice in which many participate, then it would seem belief must also be understood in this group sense.

In a sense ascribable to groups, belief does seem to necessarily follow acceptance. There are, of course, stages in the testing of a tentative hypothesis when scientists withhold final endorsement, even though predictions so far have been successful. At this stage explanations can be offered and further programs of research undertaken—all marked by the same tentativeness that applies to the hypothesis they are based on. But surely at some other stage answers are given to questions and decisions made to terminate further search for relevant evidence. Physicists have accepted as true Hubble's theory of the expanding universe and the Watson-Crick model of DNA, not simply as adequate to the existing data. but in the sense that the questions to which these were proposed as answers are no longer open in the way they once were.

To account for this it is useful to distinguish the *provisional* acceptance of a hypothesis from its *terminal* acceptance. Provisional acceptance of a hypothesis h is a decision to consider h for further testing, to include h among those hypotheses that experimental data is to decide between. The relative initial success of such a hypothesis, as Cohen notes, may be a basis for inferring from it consequences for explanations and further research, even though the period of testing of the hypothesis has not been completed. Provisional acceptance of a hypothesis h would not seem to require belief in h, though since belief admits of degrees, a relatively low degree of belief may be directed towards it even in this provisional stage. But our acceptance-belief claim is properly directed towards terminal rather than provisional acceptance, and here a decision to cease testing does seem to require belief. In fact, we do justifiably ascribe to the scientific community the belief that the universe is expanding and that DNA has a helical structure. Some individual members may not believe this, but they are discounted in our group ascription. Of course, scientific belief is fallible. Terminal acceptance certainly does not require dogmatic certainty and rule out openness to admit error if conflicting evidence were to be discovered. But it does require belief, which all sides to the dispute must concede to admit of degrees and which may fall well short of certainty. If there were widespread disbelief in a hypothesis h, or simply absence of belief, we would justifiably conclude that h had not been accorded terminal acceptance, or perhaps that this acceptance had been revoked in the face of newly observed anomalies or inconsistency with recent theories that have been accorded terminal acceptance.

Judicial Verdicts.

Considerations of a different kind can be applied to a second argument employed by Cohen. He asks us to consider a member of a jury forced to decide on the guilt or innocence of a defendant. The member may accept the innocence of the accused, basing this on instructions by the judge to acquit if the evidence for guilt is not conclusive. Nevertheless, this member may believe the accused to be guilty, perhaps because of a hunch or prejudices against the defendant, or perhaps because the belief is based on evidence of which she was aware but was not permitted to be counted as evidence by the court. Acceptance as constrained by judicial rules thus would not in such situations require belief.[9]

My reply to this is to distinguish acceptance of a proposition as true or false from a judicial verdict of guilt or innocence. The verdict is a decision that must be made; the situation requires an either/or decision to either convict or acquit. But there is no requirement that the corresponding proposition be either accepted or rejected, as there is always the option to withhold both. The juror may decide in favor of the defendant, but at the same time refuse to accept the proposition that he is innocent, leaving this still an open question in light of the available evidence. To reach a verdict is to decide to apply the law to a particular case, bringing the case under the law. To accept as true, on the other hand, is to relate the proposition accepted to the evidence on which it is based. To be sure, practical requirements force decisions such as mine whether or not to carry an umbrella tomorrow. But this only requires acceptance of a probability proposition, say the 80% probability of it raining, while the judicial question is the dichotomous one of guilt or innocence.

This distinction between acceptance of a proposition and a judicial verdict applies to the juror forced to decide whether to accept certain evidence, say the testimony of a witness, as a part of the evidence on which the overall verdict is to be based. Rules of evidence may preclude using the testimony as a basis for the verdict. The testimony may not therefore be accepted for judicial purposes, but may be believed to be true by the juror. Other evidence may be legally admissible, but not believed. Here "accept" in this judicial context also takes on a special meaning that distinguishes it from propositional acceptance. To accept testimony into evidence has the narrow judicial sense of applying the law in the form of rules of evidence to the particular evidence before the court. This seems very different from accepting what is expressed in that testimony as true.

The arguments of Stalnaker and Cohen force us to specify contents of acceptance, and to make distinctions between types of acceptance and between acceptance and judicial decision. But despite these forced qualifications, they provide, as we have seen, no convincing reasons for questioning that acceptance necessitates belief. The fact that we have such a dispute, however, should serve as a warning of the vagueness of the concepts of acceptance and belief used in formulating it. As I noted above, our conclusions about beliefs seem dictated by our understanding of the uses of belief ascriptions. In an effort to clear up some confusions surrounding our topic, I want now to take a closer look at some of these uses.

IV. BELIEF ASCRIPTION AND REALISM

Our starting with Moore's Paradox and conditions for speech acts has the effect of formulating the issue before us as a question about what we say. Is it possible to refuse to ascribe a belief to someone who has assented to or asserted a certain proposition? To extend the thesis to acceptance retains Moore's framework by posing what we loosely term a "conceptual issue" about the use of belief ascriptions. But there are some who may object to this framework. To ascribe a belief to a person, they will say, is to ascribe some state to that person. Using the persistence contrast, it would seem that this state has usually an indefinite duration, and in this sense different from acceptance as a dateable event. The problem of relating acceptance and belief should be considered, it can be argued, not as one about how ascriptions are used, but as one about the relation between the event of acceptance and belief as a persistent state. The necessary relation between acceptance and belief is thus interpreted as one of causal necessity, one to be somehow determined on empirical grounds. Is it possible for the event to not be followed by the state? This psychological question now replaces our original one about language use, and in this form the contrasts between acceptance and belief that have been formulated seem to force their separation. Given these contrasts, why must (in the causal sense) the state follow the event?

The view that belief ascriptions describe some state of affairs can be labelled the "realist" view of beliefs. It has seductive appeal, and is easily introduced into discussions. As applied to beliefs, it seems to me mistaken, and its errors—unless we take precautions to guard against them—threaten to lead to a mistaken solution to our problem.

To recognize these errors requires examining the assumption that belief ascriptions have a purely descriptive use. In typical communicative situations belief ascriptions involve a speaker (or writer) S uttering (writing) the ascription, an audience A for which it is intended, and some person or persons X to whom the ascription is being applied. In special degenerate cases S and A may coincide, as when a person notes to himself or herself what another believes. One central use of an ascription, and the only one that seems to be acknowledged by realists, is to enable A to either predict or explain some action by X when accompanied by information about X's motivational state. Thus, someone might say to another, "X believes (thinks) that the gold is hidden in the cave" as a means of predicting that X will soon travel to the cave. Where "believe" is in the past tense, as in "X believed that the gold was hidden in the cave", explanation of a past action such as traveling is enabled, assuming the audience A is aware that X wanted the gold. This *predictive/explanatory use* of an ascription is, of course, very common. We inform others of the beliefs of a third party X for a purpose, and in real life this purpose is rarely to satisfy others' idle curiosity about X's state of mind. Prediction and explanation, in contrast to information about mental states per se, are useful to us, and belief ascriptions are one of our principal means to accomplish them. Whether prediction or explanation is successful does not depend on the truth or talsity of what X believes, as false beliefs are just as efficient predictors and explainers as true ones. How do we know that a given belief ascription is intended by the speaker for prediction or explanation? One test is to apply the familiar substitution criterion that distinguishes opaque from transparent belief ascriptions. It makes a difference in predicting or explaining a person's behavior what *that person* believes, and how we specify that belief may be relevant to the success of a prediction or explanation. Hence, substitution of coreferential terms is, in general, not permissible, and the ascription provides an opaque context. Let's assume that both the speaker S and audience A know that the agent X holds a mistaken belief about the gold and that S says, "X believes that the fool's gold is hidden in the cave". This ascription with "the fool's gold" substituted for "the gold" will enable neither prediction nor explanation of X's behavior in the way that "X believes that the gold is hidden in the cave" did. How the metal is described will determine what behavior is to be expected, given knowledge of X's wants. Even though A knows of the mistake, the descriptive phrase X would use if asked about his belief, or at least a literal translation of it in the speaker's language, must occur in S's belief ascription.

This predictive/explanatory use of "believe" was the focus of Ryle's analysis of belief ascriptions as dispositional statements in *The Concept of Mind*. Critical reaction to Ryle's analysis became the basis for the prevailing of functionalist realism that a belief ascription describes a complex fact inclusive of the subject X and environmental objects to which X is causally related in relevant ways.[10] Adequate formulations of this complex fact have been notoriously difficult to achieve. Despite this, the project would be worthwhile pursuing if in fact belief ascriptions have an exclusively descriptive function.

But they do not, for there is also a second use of belief ascriptions—what can be referred to as the *interpretive/evaluative use*—that was neither acknowledged by Ryle nor by his realist critics. Here the ascription is used in a way that enables the interpretation of what X asserts and the evaluation of X's belief as true or false, justified or unjustified. X says to S, "Your next door neighbor will retire next year". If S wants to determine whether what he has been told is true, he might say to A, "X believes that my next door neighbor will retire", thus inviting confirmation or correction. Clearly no prediction or explanation of X's behavior is at issue. The focus is on *what X* believes, its content, as a means of evaluating this content, not on the fact that a certain person happens to believe this. If X's belief is false, then we might inform him of the error, thus assuming that he can voluntarily change his belief by rejecting what he had previously believed. Failing this, in correcting him S and A can avoid sharing in the error.

Such evaluative ascriptions provide transparent contexts in which substitution is permitted. Suppose both the speaker S and his audience know that S's neighbor is named Smith, though X is unaware of this. Then the substitution of "Smith" for "my next door neighbor" is permissible, as it enables an identification of the referent by A that normally would lead to confirmation or correction of the belief. Suppose also that X mistakenly believes that Smith is S's next door neighbor and both S and A are aware of the error, knowing that Smith lives across the street. Then S may correct the error with a different description, saying "X believes that my neighbor across the street will retire". Again, the substitution has no effect on determining the truth or justification of the content of X's belief, and since this is at issue, it is permitted.[11]

Functional realists propose a way of accounting for this second use of "believe" that permits substitutions. A predictive/explanatory belief ascription is said to describe a physiological fact about the subject X that provides the explanatory basis for a behavioral disposition. For some writers this includes an encoded mental representation that is identified with the content of the belief being described. Where substitution is permitted, on the other hand, they claim we employ a belief ascription describing a state of affairs including the object or objects the belief is about. In this way beliefs have what are described as "dual components," a "narrow" or "internalist" one that is physiological, the other a "broader" or "externalist" one including functional states and environment, with belief ascriptions alternating between describing first one and then the other.[12]

But this contrived solution is designed only to preserve the realist theory. When we substitute "Smith" for "my next door neighbor" in ascribing a belief to X, it seems obvious we are not shifting from describing X to describing X plus the individual Smith, nor to any more inclusive fact.[13] The role of "Smith" is to direct our audience A's attention to an intended referent as a means of A identifying this referent and possibly evaluating the truth or falsity of what is believed. It is certainly not one of shifting to a more inclusive state of affairs. The substitution marks a different *purpose* for which the ascription is being used, not a different matter of fact.

If two very different types of facts were described by the two uses of the ascriptions, as the realists maintain, it would be a mystery why the single verb "believe" would be used for both. To avoid confusions we would expect that different expressions would have evolved within our language to describe the different states of affairs. Once we recognize that the contrast between the two uses is a pragmatic one, however, the presence of a single expression is readily understood, for the two pragmatic functions of prediction/explanation and interpretation/evaluation are in practice normally combined. If a predicted action is based on a false belief, then the speaker and audience may be able to correct the subject and avert some harm. Especially for an explanation of a past action, there may be no potential relation to the subject, and it is this aspect that reinforces the view that beliefs are often beyond human control. Smith is described as having believed that wet streets were safe for high speed driving, and this explains why he crashed into the embankment. It is too late to help poor Smith in the morgue. But ascribing the belief at least allows an audience to recognize the mistake and avert a similar harm. Belief ascriptions would never seem to have the purely descriptive use assigned to them by realists, and hence there is no persistent state of affairs they are about. Instead, they have the interactive, transactional function of evaluating what others believe and through relations to predicted and explained actions enabling us to influence future conduct.[14]

It should be noted that full understanding on the part of X of what he or she says is not necessary for belief ascriptions in either their predictive/explanatory or interpretive/evaluative uses. Michael Dummett offers the example of someone who hears from her mechanic that her car' s gasket needs fixing without understanding what a gasket is and then passes this information along by asserting "My gasket needs fixing". This represents, Dummett argues, an example of assertion without belief.[15] But the ascription "She believes her gasket needs fixing" might successfully predict that person's ordering a replacement, and if addressed to a knowledgeable audience could enable evaluation of the belief's truth or falsity, even though the person herself is incapable of such an evaluation. For both uses there is a true belief ascription, despite a deficiency of understanding on the part of the subject.

The duality of pragmatic functions for third person ascriptions seems to have parallels in the first person. As we saw in Part I, normally the prefix in "I believe that p" has the role of indicating that the content p is being put forward with hesitation or with qualifications. In this use the denial by another who says "No, you don't believe p" must represent a misunderstanding. If X were to say "I believe it will rain", the rejoinder "No, you don't believe it will" would miss the point of the original utterance, and nothing could possibly be cited in support of the denial. In contrast, X might intend to describe himself by saying "I don't believe there are ghosts". Another might have observed X's behavior in haunted house type of situations, and object with "No, you do believe there are ghosts", citing the behavioral grounds for the objection. In this case, there would have been a perfectly proper denial of a description proposed by X.[16] The appropriateness of a denial here should not tempt us into thinking that denial would be appropriate where "believe" has the different pragmatic function of an illocutionary force indicator.

V. WHY THERE CAN BE NO ACCEPTANCE
WITHOUT BELIEF

If the necessity of belief accompanying acceptance is not causal necessity, then what kind is it it? It is clearly not the necessity of logical entailment, as all who have discussed this problem agree. The only remaining plausible alternative seems to be that it is a pragmatic necessity dictated by the fact that when paired with assertion or assent "believe" is invariably taken as having an expressive or interpretive use. In the first person this takes the form of Moore's Paradox outlined in Part I. If "believe" were used descriptively, it would be possible for a person to say "There are no ghosts, but I believe they exist", as he might be asserting on the basis of evidence and then describing a belief over which he lacks control. But in combination with the assertion thatp, the expressive use of "believe" invariably overrides the descriptive. A similar overriding takes place in the third person. Someone might assert "The table is four feet long" and based on behavioral criteria at some later time we might describe this person as believing that the table is 3 feet 11 and 7/16 inches long. But this predictive/explanatory use of "believe" would again be overridden if the assertion were paired with the belief ascription, for where there is spatial/temporal proximity we regard the ascription as an interpretation of what has been asserted.[17]   Those insisting on detaching belief from acceptance might respond this way: "Look, we just saw X measuring the table with an accuracy to the sixteenth inch. Therefore, we know our exact belief ascription to be true, that is, we know it accurately describes X's psychological state." But this reply simply restates the realist assumption that the belief ascription has a purely descriptive use, an assumption I have been arguing to be false.

Similar considerations would seem to apply to those who might be tempted to follow Cohen in inferring from scientific practice (o the possibility of acceptance without belief. Suppose we find scientists publishing papers announcing that a certain hypothesis h has been conflrmed by experimental tests, agreeing with each other about these results, and   using h as an assumption in the testing of other hypotheses. Provided these scientists have open, inquiring minds, and are aware of the fallibility of all empirical propositions, Cohen suggests we should conclude that they don't really believe h to be true. But why should we say such a thing? The point of belief ascription is to interpret what a person says as a means of evaluating an possibly correcting it. In this case, we as observers would have absolutely no basis for evaluation and correction, and thus no grounds for a belief ascription inconsistent with what is assented to and asserted.

It seems to me, therefore, that we should conclude that there can be no acceptance without belief. The reasons to the contrary seem weak, and the realist assumptions underlying them are consistent with the use of belief ascriptions to both interpret and evaluate.

NOTES

[1] I am using the version of the paradox stated by Moore in *The Philosophy of G. E. Moore*, P. Schillp, ed. (New York: Tudor, 1952), pp. 542, 543. Here the example is "I went to the pictures last Tuesday, but I don't believe that I did". Not so obviously paradoxical is the form "I believe that p, but not p" stated by Moore in *The Philosophy of Bertrand Russell*, P. Schillp, ed. (New York: Tudor, 1952), p. 204, for it seems quite possible for someone to be aware of a belief they cannot rid themselves of, say a belief in ghosts, but realize as based on evidence that this belief is false. This person might then report the belief to us, but deny its truth. Moore usually states the paradox in the first person, but in the Russell volume he states this third person version: "A hearer who hears me say "He has not gone out", will, in general, assume that I don't believe that he has gone out" (p.204).

[2] Some might claim that community acceptance can be determined from assent or assertion by the proportion of individual members performing the speech acts or perhaps from assent by those in prestigious positions. Such issues are irrelevant to my claims, and I ignore them.

[3] Confusions about probabilities as objects of acceptance are responsible for Michael Bratman's argument for the possibility of acceptance without belief in his "Practical Reasoning and Acceptance in a Context," *Mind*, 101 (1992): 1-15. For criticisms of Bratman's view see my "Does Acceptance Entail Belief?", *American Philosophical Quarterly*, 31 (1994): 145-55.

[4] L. J. Cohen, *Essay on Belief and Acceptance* (Oxford: Clarendon Press,1992), Sec. 4.

[5] Ayer claims no distinction between acceptance and belief with regard to control; both the acceptance of the table as brown and the belief that it is are equally

determined effects of causes. See his "Reply to My Critics" in *The Philosophy of A. J. Ayer*, L. Hahn, ed. (Peru: Open Court, 1992), p. 126. But this ignores the fact that we criticize others for accepting prematurely and failing to gather sufficient evidence, a type of criticism that implies responsibility.

[6] Bernard Williams, "Deciding to Believe" in *Problems of the Self* (Cambridge: Cambridge University Press, 1972).

[7] See Searle, *The Rediscovery of the Mind* (Cambridge: MIT Press, 1992) and "The Connection Principle and the Ontology of the Unconscious: A Reply to Fodor and Lepore," *Philosophy and Phenomenological* Research, 54 (1994): 847-855).

[8] This point is stated both by Williams and by William Alston in "Concepts of Epistemic Justification," *Monist*, 68 (1985): 57-83.

[9] See Robert Stalnaker, *Inquiry* (Cambridge: MIT Press, 1984), p. 93.

[10] Essay on *Belief and Acceptance*, p. 88.

[11] Ibid., Sec. 20.

[12] The transition came by way of David Armstrong's central state materialism in *A Materialist Theory of Mind* (London: Routledge and Kegan Paul, 1968). All dispositions, reasoned Armstrong, have a categorical basis, and for beliefs these are neural states. Applying the identity theory, Armstrong concluded that a belief is a brain state. Functionalism arose through Putnam's thought experiment in "The Meaning of Meaning" in *Mind, Language and Reality* (Cambridge: Cambridge University Press, 1981) describing a situation in which there could be sameness of physiological states for two individuals but differences in belief ascriptions. Since the differences are traced to differing environments, functionalists conclude that a belief is a relational state between a person and objects to which the person is causally related.

[13] That the de re/de dicto distinction has no applicability to the question of substitution is noted by Tyler Burge in "Individualism and the Mental" in *Midwest Studies in Philosophy*, Vol IV, P. French et al., eds.

[14] That it is clearly false for normal uses of first person ascriptions has I think been successfully shown by Arthur Collins in *The Nature of Mental Things* (Notre Dame: University of Notre Dame Press, 1987), Ch. II. See also his " Reply to Commentators," *Philosophy and Phenomenological Research*, 54 (1994): 901-04. For me to say "I believe that p", argues Collins, cannot for me be simply a description of my internal state, since I am usually claiming by this sentence the correctness of p, and the question about the presence of an internal state is independent of p's correctness. The dual use theory of "believe" outlined here extends this reasoning to third person ascriptions.

[15] This example is used by Michael Dummett in arguing that there can be assertion without belief. See his *Origins of Analytical Philosophy* (London: Duckworth, 1993), p. 147.

[16] That denial can be appropriate is noted by David Rosenthal in "Thinking That One

Thinks" in M. Davies and G. Humphreys, eds., *Consciousness* (Oxford: Blackwell, 1993). In terms of this duality of pragmatic function in the first person we can explain the example of the mad patient given in Jean-Pierre Dupuy's *"Mauvaise Foi and Self-Deception"* in this volume. In effect, Dupuy's patient says, "I believe I'm mad, but I also believe I'm not mad", with the first occurrence of "believe" used descriptively of himself based on behavioral evidence and the second used expressively. Because the second use dominates, the person remains uncured.

[17] This requirement of temporal proximity was pointed out by Elie Zahar during discussions at the Caen Workshop.

WHY ACCEPTANCE THAT *P* DOES NOT ENTAIL THAT *P*

Jonathan Cohen
The Queen's College, Oxford

I have no objections to make to the distinction between different uses of belief-ascriptions that Professor Clarke draws in Part IV of his very stimulating paper. But I do not think that what he says there helps —as he claims it helps—to strengthen arguments against separating belief from acceptance. He points out in that part of his paper that an ascription of belief has two different possible uses: first, to provide a basis for predicting or explaining the behaviour of the alleged believer, and secondly, to provide a basis for evaluating the truth of the proposition that is said to be believed. But an analogous distinction could be drawn among ascriptions of acceptance, or indeed among ascriptions of indefinitely many other content-oriented mental attitudes, states, policies or acts (such as fearing, expecting, inferring, denying, assuming, intending, being glad, being sad, etc. etc.). So the issue about whether or not acceptance that *p* entails belief that *p* is left quite untouched by the fact that Clarke's distinction can be drawn in the case of belief-ascriptions. Clarke says that without having the right kind of belief-ascriptions available we should lack any basis for evaluating and correcting a scientist's state of mind. But my answer to him is that we can use instead the right kind of acceptance-ascription.

II

Clarke seems to think that, while "What is a belief?" is a straightforward question about how belief ascriptions are used in ordinary language, "we lack a basis for claims we might want to make about the propositional content of an acceptance, about exactly what a person is accepting as true". In particular, according to Clarke, we certainly don't want our usage of the expression "accepts that p", which we are taking as our object of philosophical analysis, to carry with it the suggestion of regret or resignation that it makes in ordinary speech. But Clarke is mistaken in claiming that some suggestion of regret or resignation is indeed always present. There is nothing self-contradictory, for example, in the ordinary-speech meaning of the sentence "X has always willingly accepted that p", as there should be if Clarke's claim were valid. Similarly in ordinary language the question "Do you accept that p?" does not ask you whether you are reluctant or resigned about the issue but only whether in appropriate contexts you do take it as one of your premises that p. Nor is it satisfactory to treat acceptance as, in Clarke's words , "a kind of internalized assertion or assent to sentence-tokens that may or may not be given public expression". When the term "assertion" is used in ordinary language (and not in philosophers' jargon) it implies, as "acceptance" does not, the declaration of a claim and some expectation of its recognition or some insistence on its validity. And it is no accident that, while "accept" introduces indirect discourse quite smoothly, as in sentences of the form "X accepting that p", the term "assent" does not. One assents to a proposal or a request rather than to a premiss, and there is something awkward about describing a person as assenting that something is the case.

Moreover, even if acceptance were an internalized form of assertion or assent (which I have given reasons for denying), it still would not follow, as Clarke claims, that "acceptance presupposes belief, just as do assent and assertion". For, if acceptance were an internalized act of assertion or assent, it would be as voluntary as any speech-act of assertion or assent, and then the belief that was presupposed by this act would have to be equally voluntary, whereas Clarke agrees that belief may be wholly involuntary. Indeed the point at issue here can be generalised. It holds good just so long as acceptance is held to be voluntary. For example, if a person ought to do act A, and doing A entails or presupposes doing A', then that person ought to do A'. For example, if you ought to return the book at noon on Tuesday, this presupposes you will have borrowed the book before then, and entails that you ought to return the book at noon on the day after Monday. It follows that if X accepts that *p*, and accepting that *p* entails or presupposes believing that *p*, then X ought to believe that *p*. But if belief is involuntary no-one can have a duty to believe anything, since no-one can have a duty to do what he is not free to do or to become what he is not free to become. Consequently accepting that *p* cannot entail or presuppose believing that *p*.

III

I have argued elsewhere (*An Essay on Belief and Acceptance*, pp.88-100) that the canonical attitude of a scientist, towards a proposition that he or she takes to express a physical law or some other kind of natural uniformity, is an attitude of acceptance, not belief. The scientist must be willing to go along with that proposition, and with anything that it is seen to entail, as a premiss—one among many—for his predictions, explanations, further research, etc. Moreover, even when we regard a physical law as a simplification or idealisation, we can use it as a premiss for predictive or explanatory calculation about the actual world, if we make appropriate allowances and corrections. So in this sense we can accept the law even when we do not believe it to be true, and in fact believe it to be false, of the actual world. This is not to deny that a scientist may often believe the proposition. Indeed perhaps in many cases there is not much harm done if in the end the scientist believes the proposition as well as accepting it. But in principle he should be more detached and thus readier to change his mind if new evidence or a better theory becomes available or is being actively sought. And certainly, if a scientist is content to have attained belief in his establishment of a physical law or natural uniformity, some factors might be influential in the black box of his sub-conscious mind that he would reject as influential or prejudicial if they came up for consideration before the tribunal of conscious acceptance.

The question arises, however, whether a scientist needs only to accept the experimental or observational data that he cites in support of accepting his favourite hypothesis, or needs also to believe them. Acceptance is certainly needed here because a report of the data is the premiss for the inductive justification of the theory. But, where an experimenter or observer is to be trusted as an original authority for the correctness of the report, he should also be taken to believe that the report is correct. Indeed, if acceptance alone were to operate here, or if belief were to operate here only because acceptance entails or presupposes it, then the content of scientific knowledge would be wholly a matter for human decision.

Clarke's response to all this is to admit that the personal beliefs of individual scientists are irrelevant to their practice of proposing and testing hypotheses. But he claims that, since it is acceptance by the scientific community as a whole, rather than by individual scientists, that I have in mind when I talk about acceptance, it should be the community's belief, not individual beliefs, that I have in mind when I talk about belief. And then, Clarke claims, with only *communal* attitudes at stake, there would be no ground for objecting to the thesis that acceptance entails belief. But my answer to Clarke is that in this context I do not talk about communal attitudes at all, only about individual ones. My claim is that an individual scientist's acceptance that p does not entail his or her believing that p, not that the scientific community's acceptance that p does not entail individual scientists' believing that p. So Clarke's argument against me here has no foundation. Moreover it would do his cause no good if he were to say: "Well, even if an individual's acceptance that p does not involve his believing that p, at least a scientific community's acceptance that p does involve its believing—i.e is normally accompanied by—that p". The truth is that what is at stake here is not the factual or causal linkage of attitudes but their conceptual entailment. So, even if there were a factual or causal linkage at the communal level, as Clarke suggests, this still would not serve to support the thesis that he defends.

IV

Another argument of Clarke's also revolves round a distinction between different kinds of acceptance. Provisional acceptance of a hypothesis *h*, he says, "is a decision to consider *h* for further testing, to include *h* among those hypotheses that experimental data is to decide between". And provisional acceptance of *h* obviously does not require belief in *h*, except perhaps at some very low level of belief. But the entailment thesis, Clarke claims, is about terminal, not provisional, acceptance and "a decision to cease testing," he says, "does seem to require belief", even though attainment of such belief does not rule out openness to the admission of error if conflicting evidence is discovered. Unfortunately, however, many different factors may influence a scientist's decision to cease testing a particular hypothesis. For example, the scientist's grant may run out, or he may get ill, or he may wish to switch to a more exciting line of research, or another scientist may have anticipated him, etc. So, *pace* Clarke, even terminal acceptance does not presuppose belief, while what he calls "provisional acceptance, is more like assuming or hypothesising than it is like acceptance.

V

Clarke also argues (pp. 13-14) that "if there is widespread disbelief in a hypothesis *h*, or simply absence of belief in *h*, we would justifiably conclude that *h* had not been accorded terminal acceptance, or perhaps that this acceptance had been revoked in the face of newly observed anomalies." But we have to ask here whether this allegedly justifiable conclusion is to be understood as a factually or conceptually based inference. As a factual inference it might very well be true in a particular situation: that is, with so few scientists holding the relevant belief we might well infer that few or none had terminally accepted it. But, because this inference is a factual one, it gives no support to the thesis that acceptance entails belief or to the thesis that disbelief, or the absence of belief, *entails* non-acceptance. And, if we understand the inference in question as being one that purports to express a conceptual linkage which it must do if it is to support the entailment thesis—then the inference is clearly invalid. It is conceptually possible, for example, however unlikely, that first, though there is actually widespread disbelief in *h*, nevertheless each member of the community believes all the other members to believe in *h*, and secondly, at the same time, that influenced by this there is in fact widespread terminal acceptance of *h*. So we have any number of possible cases of acceptance without belief, and the entailment thesis collapses.

VI

Another objection to the entailment thesis arises from what happens in certain legal systems. We need sometimes to be able to describe how in a court of criminal law members of a jury, or other fact-finders, may be in a situation in which they accept or ought to accept a proposition about the defendant but nevertheless do not believe it. For example, it may be a rule of law in their legal system that anyone who, according to valid testimony, has been found in possession of a narcotic substance without good excuse, should be deemed to have had guilty knowledge of this possession (and thus to have committed a felony). So in a particular case the jurors may accept, as instructed by the judge, that the defendant had such knowledge even though they do not in fact believe that he had. Or the advantage of the distinction may lie in the other direction. Perhaps the jurors accept that the defendant did not commit the crime of which he is accused, because the only evidence against him comes from the uncorroborated testimony of a child witness, whereas it is a rule of law that a child's testimony always requires corroboration. In such a case the jurors may be described as accepting but perhaps not believing that the defendant did not do what he is accused of doing.

Clarke's response to this line of argument distinguish acceptance of a proposition as true or false from a judicial verdict of guilt or innocence... To reach a verdict is to decide to apply the law to a particular case, bringing the case under the law. To accept as true, on the other hand, is to relate the proposition accepted to the evidence on which it is based'. But accepting that *p*, as I define it (*An Essay on Belief and Acceptance*, p.4), is to have or adopt a policy of deeming, positing or postulating that *p*—i.e. of including that proposition or rule among one's premises for deciding what to do or think in a particular context, whether or not one feels it to be true that *p*. So my thesis is not refutable by Clarke's argument that '"accept" in this judicial context... takes on a special meaning that distinguishes it from propositional acceptance'. Any juror who accepts, in my general sense, that the defendant or innocent, as the case may be, is in effect laying down a premiss in his mind from which, along with other premises, he can infer what to say when asked to declare his verdict. So it would be wrong to identify the verdict that with what is accepted—in some specially restricted sense when a juror accepts that *p*. A juror or jury *gives* a verdict and does not *accept* it. And this is not a trivial point, because the utterance of the verdict is a quite different kind of act from that of laying down the premises on which the verdict is based, not least because giving a verdict (unless we are using the term metaphorically) is a public speech-act, while accepting a proposition can be a private mental act.

Of course, accepting that X was a drug-dealer within the context of courtroom reasoning about matters of fact in A's criminal trial is different from accepting that A was a drug-dealer within the context of a professional historian's or detective's reasoning about A's mode of livelihood. But even the latter kind of acceptance, backed by ideals of accuracy in factfinding, does not entail believing that A was a drug-dealer. For you may have to accept, as a responsible historian or detective looking at all the evidence, that your old and dear friend X was a drug-dealer, while you still have a very strong conviction that he was not. There may be a deep, Proustian conflict here between the outcome (viz. acceptance that *p*) of your careful and deliberate analysis of the evidence and the outcome (viz. belief that not-*p*) of your generous and affectionate sympathy. But it does not follow, because of the mental anguish caused by the clash of these two states of mind, that their combination is conceptually impossible. And, if acceptance that *p* is thus in principle combinable with belief that not-*p*, it is clear that acceptance that *p* is in principle combinable with the absence of belief that *p*: acceptance does not entail belief.

Clarke's strategy here, when he is dealing with acceptance in courtroom reasoning, is the same as when he is dealing with acceptance in scientists' reasoning. In both types of context he tries to show that we need to distinguish between what he calls the ordinary language sense of the term "acceptance" and some other, philosopher's sense, so that the apparent occurrence of cases of acceptance without belief may be explained away by being attributed to some special sense of the term while in the ordinary-language sense of the term "acceptance" is seen always to entail or presuppose belief. Thus in courtroom reasoning giving the verdict that *p* is to be distinguished from accepting that *p*, and in scientists' reasoning provisional acceptance that *p* is to be distinguished from terminal acceptance that *p* and an individual scientist's acceptance that *p* is to be distinguished from a scientific community's acceptance that *p*.

But in fact it would not affect the substance of my point if the current ordinary-language use of the term "acceptance" were different from that which I am assuming it to be. What matters is that in order to be able to describe our intellectual activities and attitudes adequately we need to characterise a concept that has the same presuppositions and entailments as those which I have attributed to the term "acceptance", and another concept which has the same presuppositions and entailments as those which I have attributed to the term "belief". When we have such concepts we are in a position to do justice to the complexities of jurists' or scientists' reasoning: when we lack them we are not. And it is not only to analyse *those* types of reasoning for which we need this pair of concepts. We need the same pair of concepts in order to resolve quite a number of other analytical issues. For example, there are relevant issues about the purposes of animals, infants and adults, about the purposes of organizations and artefacts, about credal feelings (feelings of disbelief, suspicion, doubt, surprise, expectation, confidence, conviction, certainty, etc.), about the foundations of subjective probability, about the implications of intentions, about self-deception, about what Aristotle called *akrasia*, and so on. The ability to deal helpfully with those other issues is also part of the argument for the distinction that I have drawn in terms of the difference between belief and acceptance (*An Essay on Belief and Acceptance, passim*), but I can't discuss those issues here.

MOORE'S PARADOX

Laurence Goldstein
University of Hong Kong

I. MISSIONARY ZEAL

There is no doubt that the distinction drawn by Jonathan Cohen between the concepts of belief and acceptance is an important one.[1] Certain long-standing philosophical problems seem remarkably more tractable once this conceptual clarification has been achieved, and I should go so far as to say that Cohen's book is testimony to, and a great advertisement for, the utility of analytical philosophy. For example, the phenomenon of self-deceit (a real phenomenon rather than a philosophical contrivance) is extremely curious and recalcitrant both philosophically and psychologically. But, once we see, with Cohen, how a belief that p can be put on the back burner while at the same time a person is accepting not-p, the matter of self-deceit becomes vastly clearer (p.141 ff.). Typically, a person who plays the stock market believes, deep down, that the only person likely to win is the stockbroker, yet, driven by greed, accepts the stockbroker's forecast that he, the punter, will make stupendous financial gains. And one could use Cohen as a guide to good parenting: accept what your child says, even though you don't believe a word of it. Again, the use that Cohen makes of his distinction to mollify both sides of the modern dispute between symbolic and connectionist modellers of the mind (p.53ff.) is, to my mind, greatly illuminating. And yet.......

When Plato discovered the Forms, he became enamoured of them, and we find them figuring in his account of all manner of things, including number, love, how best to run a state, the relation of belief to knowledge and the metaphysically basic structure of the universe. Now Cohen is likewise excited by his discovery and he wants to bring it to bear on a tremendously wide range of issues, including the structure of scientific knowledge, subjective probability and judicial fact-finding (p.3). But remember what happened to Plato's theory. Nowadays some people are still attracted to the idea that mathematics is about relations between Forms, but most of the other applications of the doctrine do not attract many buyers. My view is that Cohen, too, has got over-excited, and I want to consider one case, that of Moore's Paradox, where the belief/acceptance distinction does not do the work he claims it does.

II. COHEN ON MOORE

Let me say, straight away, what I don't like about Cohen's solution to Moore's Paradox. Recall that this paradox concerns anomalous utterances, with forms such as

i. p, but I don't believe that p.

ii. Not-p, but I believe that p

Clearly, any decent solution is going to have to tell us something about what belief is, and I believe that some of what Cohen tells us is wrong. Second, Cohen, like almost everyone else who writes about this subject, accepts and believes that, when someone says

It is raining, but I do not believe that it is raining

"the two clauses of such an utterance are not logical contradictories of one another, since both could well be true" (p.68). I disagree. Third, having constructed a case in which the utterance of a sentence of the form "p, but I don't believe p" might be quite appropriate—a case in which the utterance of the first "p" indicates acceptance rather than belief—Cohen goes on, via the fallacy of hasty generalization, to conclude that the Mooronic sentences "cannot be quite as odd or anomalous as most philosophers who have discussed them have supposed" (p.72). Fourth, after proceeding to construct what he takes to be a strengthened version of Moore's Paradox, namely

It is raining but I neither accept nor believe that it is raining (p.73),

Cohen stops short, without so much as hinting at a solution of this version of the problem. This is extremely frustrating. All the interesting work on the Liar paradox has, in recent years, focused on strengthened versions, for if a purported solution doesn't eliminate a new strain, then clearly it has not got to the nub of the problem. After reaching the point in Cohen's book where the strengthened Moore appears, I read on avidly, but in vain; Cohen interrupts his discussion at this point, and never returns to the paradox. Just as the Liar is a testing ground for theories of truth so, I believe, its capacity to handle Moore's paradox is a test of the adequacy of a theory of belief, so this is a bad time for Cohen to pull out of the discussion.

III.   APRIL IN PARIS

In what follows, I shall return to these remarks about Cohen in the course of advocating a different line on the Moore paradox. I say "line", but it's not a straight one, more of a circuitous path. My point of departure is Paris.

When I flew into Paris from Hong Kong a couple of days ago, and was about to leave the airport, a Chinese woman, who looked lost, came up to me and, in perfect English, asked me the way to Tower Bridge. Naturally, I thought that she meant the Eiffel Tower, so I took her to the airport bus, we both got on and were soon speeding towards the centre of town. We chatted. Her name was Mei-Li and this was her first trip outside China; she knew virtually nothing about Europe. I gathered from her that she had learned spoken English but had never learned to write the language; in fact she did not even recognize the letters of the alphabet. As we passed through the outer suburbs, she became animated, and kept pointing out of the window exclaiming "London is beautiful". This struck me as curious but I didn't disabuse her, already feeling rather uneasy at the thought that it really was Tower Bridge she was after, and that I had led her astray. Unfortunately, this turned out to be the case. Further conversation revealed that she had booked a ticket from Beijing to London and thought that it was London that we were now driving through. But I was beginning to enjoy her company so, for the rest of the day, I showed her the sights of Paris—Notre Dame, Montmartre, the Louvre... —and enjoyed her gasps of pleasure and delight. It was especially amusing to hear her exclaim "London is so beautiful", so I just nodded in agreement. "What about Tower Bridge?" she eventually asked. "Strange, they must have sold it to the state of Arizona", I replied.

In recent discussions of belief-ascription, there seems to be little consensus about how, in various contrived cases, the beliefs of a believer are to be characterized. The above story of Mei-Li (which I told as fact, but which, in fact, is fantasy) is different in that nobody (in their right mind) would deny that Mei-Li believes that Paris is beautiful and that a significant part of our evidence for thinking she believes Paris beautiful is her declarations "London is beautiful". About London, however, she had not had the opportunity to form an opinion.

When I am engaged in conversation, it is my responsibility to use words in a way which, to the best of my knowledge, is correct, and I am aware that my hearer will normally interpret my words on the assumption that I am so using them. So when I (a Londoner, as it happens) use the word "London", my audience will take me to be referring to London. Hence, unless I wish to tell a lie, I shall refrain from saying "Mei-Li believes that London is beautiful". In a moment of absent-mindedness, my thoughts drift to London (the real London), in particular to the rather shabby area in which I grew up. Wistfully, I say to Mei-Li "London is not a beautiful place" but, with some vigour, she disagrees, and retorts "Well, that's your opinion; I believe that London is beautiful". Yet Mei-Li's meagre fund of beliefs about London did not increase at all in the course of our day together, although she discovered a great deal about the place she has been calling "London", namely Paris. Her words are not to be taken "at face value" as an indicator of what she believes. We could say, without implying moral condemnation, that she is not to be taken at her word.[2]

When reporting the speech of another person to a third, we are required by the Gricean conversational maxims to say what's needed in order not to mislead our hearer. Now, suppose that the American ambassador to Moscow believes that a member of his staff is spying for the Russians. The ambassador points the man out to me and asks me to investigate. I track the suspect and follow him into a Turkish bath, where, in the steam room, I observe him remove what appears to be a mole on his butt, but which must really be a microdot, and hand it to a shifty looking attendant, who gives him a microdot in return which the suspect puts back in the same place. Intrigued, I say to the person standing beside me "The American ambassador believes that the guy over there with a mole on his butt is a spy". Now obviously this description of the mole with the mole is not one under which the American ambassador knows the suspect.[3] In reporting a person's belief, the default value might be to report that belief in words very similar to those which the person himself would use to express the belief—this may be a Grice-like injunction[4]—but, as we have seen, it is over-ridden when to use those words would be to mislead or under-inform our hearer. This is why, in telling you about Mei-li, I used the word "Paris" to retail her belief, even though she herself never mentioned the word "Paris" and may not even know of its existence.

Mei-Li thinks that Paris is beautiful. This is how I describe what she thinks. But Mei-Li herself gives expression to this belief when she says "London is beautiful". Her words, we might say, are the product of the two beliefs that Paris is beautiful and that the name of Paris is "London". There is, then, a mismatch between what she thinks and what she says. The complexity of her thought is masked by the simplicity of her words. This does not imply that she is not first-person-authoritative about what she thinks; it just means that somebody who does not know her situation cannot read off her thoughts from her words. We could conclude either that her thoughts are verbal, but that the mental words in which they are couched do not match the words she utters, or that her thoughts are non-verbal. The

first option is implausible, so it is, no doubt, the one that J. Fodor
would espouse. Cohen, rightly in my view, insists that while with
acceptance there is "an a priori conceptual requirement that what is
under consideration is tied to some type of linguistic formulation"
(p.12), the same is not true of belief. In Cohen's book, the objects of
beliefs are propositions, so propositions are non-linguistic—a position
that Professor Stalnaker and others have defended, as have I.[5]

IV. THOUSANDS OF WAYS TO DO IT WITH WORDS

It is one thing, however, to agree with part of an author's view of
propositions, but quite another to go along with the argument that he
uses to support it. The argument, as I have sketched it above, starts
from a conception of the nature of belief. Cohen contends that we have
"credal feelings" associated with "this or that proposition that somehow
comes before our mind" (p.11), that "beliefs ... actually occur in
people's minds" (p.79). Cohen's position here seems to be a Cartesian
one.[6] We may need the notion of a proposition in order to understand
the concept of belief, but we should hope for something clearer than the
image of a believer reading or feeling propositions floating around in
his mind. What we need is a general framework for understanding the
relationships between an agent's thoughts and beliefs, his statements
and the propositions he expresses.
    Such a framework can be extrapolated from what many people will
think is a most unlikely source: J. L. Austin's now neglected *How to do
things with Words*. Towards the end of that book, Austin remarks:
"The total speech act in the total speech situation is the only actual
phenomenon which, in the last resort, we are engaged in elucidating"[7].
Up to that point he had been elucidating such acts as the phonetic,
phatic and rhetic which are, in some sense "less than" the total speech
act. Austin's prescription for dissecting the total speech act can be
developed into a theory that clears away a mountain of problems that
has beset philosophy for centuries. The basic idea is that the total
speech act in the total speech situation is an enormously complex
phenomenon and, for various theoretical purposes, we isolate or

abstract certain features.[8] A normal speech act consists of the making of sounds where these are the sounds of words which are part of a language with its particular vocabulary and grammar. The words are used with intention, for example, we intend to mean something by them; we intend them to have an effect on our audience; the words are uttered in particular surroundings both physical and social. Now, if we ignore all of these features—the surroundings, the intentions, the grammar etc.—and consider just the sound made by the speaker (as a studio sound technician does), then we are considering the phonetic act. Likewise, other acts or, as I prefer to call them, aspects, are identified according to the feature or set of features focused upon. So, for example, a proposition, in one sense of that notion, is the result of taking the total speech act, ignoring sound and language which are irrelevant to the identity of propositions, while focusing on features relating to the speaker's meaning and to the surroundings in which the utterance is made. (The identity of the proposition expressed in an utterance "I am anxious" will depend on who the speaker is; another utterance of the same type by a different person would be the expression of a different proposition.)[9] To take one of Austin's own examples, the criteria of identity for the phatic act are sound and grammar, with other features such as intentions and context ignored. So if I read out of my grammar book "La plume de ma tante est dans le bureau de mon oncle", it would be not just a mistake, but a category mistake for you to ask me "What pen do you mean?" Reference and meaning are not the sorts of things that phatic acts possess.

What we have, then, is the apparatus for distinguishing thousands of aspects of the speech act (for n features, there will be $(2^n - 1)$ aspects, i.e. if there are 12 prominent features of a speech act, there are close to 5,000 aspects, so Austin named only a tiny fraction of the total)[10] and hence, of course, for accounting for the disputes that have arisen from philosophers talking at cross-purposes: with so many closely related notions, it is no wonder that such confusions have arisen.[11] Consider, for example, the doctrine of externalism. Putnam and other externalists insist that meanings are not in the head; opponents say that they must be, and talk of "narrow content". The resolution is simple: there are two notions of meaning involved here.

The criteria of identity for one include the surroundings in which the speech act occurs; meaning, in this sense, is a function of the speaker or believer and his environment; the criteria of identity for the other exclude the external environment. Small wonder that, on the first conception, it will matter to identifying the meaning of what a speaker says whether he says it on Earth or on Twin-Earth.

V. BELIEF AND THE VERBAL EXPRESSION OF BELIEF

According to a venerable tradition, thoughts just are unvoiced assertions. This conception of a thought is entirely legitimate. In terms of our Austinian theory, a thought, in this sense, is simply an act of speech minus the sound (where it is the theoretician's mind that does the minusing) (just as the phonetic act is the result of minusing from a speech act everything except the sound).[12] Thoughts so conceived clearly are linguistic creatures and seem pretty close to what Cohen calls an acceptance, "an interiorization of the corresponding speech-act" (p.79). If thinking is a matter of having thoughts of this kind, then we could, with Plato, regard thinking as the soul's inner dialogue with itself. Conversely, an assertion would be regarded as a thought-out-loud. Clearly, if this were the only legitimate conception of thought, then we should have to say that Mei-Li was really thinking about London, and that Kripke's Pierre, who makes contradictory assertions, is inconsistent in his thinking, despite being an excellent logician. We don't want to say these things, so we need some way to maintain that their thinking is coherent, even though their thoughts (the linguistic kind described above) are patently false (Mei-Li) or inconsistent (Pierre). There is an obvious way to do so: deny that thinking is the having of such thoughts.

It is customary to distinguish between the act of thinking—a burst of neuronal pandemonium—and what is thought, also termed the content of such an act. When we report our, or someone else's thinking we, perforce, use language to do so. Language is the vehicle for making manifest what a person is currently thinking. But to conclude that the thinking is itself linguistic (e.g. that a stream of thinking comes in sentence-like chunks) is to transfer properties of the vehicle of expression onto what it is that is being expressed—an unwarranted move.[13] I may report what a person is thinking by using a sentence, but the report must not be confused with what is reported. When assessing the rationality of Mei-Li or Pierre, it is their thinking in which we are interested, and we may need to discount some of the linguistic clothing in which that thinking is dressed when it is, in Clifford Hooker's phrase, "fed to the tongue". Labov did some well known work showing how the linguistic deficit of a minority group was no indication of an underlying reasoning deficit.[14] And Einstein's thinking, according to Einstein, was not done in language.[15] The idea that thinking is non-linguistic seems pretty well established outside of philosophy.

We have already seen that beliefs are non-linguistic, so it now appears that we have an appropriate notion for the analysis of belief: I propose that to believe that p is to have the settled disposition to think that p. This is, of course vastly different from having a disposition to think "p". Mei-Li thinks that Paris is pretty, although the sentence "Paris is pretty" never crosses her lips or her mind. Our analysis is, for example, compatible with adverbialism which claims that to think that p is to think p-ly, where there is no "object" of thought.[16] Cohen doesn't seem uncomfortable with the idea that to believe is non-metaphorically to feel, but somehow it feels all wrong to me. The above account maintains the proper distance between cognition and sensation, and survives all the caveats and glosses that Cohen lists at the beginning of his essay.

VI. MOORONIC ANIMADVERSIONS

When I ascribe a belief to you, I do so on the basis of evidence, commonly the evidence of what you say. So my ascription is a result of an inference as to your disposition to think that p. When I ascribe to myself a belief that I once held, this may, again, be based on evidence, evidence of what I once wrote, or on my memory of views I once held. But when, here and now, I say "I believe..." I am not drawing on evidence, nor inferring anything about my own dispositions, I am expressing a belief, not reporting one. If to say, "I believe that it is raining" is to express the belief that it is raining, then, from a logical point of view, it cannot be so different from my assertion "It is raining" with which I normally express that belief. There will be a rhetorical difference: the prefix "I believe" may indicate a certain hesitancy or guardedness on my part; in other conversational contexts it may indicate the opposite—complete confidence in my claim. Such indeed was Mei-Li's use of her "I believe that London is beautiful" in response to my expression of the contrary view. But, from a logical point of view, the utterances "p" and "I believe that p" are on a par.[17] I contradict myself if I say "I believe that p" but then immediately follow up by saying "But p is not the case", whereas there's no contradiction in my saying "I believed p" and then adding "But it's just not the case that ". So the "logic" of "I believe ..." is different from that of "He believes ..." or of "I believed ..." This observation is the basis of Wittgenstein's solution to Moore's paradox, a solution which I believe to be almost exactly right.[18] The "logic" alluded to here is the logic of language-in-use, the study of real linguistic behaviour, not of "some non-spatial, non-temporal phantasm".[19]   As Strawson emphasized, it is the uses of sentences that have truth value, not the sentences themselves.[20] If we step away from the Mooronic sentence "It is raining, but I do not believe that it is raining" and comment on it, then the circumstances described in the sentence certainly could co-exist—me not believing that it's raining when in fact it is. But under those circumstances, I certainly would not candidly assert that it is raining, I would not use the Mooronic sentence there-then, nor would any other sane person similarly situated. There is a rather interesting counterpart to this phenomenon in the strengthened Liar paradox. Someone utters

    S: S is not true

I, wise to the ways of paradox, see that to assert either that this is true or that it is false is going to lead me to the opposite conclusion, so I say that S is neither true nor false. But, if it's neither true nor false then a fortiori, it is not true, so I say "S is not true", and count this other-referring token as true, while still content to count the previous equiform self-referring token as truth-valueless. I can use the second token to express a true reflection on the first.[21]

"I believe that *p*" is an expression (Ausserung) of belief, not a description of one. Similarly, a speaker who says "I don't believe that *p*" is denying that *p* or is expressing his refusal to accept the proposition. Thus a speaker who says "*p*, but I don't believe that *p*" is, or purports to be, simultaneously putting a proposition forward and taking it back. So what is absurd about a Mooronic utterance is just what is absurd about the utterance of a straight contradiction. The Mooronic utterance is not a formal contradiction in that it is not of the form "*p* and not-*p*", but, in making such an utterance, a speaker is contradicting (speaking against) himself and is thus acting absurdly. That is why Wittgenstein says, in his letter to Moore immediately after Moore's talk to the Moral Sciences Club, "... this just shows that logic isn't as simple as logicians think it is. In particular: that contradiction isn't the unique thing people think it is. It isn't the only logically inadmissible form.".

Wittgenstein has several arguments in favour of his solution to the Moore paradox. His simplest is one we have already made use of. Consider the following dialogue:

A: I believe it's raining

B: I don't believe so.

If each of these statements were about its utterer or his mind, then the speakers would not be contradicting each other; and clearly they are[22] —perhaps even more clearly were B to say "I believe that it's not raining". Of course, my statement "I believe that it is raining" throws light on my state of mind, but so does my statement (i.e. my use of the sentence) "It is raining".[23] It does not follow that either statement is a report or description of my inner state.

I can mistrust my own senses, but not my own belief. While it may be appropriate to say "He seems to believe ...", there is not normally the occasion to say "I seem to believe ..."[24]. So, in Wittgenstein's terms, the "grammar" or "logic" of the verb "believe" is different from that of, say, "write" or "chew".[25] In saying "I chew", I am describing the same sort of activity (or disposition, in the case of tobacco) that I describe by saying "He chews". The word "wish" is more similar, in its first person present singular use, to "believe" than to "chew". If I say "I wish you'd go away", I'm not describing my inner state, but inviting you to disappear.[26] It is certainly possible for me to wish you to go away, while encouraging you to stay—maybe you're a pain in the neck, but I fear that, if I'm not nice to you, you'll go off and do serious damage to yourself or others—but that in no way detracts from the absurdity of my saying to you "I wish that you'd go away, but please stay". Here the manouevre of, as I called it, "stepping away" from the utterance and describing circumstances in which both clauses could be true or sincere is transparently misleading. It is obvious, in this case, that giving voice to them would subvert my good intentions.

Wittgenstein's solution to Moore's paradox could be called a "pragmatic" one. It starts by observing that, in actual use, the first person singular present tense of the verb "to believe" does work different from what it does in all other inflexions. One clear proof of this is that you can change a Mooronic to a non-Mooronic assertion simply by changing the tense or person of the verb. The job done by my utterance of "I believe that p" is roughly that done by my simple assertion `$p$'. Hence the absurdity of a Mooronic assertion of the form `Not-p, but I believe that p' is equal to the absurdity of my giving expression to a contradictory thought by uttering a contradiction. This is a very simple solution, but a very powerful one. I have elsewhere argued that it allows us to escape the Hangman (the Surprise Examination) as well as Gregory Kavka's toxin puzzle.[27]

VII. COHEN'S OBJECTIONS

Cohen has two objections to this sort of solution. The first he made to me several years ago in conversation, and maybe he would not now be inclined to raise it. The objection derives from the Frege-Geach point that "a proposition may occur in discourse now asserted, now unasserted, and yet be recognizably the same proposition".[28] If utterances of the form "I believe that *p*" are expressions of belief—assertions—then we could not account for how they feature unasserted in, say, the antecedents of conditionals.

This objection, it seems to me, rests on the "phantasm" picture of language mentioned earlier. We really have to disabuse ourselves of the notion that a bit of language serves the same function in whatever context it occurs. As we have seen, "believes" works differently in "He believes" and in "I believe"; and it works differently in "I believe" and in "If I believe". In fact, it is in terms of the latter difference that Wittgenstein sets up the problem, both in his letter to Moore, and in the Philosophical Investigations. Respectively:

> It makes sense to say "Let's suppose: *p* is the case and I don't believe that *p* is the case", whereas it makes no sense to assert "*p* is the case and I don't believe that *p* is the case"

Moore's paradox can be put like this: the expression "I believe that this is the case" is used like the assertion "This is the case"; and yet the hypothesis that I believe this is the case is not used like the hypothesis that this is the case.[29]

Cohen's second complaint is that, in some circumstances, saying something does not imply belief in that thing (p.69), so in such circumstances, there is nothing particularly untoward in saying that thing and adding that you don't believe it.

Again, this objection would not worry Wittgenstein. Only a "craving for generality" of the sort he disdains would lead one to hold that the behaviour of "I believe" is the same in all circumstances.[30] Cohen gives an example in which the use of "I believe" implies acceptance and not belief—but Wittgenstein himself gives several such examples, such as that of the announcer at the train station who announces that a train is on schedule, but—perhaps groundlessly—is convinced that it won't arrive, and who therefore says "Train No. ... will arrive at ... o'clock. Personally I don't believe it".[31] Or a Mooronic utterance can be made because of some pathology, such as a split personality. In a case like that, Wittgenstein says that the speaker "no

longer play[s] the ordinary language-game, but some different one".[32]
There are these cases where Mooronic assertions are apt, just as there
are instances where the utterance of a contradiction is intelligible. In
such cases there is some story to be told, against which background an
utterance which, when viewed "cold" or context-less looks odd, makes
perfectly good sense. Applied linguists who advocate the
"communicative approach" to language learning are fond of making
this point. If I may be allowed a personal example: my wife once said
to me "She's up with her ear". In the context in which she used these
words (which I won't bore the reader by describing) they gave me
information I needed to know.

These examples of Mooronic assertions in which there is some
story to be told are the easy cases, where the utterances are
non-paradoxical. The difficult examples are those in which a speaker
makes an assertion of the form "I believe p, but not-p" when we have
not been given any surroundings against which that utterance can be
viewed as non-absurd. In such cases the unacceptability of the
utterance is, we have argued, just the unacceptability of a contradictory
utterance. If you say to me, in all seriousness "Today is Tuesday and
it isn't", I'll just shrug my shoulders, and call the asylum.

VIII.   THIS IS THE CONCLUSION.   NO, IT ISN'T.

The solution to Moore's paradox just offered rests on the
assumption that we cannot believe contradictions and that it is,
generally, absurd to make Mooronic assertions. The first of these
assumptions could be challenged, in light of the fact that one possible
answer to Kripke's Pierre puzzle is that Pierre (and we) do have
contradictory beliefs. It would need another paper to meet that
challenge.[33] The second assumption too might give cause for concern
not only because of Cohen's arguments but because, in a recent paper,
Mark Crimmins has attempted to show that it would be quite natural
sometimes to say "I falsely believe that p", which is just a shrunken
version of a Mooronic assertion. Wittgenstein, by contrast, says "If

there were a verb meaning 'to believe falsely' it would not have any significant first person present indicative."[34]

I cannot go into the matter here, but I think that both the Kripke puzzle and the Crimmins rest on a fallacy that I have dubbed "the fallacy of the simple question".[35] Here is Crimmins' example: An intelligent and trusted friend informs me that, for some years, he has switched between two guises (like Batman/Bruce Wayne), and that whenever I encounter him, or even just think of him under the other guise (he persists in giving me no clue as to what that guise is) I think he's an idiot. I believe what he tells me, so I say to him "O.K., I falsely believe that you are an idiot". My response is that just as we should refuse to answer Kripke's simple question "Does Pierre or does he not like London" after we have given a full account of Pierre's likes and dislikes, so too, having told Bat-Bruce when we think he's an idiot and when not, we are right not to allow ourselves to be drawn into answering his simple question "Yes, but tell me straight, do you or don't you believe that I'm an idiot". But obviously this is not the end of that.

IX. RESPONSE TO STALNAKER

Robert Stalnaker, in his useful commentary (this volume) pushes the discussion in a number of interesting directions. One of his points against me is undoubtedly correct and I shall come to this in a short while. First, though, I'll take another glance at the question of propositional attitudes, which Professor Stalnaker charmingly describes as scenery on the route to our main concerns. The debate, recall, centred on how we should best characterize the beliefs of Mei-Li who was unfortunate enough to have had me as an escort on her unplanned trip to Paris (She thought that she'd arrived at her destination, London.) Professor Stalnaker agrees that it would be correct to say that Mei-Li believes that Paris is beautiful. If you asked her why she so liked the town she was in, she might well reply "Mainly because of that big cathedral, Notre Dame, in the middle of the Seine". But, according to Professor Stalnaker (and I feel a strong pull to say so as well), Mei-Li believes that Notre Dame is in London. Clearly something strange is going on.

Let's try some intuition-pumping. Suppose, at a conference in Caen, I go up to Professor Stalnaker, start talking to him in Cantonese, offer him a lift on my motorbike from the conference hall to his hotel, and suggest that we all go eat tonight at the Tsing Tao restaurant on Yee Wo Street. Pascal Engel, the organizer of the conference, overhears all this; he knows that my bike is in Hong Kong and so, nervous, he says to a friend "Tiens, Laurence thinks he's now in Hong Kong". Now, we don't have such doubts about Mei-Li. She's not crazy, like Laurence. She believes the evidence of her own eyes, and so thinks that the town she is in is the one containing Notre Dame, the Louvre, and those peculiar little structures on the pavement into which men disappear for a minute or two. That town is Paris—it's just that Mei-Li thinks that the name of Paris is "London". Of course, it seems natural to explain her strange verbal behaviour by saying "She thinks she's in London", but it seems to me that is either a misleading, shorthand way of saying what I just said, or else it is a false description that would be given by someone who hadn't properly thought through what "thinking that she is in London" entails. I believe that Professor Stalnaker himself, in the alternative scenario he provides, in which Mei-Li had never before heard of London or Paris, but had been told that the town she is in is called "London", would be disinclined to say that Mei-Li thinks that she's in London.

So what does "thinking that one is in London" amount to? We don't have beliefs (true or false) without evidence. Without any evidence about London, Mei-Li doesn't have any beliefs about the town. That's what I say. Professor Stalnaker demurs, and warns that "it is not so easy to separate beliefs about things from beliefs about their names". He makes the intriguing suggestion that, although the contents of belief are nonlinguistic propositions, "in some cases we have access to these nonlinguistic propositions only through the names of what they are about". Although I'm against doing tests on animals, let's try this one out on a dog. Consider a stowaway dog from China who, having evaded airport security, is now roaming the streets of Paris. If it kept returning to La Place Pigalle, where it met up with other strays, we'd have little trouble attributing to it the belief that Pigalle is a good place to meet dogs. That it didn't know the name "Pigalle" would not inhibit our attributions. To believe that p is to be disposed generally to act in a way consistent with p's being true, and that's just how this dog is acting with respect to the sentence that I am using to record its belief. However, Professor Stalnaker didn't say that in all cases we need to know what name an agent gives something in order to determine that agent's belief, but only that there might be some such cases. Here's one possible case: We'd be disinclined to say that the dog knows that it is in Paris. The reason is that to believe you're in X entails that you have, or had, a name for X. But even this case is not clear-cut. Suppose you took the dog and set it down in Twin-Paris[36] and it started heading for Twin-Pigalle. I'd be strongly inclined to explain its behaviour by saying "It thinks it's in Paris".

Well, this one could run and run. I must say that I am rather attracted to Professor Stalnaker's idea that what belief we attribute is, in some way, context-dependent, but I'm not sure whether my way of cashing that idea would meet with his approval. My theory is that if we really get a hold of the notion that thinking and believing are not the manipulating of words or other symbols,[37] then we shall see that there has to be a loose fit between, on the one hand, beliefs, and, on the other, belief-expression or belief-attribution.[38] Spoken language comes in sentence-sized chunks, but that is for the benefit of the lungs, not the mind; thinking and believing do not come so neatly bundled. In reporting the thinking of a non-human animal, or of a young human child, or of a person whose experiences are remote from our own, it is particularly clear that our sentences are not faithful reflections of the contents of those minds. When I tell you that the dog thinks that the cat is up the tree, I am using your categories, not the dog's. The most appropriate expression or attribution is going to depend on contextual factors, such as the knowledge possessed by addressees and our knowledge of that. In any conversation, our primary concern is to make ourselves understood by those we are addressing. The form of words we use in attributing a belief will depend both on the attributee and the addressee.

Turning now to Wittgenstein's treatment of Moore's paradox, I was alarmed to find Professor Stalnaker reading a crucial passage in quite the opposite way that, for years, I assumed it ought to be read. This is where Wittgenstein, in his letter to Moore, says that the lesson of the paradox is that "contradiction is not the unique thing that people think it is. It isn't the only logically inadmissible form". As Professor Stalnaker reads it, this means that a Mooronic sentence has a logical form different from a contradiction. I think it's fair to say that Wittgenstein's clumsy phraseology is responsible for this divergence of interpretations. What I take him to be saying is that contradiction manifests itself in many guises, related (perhaps in the family way) to "straight" contradiction. Earlier in the letter, Wittgenstein says that the Moorean absurdity is "similar to a contradiction, though it isn't one" (his emphasis). He elaborates:

> This means roughly: it plays a similar rôle in logic. You have said something about the logic of assertion. Viz.: It makes sense to say "Let's suppose: p is the case and I don't believe that p is the case", whereas it makes no sense to assert "p is the case and I don't believe that p is the case". This assertion has to be ruled out and is ruled out by "common sense", just as a contradiction is.[39]

Perhaps, as Professor Stalnaker suggests, there is only a terminological difference between us, but I think that there is one point on terminology that might help clarify the interpretational problem. When Wittgenstein talks about logic, he does not mean the sort of formal logic that is now part of any (decent) philosophy curriculum—he condemns such logic as "dull and useless" and names Russell as one of its misguided exponents.[40] In his later writings, Wittgenstein uses the word "logic" to mean the logic of language, specifically, the logic of language-in-use. He holds that only in use (i.e. in language-games) do sentences have sense, and he calls the failure to see this "the main mistake made by philosophers of the present generation"[41] Interestingly, when he said this (in 1937) he specifically included Moore in the generalization, so it is not surprising that he was so pleased to find Moore, in 1944, making a contribution to the logic of assertion, i.e. to the logic of language-in-use. Wittgenstein holds that mostly (but not always) sentences of the form "*p* and not-*p*" have no use ("a contradiction prevents me from getting to act in the language game")[42] and hence have no sense and a fortiori are not false. Although this is a view that he held throughout his philosophical career, it is not widely known that he did.[43] It is in the light of these views on contradiction that we should see what Wittgenstein is claiming when he says that a Mooronic utterance is "similar to" a contradiction. It is a quasi-contradiction; it has no sense. Using the example "I believe he'll come, but he certainly won't come", Wittgenstein remarks

> If I say that to someone, it tells him that he won't come but that nevertheless I am convinced of the opposite and will act according to this belief. However, by the very fact that I am reporting to someone else that he won't come, I am not acting according to this belief.[44]

In other words, the speaker is undermining himself in a way that renders his behaviour unintelligible in that we cannot figure out what he could mean by his words. To perform the speech-act of reporting that a particular person won't come is not consistent with acting out a sincere conviction that he will come. To assert a straight contradiction (were that possible) would be to take back what you put forward. This is perhaps the most dramatic way of undermining oneself. Making a Mooronic assertion is another way. Uttering a Liar sentence is another, for when one asserts (or purports to assert)

S: S is false

one is asserting S and, in so doing, denying S (claiming it to be false). Someone who issues a Mooronic utterance doesn't make any sense to us, "we should regard him as demented"; "if he seemed to be serious, I would be stunned", I might say "Run that by me again" and if he did so I should conclude that he had a linguistic disorder.[45] Similarly, we wouldn't know what to make of someone who, without intending to joke, said "I am immensely modest" or "I've forgotten that my best friend's name is Harry".[46]

So much for Wittgenstein exegesis; the important question is whether his views on Moore's paradox are correct. I think that they very nearly are while Professor Stalnaker holds that they are not, so my task is to tackle Professor Stalnaker's criticisms.

Professor Stalnaker raises the question of just what the problem of Moore's paradox is. He says "If someone were to say something of the form 'p but I don't believe it' he would be saying something paradoxical, but that is a fact, not a problem". Now, it is always salutary, when embroiled in a dispute, to step back and ask "What is the problem?", but, in this case, I can't really see why Professor Stalnaker has a problem with the problem. Here is one recent attempt to say what's problematic: How could I agree that I could not coherently believe something which I can clearly see could be true?[47] Substitute "suppose" for "see" and we have a formulation of the problem quite close to Wittgenstein's. He takes a Mooronic utterance to be senseless, so his problem is how to account for the fact that it makes no sense to say something like "It is raining and I don't believe that it is", whereas it makes good sense for someone to say it of me (putting my name in place of the "I").

As in the case of all paradoxes, the challenge is to explain how, starting from an apparently true premise and proceeding by apparently valid steps of argument, we arrive at a crazy conclusion. In the case of the Moore paradox, we begin with the reasonable assumption that if some proposition could be true and is intelligible to a speaker, then that speaker can intelligibly assert that proposition. Now the proposition—that the Earth moves in an elliptical orbit yet that fact is not believed by me—could be true, and I understand it perfectly well. So anyone, and, in particular, I myself, should be able, perfectly sensibly, to assert that proposition. And this is precisely the crazy, or unacceptable conclusion, for in fact it would be absurd for me to assert that proposition. My account of why it's absurd is that there is a difference between anyone else asserting of me that I believe p and my asserting that I believe p, the difference being that they are ascribing a belief to me—describing my state of mind—whereas I am not ascribing a belief but expressing one, an act not dissimilar to just asserting plain "*p*". So, as Wittgenstein says, there is something similar to a contradiction in the first-person case—in Professor Stalnaker's terms, it is a semantic contradiction and this is because of the pragmatic fact that a first-person present use of "believe" serves a different purpose from other uses of this verb. I can't accept the choice Professor Stalnaker is offering me between a semantic and a pragmatic solution. These are not alternatives; meaning is use.

In most, but not all circumstances, when I say "I believe *p*" I am not furnishing an introspective report—a description of my inner state. It is important to stress the qualification. Only what Wittgenstein termed a "craving for generality" would drive me to concoct a theory which attempted to force all belief-talk, or even all first-person-present belief talk, into one mould. We must distinguish between the expression of an opinion by a speaker, and that speaker's describing the opinion he holds. These are easy to confuse, because sometimes the same sentence can be used for both jobs.[48] There are, as Wittgenstein acknowledges, surroundings (his word) in which a first-person-present use of "believe" does serve to describe a belief. Professor Stalnaker hits upon one such circumstance. He imagines someone reflecting about his own obligations: "If I believe that it would be better for France if Jospin were to win, then I ought to give money to his campaign .... Crikey, I do believe that it would be better for France if Jospin were to win, ergo ...." The "do" here is Professor Stalnaker's addition to the standard Moore formula; the "crikey" is mine. Here we have someone reflecting on his own belief state and using words to announce a discovery about himself.

I agree with Professor Stalnaker too when he claims that if someone speaking about him says "Bob believes that Balladur will win" but Bob, overhearing this, corrects him by saying "No I don't; I think it will be Chirac" then Bob (Professor Stalnaker) is contradicting the speaker and so is denying that he is in the state of mind that the speaker said he was in. This example is valuable because, while Wittgenstein gives the impression that first-person-present uses of "believe" describe the person's state of mind only under strange, unusual circumstances, Professor Stalnaker shows that the verb can be so used in perfectly ordinary situations. And this is where we come to the crunch, where Professor Stalnaker has exposed a serious defect in my paper: given that "I believe ..." can often be used by me to describe what's on my mind then a Wittgensteinian solution, even if it is perfectly correct for the "avowal" cases (there's no reason to suppose that there must be a unified solution to cover every kind of case) is not going to apply to those Mooronic utterances where it is so used for describing my state of mind. For, in such cases, it is still absurd for a speaker to make an assertion of the form "I believe p, but p is not so", and we still have the problem of explaining why it's absurd. Norman Malcolm considers one such case[49] but he does not treat it seriously enough. He says that the speaker, is speaking of himself, but speaking as if he were another person. Yet the examples of Professor Stalnaker's that I have cited do not fall under this description.

The root problem, as Professor Stalnaker points out, is not about speaking but "about belief itself, and a person's relation to his own beliefs". I think that, for the cases we are considering where an individual is describing his own belief, a solution is straightforward. If I say of someone "he believes that p is true, but it isn't", I am accusing him of misjudging: I judge p to be untrue, but he (perhaps because he doesn't have such good evidence as I do, perhaps because he's stupider etc.) judges that p is true; there's some difference between me and him which is responsible for the fact that we judge differently whether p is true. Now, obviously, the first-person analogue is absurd, because I can't have less evidence than I, I can't be stupider than I, there can't be a difference between me and me. This is why we not only cannot assert Mooronically but also cannot believe Mooronically; why we cannot have a Mooronic attitude. As we said before, to believe that p is to be disposed generally to act in a way consistent with p's being true. So, to believe: (p is not the case but I believe that p) is to be disposed to act as if it were true that not-p while at the same time being disposed to act in a way consistent with p's being true. Can't be done. The fundamentum in re is an incompatibility of action.[50]

It may be rational now to believe that my opinions or desires with regard to some event are going to be different at some time in the future. So it might be sensible for Ulysses to bind himself to the mast while he's still only mildly excited by the thought of the Sirens, knowing that he could be fatally overcome by lust when he hears them singing.[51] Future tense Mooronisms "*p*, but I shall come to believe not-*p*" present difficult epistemological problems, but the present tense cases are easy.

In the closing section of his response to me, Professor Stalnaker gives a very nice example. He imagines that someone says to him "Chirac will win, but you won't believe that he will" and that he (Professor Stalnaker) at least initially regards that person as an authority both on French politics and on human psychology. So, as Professor Stalnaker points out, if he accepts what the expert says, then he, Stalnaker, would have to be prepared to believe a Mooronic sentence. He then, entertainingly, documents the inner turmoil to which this reflection leads. The fun starts when Professor Stalnaker appropriates the second-person assertion of the expert and "makes it his own" by transposing to the first person. And that, according to me, is exactly the pathology of the surprise examination paradox. The teacher says to her class "There will be an examination some day next week, but you won't believe it until it happens". Things go awry, and a contradiction ultimately emerges when one smart-alec student first-personalizes the teacher's claim and accepts "There will be an examination some day next week, but I won't believe it until it happens". From a contradiction or quasi-contradiction, no proposition follows (another controversial Wittgensteinian thesis). Similarly, the crucial move in Greg Kavka's toxin puzzle is from "... you intend to drink the poison" to "...I intend to drink it".[52] What makes the Moore paradox fascinating for me is that it's an apparently trivial, even stupid puzzle, yet resolving it provides the key to solving deep and serious enigmas.

NOTES

[1] L.J. Cohen, *Belief and Acceptance* (Oxford, Oxford University Press, 1992). Further citations of this opus will be by page number only. I have taken the opportunity, in Section IX of this paper, to respond to helpful criticisms made by

Robert Stalnaker at the Caen workshop.

[2] See also Cohen on *de dicto* interpretation (p.50).

[3] See also Robert Stalnaker, "Propositions", in MacKay, A.F. and Merrill, D.D., eds., *Issues in the Philosophy of Language* (New Haven, Yale University Press, 1976), pp.79-91.

[4] See also the case of Dostoyevsky and the rubber ball in Jacob Mey, *Pragmatics* (Oxford, Blackwell, 1993), pp.66-67.

[5] Stalnaker, op. cit., note 3.

[6] See also Pascal Engel, "Davidson on Believing, Holding True and Accepting" TS p.4, fn.13. Arguably, it was Kant who first rejected this "objects before the mind" picture. Richard Aquila, in his Representational Mind: A Study of Kant's Theory of Knowledge (Bloomington, Indiana University Press, 1983) writes "Kant discovered (or perhaps he invented) the notion of a cognitive state. What might be called 'cognitive states' among Kant's predecessors were really nothing more than would-be mental or cognitive relations of various sorts. Cognitive states, in the sense that was new with Kant, are not cognitive relations with objects, nor are they themselves peculiar objects supposed to mediate the occurrence of cognitive relations. They are simply the perceiver's awareness of possible objects" (p.xi). See also H. Ishiguro, "On Representations", *European Journal of Philosophy* 2 (1994), pp. 109-124.

[7] John L. Austin, *How to do Things with Words* (2nd ed.) (Oxford, Oxford University Press, 1975), p.148.

[8] Austin says "in general the locutionary act as much as the illocutionary is an abstraction only: every genuine speech act is both. (This is similar to the way in which the phatic act, the rhetic act, &c., are mere abstractions.)"

[9] Gabriël Nuchelmans, *Theories of the Proposition: Ancient and Mediaeval Conceptions of the Bearers of Truth and Falsity* (Dordrecht, North-Holland, 1973) is a three-volume work devoted to revealing part of the chequered history of the term "proposition". For some of the recent history, see Walter Edelberg, "Propositions, Circumstances, Objects", *Journal of Philosophical Logic* 23 (1994), pp.1-34.

[10] For further discussion, see my "Linguistic Aspects, Meaninglessness and Paradox–A Reply to John David Stone", *Linguistics and Philosophy* 4/4 (1981), pp.579-592.

[11] For an interesting attempt to remedy the tendency to confuse conventional linguistic meaning, ideolectic linguistic meaning and Fregean Sinn, see Tyler Burge, "Frege on Sense and Linguistic Meaning" in D. Bell and N. Cooper (eds.), *The Analytic Tradition* (Oxford, Blackwell, 1991), pp.30-60.

[12] Austin, op. cit., note 7, pp.92-6.

[13] Discussed by Ruth Garrett Millikan, "Perceptual Content and Fregean Myth", *Mind* 100 (1991), pp.439-459 and Laurence Goldstein and Hartley Slater, "Wittgenstein, Semantics and Connectionism", forthcoming in *Informatica*.

[14] W. Labov, "Objectivity and Commitment in Linguistic Science; the Case of the Black English Trial in Ann Arbor", *Language in Society* 11 (1982), pp.165-201.

[15] Roger Penrose, *The Emperor's New Mind* (Oxford, Oxford University Press, 1989)

[16] See my "The Adverbial Theory of Conceptual Thought", *Monist* 65/3(1982), pp. 379-392 and Michael Tye, *The Metaphysics of Mind* (Cambridge, Cambridge University Press, 1989).

[17] Under pressure from Stalnaker (see his paper in this volume) and Recanati (in discussion), I should now wish to qualify this remark. See Section IX below.

[18] Ludwig Wittgenstein, *Philosophical Investigations* (Oxford, Blackwell 1953), pp.190 ff.; Ludwig Wittgenstein, *Remarks on the Philosophy of Psychology* (Oxford, Blackwell 1980), Vol 1, "460-504. Henceforth, I shall refer to these works as PI and RPP respectively. Wittgenstein says of a Mooronic utterance that it is similar to a contradiction in that it "plays a similar rôle in logic". He credits Moore with having "said something about the logic of assertion". See Ludwig Wittgenstein *Letters to Russell, Keynes and Moore* (Oxford, Blackwell, 1974), p.177 (Wittgenstein's emphases.) I do not, however, believe that all the considerations that Wittgenstein advances are compelling. See my "Wittgenstein's Late Views on Belief, Paradox and Contradiction", *Philosophical Investigations* 11/1 (1988), pp. 49-73. Wittgenstein's point is that, in normal utterances in the first person present, the use of "believe" is quite different from its use in other persons and tenses. Jane Heal has used this point to refute functionalism. She says, "It is very important to functionalism that the meaning of 'believe' is uniform" (Heal 1994, pp. 13, 18, 19) for functionalism defines belief that *p* just as a state which, together with a person's desires, will normally cause behaviour which satisfies those desires only if *p*. So, for a functionalist, the Mooronic assertion "I believe that it is raining, and it isn't" would have the form "There is some state within me, and there's something going on in the world outside". In other words, if functionalism were true, then the Mooronic assertion would not be absurd. So, by modus tollens, Heal is able to refute functionalism, because, of course, the Mooronic assertion is absurd.

[19] Wittgenstein PI, '108. The crucial passage is RPP Vol.1, '488: "It would produce confusion if we were to say: the words of the ...sentence...have a definite sense, and the giving of it, the 'assertion' supplies something additional. As if the sentence, spoken by a gramophone, belonged to pure logic; as if here it had the pure logical sense; as if here we had before us the object which logicians get hold of and consider– while the sentence as asserted, communicated, is what it is in business. As one might say: the botanist considers the rose as a plant, not as a decoration for a dress or for a room or as a delicate ornament. The sentence, I want to say, has no sense outside the language-game. This hangs together with its not being a kind of name. As though one might say '"I believe ...' – that's how it is" pointing (as it were inwardly) at what gives the sentence its meaning."

[20] Peter F. Strawson, "On Referring", Mind 59 (1950), pp.320-344.

[21] How to get away with this is another story. See H. Gaifman, "Pointers to Truth", The Journal of Philosophy 89 (1992), pp.223-261, my "'This statement is not true' is not true", Analysis 52 (1992), pp.1-5 and Keith Simmons, Universality and the Liar (Cambridge, Cambridge University Press, 1993).

[22] Wittgenstein, RPP Vol.2, '420.

[23] PI, p.191.

[24] PI, pp.191-192

[25] RPP Vol. 1, '472.

[26] See RPP vol 1, '477.

[27] "Inescapable Surprises and Acquirable Intentions", Analysis 53 (1993), pp.93-99.

[28] P.T. Geach, "Assertion", reprinted in his in Logic Matters (Oxford, Blackwell, 1972), pp.254-269; see p.254.

[29] Letters to Russell, Keynes and Moore, op. cit., note 18, p.177; PI, p.190. See also RPP Vol.1, '478.

[30] Richard Moran, "Interpretation Theory and the First Person", Philosophical Quarterly 44 (1994), pp.154-173, says that Wittgenstein explores the theory of belief-ascription discussed here but that it is "ultimately rejected by him as a general account". See p.156, fn.3. This is a serious misreading of Wittgenstein. In his later works, Wittgenstein rejects the ambition to produce general theories for this blinds us to the careful weighing of the linguistic facts.

[31] RPP Vol.1 '486

[32] RPP Vol.1 '820. A further illustration is given at RPP Vol.1 '495 involving the claim "He's coming, but I don't believe it". Wittgenstein comments: "It is possible to think out a language-game in which these words would not strike us as absurd".

[33] Richard Foley has written one: "Is it Possible to have Contradictory Beliefs?", Midwest Studies in Philosophy X (1986), pp.327-355.

[34] See Mark Crimmins, "I Falsely Believe that p", Analysis 52/3 (1992) 191. Wittgenstein, PI, p.190.

[35] "The Fallacy of the Simple Question", Analysis 53 (1993), pp.178-181.

[36] This is the capital of Twin-France on Putnam's Twin-Earth.

[37] To see what an alternative might look like, check out Tim van Gelder, "What Might Cognition be if not Computation?", The Journal of Philosophy 92/7 (July, 1995), pp.345-381.

[38] This idea of a loose fit goes back to Frege. He takes the view (with which I disagree) that the fit can be tightened by constructing a perfect language. In a letter to Husserl in 1906, Frege writes "It cannot be the task of logic to investigate language and determine what is conained in a linguistic expression. Someone who wants to learn logic from language is like an adult who wants to learn how to think from a child. When men created language, they were at a stage of childish pictorial thinking. Languages are not made to match logic's ruler". See G. Frege, Philosophical and Mathematical Correspondence eds. G. Gabriel et al. (Oxford, Blackwell, 1980), p.67.

Burge (op. cit., note 11) gives a splendid account of Frege's conception of the relation of language to thought, and related matters.

[39] Wittgenstein, Letters to Russell, Keynes and Moore, op. cit., note 18, p.177.

[40] See Ludwig Wittgenstein, Wittgenstein's Lectures, Cambridge, 1932-35, ed. A.Ambrose (Oxford, Blackwell, 1979), p.139.

[41] Ludwig Wittgenstein, Lectures and Conversations on Aesthetics, Psychology and Religious Belief (Oxford, Blackwell, 1970), p.2.

[42] Ludwig Wittgenstein, Remarks on the Philosophy of Psychology (Oxford, Blackwell, 1980), vol.1 '44, vol.2 '290, and Zettel (Oxford, Blackwell, 1967), '685.

[43] For the full story, see my "Wittgenstein's Late Views on Belief, Paradox and Contradiction", Philosophical Investigations 11 (1988), pp. 49-73, esp. pp.67-68.

[44] Ludwig Wittgenstein, Last Writings on the Philosophy of Psychology (Oxford, Blackwell, 1982), '142.

[45] These three quotations are from, respectively, Ludwig Wittgenstein, On Certainty (Oxford, Blackwell, 1974), 155; Norman Malcolm, "Disentangling Moore's Paradox" in R. Egidi (ed.), Wittgenstein: Mind and Language (Dordrecht, Kluwer, 1995), pp.195-205; Rogers Albritton, "Comments on 'Moore's Paradox and Self-Knowledge'", Philosophical Studies 77 (1995), pp.229-239. Wittgenstein, Malcolm and Albritton take the view that, in the absence of any background story which shows its point, a Mooronic utterance is an Unsatz, a view which I too defend in "Wittgenstein's Late Views on Belief, Paradox and Contradiction", Philosophical Investigations 11 (1988), pp.49-73.

[46] This last example is due to Foley, op. cit., note 33.

[47] Bas C. van Fraassen, "Belief and the Problem of Ulysses and the Sirens", Philosophical Studies 77 (1995), pp.7-37; see p.27.

[48] See Van Fraassen, op. cit., note 47, pp.26-27, my own "'This statement is not true' is not true", Analysis 52 (1992), pp.1-5, where I point out that the doing/describing distinction applies to other speech-acts, and Jean-Louis Gardies, Esquisse d'une grammaire pure (Paris, Vrin, 1975), p.157, in which credit is given to Husserl. For the latter reference, I'm very grateful to Daniel Schulthess.

[49] Malcolm, op. cit., note 45, p.204. Malcolm's paper was delivered at a conference in Rome in 1989, but it was printed in 1995 and I came across it only after giving my talk at Caen. Had Malcolm come across my 1988 paper (op. cit., note 18) he could have spared himself the effort of working out most of his.

[50] This is a point that Aristotle makes at Categories 12b5-12b15: "For in the way an affirmation is opposed to a negation, for example 'he is sitting'–'he is not sitting', so are opposed the actual things underlying each, his sitting– his not sitting."

[51] This example inspired the title of Van Fraassen's paper, op. cit., note 47. The general principle that Van Fraassen defends in that paper is: "My current opinion about event E must lie in the range spanned by the possible opinions I may come to have about E at a later time t, as far as my present opinion is concerned" (p.16). It

seems to me that one practical upshot of Van Fraassen's discussion is that we may be in a better position to formulate a sensible policy on those wills wherein an agent requests euthanasia under specified future circumstances and that this request should over-ride any contrary wishes he expresses at that later time.

[52] See my "Inescapable Surprises and Acquirable Intentions", *Analysis* 53 (1993), pp.93-99.

ON "MOORE'S PARADOX"

Robert Stalnaker
Massachusetts Institute of Technology

In my comments, I will spend most of my time on Moore's paradox—I want to raise some questions, first about just what problem the paradox poses, and what counts as a solution to it; second, about what solution to the problem is being proposed, and how it relates to what Wittgenstein said and thought about Moore's paradox. But as Professor Goldstein says, he follows a circuitous path in his paper, and I can't resist a brief comment about a bit of the scenery that he passes by on his route to his solution to the paradox. So before getting to Moore's paradox I will first take a look at the story of Mei-Li.

Mei-Li, it seems to me, has confused London with Paris. But that is not how Professor Goldstein thinks the situation should be described. According to him, her relevant beliefs are all about Paris and not about London at all, since London is a city about which "she has not had the opportunity to form an opinion." Her mistake is a purely linguistic one—she believes that Paris is called "London"—but terminology aside, he seems to be suggesting, she has a pretty accurate conception of the state of the one European city that she is in a position to have opinions about. Now I can imagine a situation for which we can agree that this would be the right description: Suppose Mei-Li had arrived unexpectedly in a city, in fact Paris, whose name she did not know. Suppose further that she had never heard of either London or Paris. She asks, "what is the name of this city?" and someone replies "it is called 'London'." But Professor Goldstein's story is not like this. In his story, Mei-Li, before arriving in Paris, had the expectation of arriving in London. She did not know much about London, but she had heard of it (the city, not just the name), and had some beliefs about this city, such as the belief that she was traveling to London, that London is a

93

city in Europe, and that there is a bridge called "the Tower Bridge" in London. The first of these beliefs (that she was traveling to London) was false, but she didn't learn, on arriving in Paris, that it was false. After her arrival, and throughout the day, she believed falsely, I think it is perfectly reasonable and natural to say, that she was in London, and as a result she formed many false beliefs about London—that Notre Dame cathedral is there, for example. Of course it is also reasonable (though perhaps not in the same context) to attribute beliefs about Paris to Mei-Li. Asked by another tourist that they meet on their travels what Mei-Li thought of Paris, Professor Goldstein would certainly have been correct if he said that she liked it—that she thinks Paris is quite beautiful.

Well, which is it, Paris or London? Which is the city that is the one European city that Mei-Li believes she has visited (it is clear that she believes she has visited only one European city)? Which is the city that she believes is pretty, and that contains Notre Dame and the Eiffel Tower, and that used to contain the Tower Bridge before they moved it to Arizona? Professor Goldstein ought to agree with me that we don't need to answer this question—to require an answer would be to commit his fallacy of the simple question. It depends on the context in which the belief is being attributed. So I think we should resist Professor Goldstein's answer to the question that it is Paris and not London that her beliefs are about. It is, I think, not so easy to separate beliefs about things from beliefs about their names. We can agree that the contents of belief are nonlinguistic things, propositions that are expressed by sentences, but distinct from the forms of words used to express them. But it still may be that in some cases we have access to these nonlinguistic propositions only through the names of what they are about.

Now to the main topic: Moore's paradox. My first question is, what is the problem? Professor Goldstein talks about solutions to the paradox—one that he defends and others he doesn't like—but I am not sure what the paradox is. We're told that the paradox concerns anomalous utterances with certain forms, but we are not told just what it is concerning these utterances that poses a problem. If someone were to say something of the form, "P but I don't believe it," he would be saying something paradoxical, but that is a fact, not a problem. The speaker of the Moorean sentence will have some explaining to do, but what do we have to explain? What is it about the fact that the Moorean sentence is paradoxical which creates a paradox for which we need a solution? It is not that I want to suggest that there is no problem—Moore's example may pose a number of problems. But I think there is some work to be done saying what the problem is before we start work on solving it.

Here is one way to make explicit a problem that might be taken to be posed by these sentences: First, it seems obvious that there is some kind of impropriety In a statement of the form "P, but I don't believe that P," and that the impropriety arises from the form and meaning of the sentence. There is no problem with the two sentences that are conjoined in the paradoxical utterance, when they are taken separately. The problem is that one conjunct seems to contradict the other. Second, it is equally clear that there is no comparable impropriety in sentences of the form, "P, but I didn't believe that P," or "P, but he doesn't believe that P," or "If it were the case that P, but I didn't believe that P, then Q". It seems that sentences of these forms might be appropriately used to say something true. So it is clear that with these sentences and clauses, the first conjunct does not contradict the second. But third, it seems that sentences of the first, problematic, kind—the sentences that appear to be contradictory—can be used to express the same propositions as the sentences of the second, unproblematic kind. That is, it seems that when you say, referring to me, "it is raining, but he doesn't believe that it is raining," what you say will have the same content as the content of what I would be saying if I said (at the same time) "it is raining, but I don't believe that it is raining." So how can your statement be true, while mine would be a contradiction?

The most straightforward response to this problem is to explain the conflict in the Moorean sentences as some kind of pragmatic conflict—to locate the problem not in a contradiction between the propositions expressed by the conjuncts, but in the act of asserting those propositions in a certain context. For example, if we assume that an act of assertion is, among other things, an act of representing oneself as believing the content of the assertion, then it will follow that an assertion using a Moorean sentence would represent the speaker has having a certain belief, while at the same time explicitly denying that he has that belief. The strategy is to explain the appearance of a contradiction in Moorean sentences while holding onto the thesis that the third person and past tense sentences and conditional clauses express the same propositions as the of the corresponding Moorean sentences would express.

The details of the explanation of the pragmatic conflict may differ from one theorist to another, but most responses to Moore's paradox have taken this form. One might, however, respond in a different way: by accepting that the source of the conflict really is a contradiction in the content expressed in the Moorean sentence, but by rejecting the assumption that the third person, past tense, and conditional analogues have the same content as that expressed by the Moorean sentences themselves. Some things that Professor Goldstein says suggest that he wants to defend this more radical solution. If he is, then I don't think his solution is plausible. On the other hand, if his solution is better described as a solution of the first kind, then it is not clear to me that he is disagreeing with some of the people who he is arguing against. The reason I am not sure just what solution to this problem is being proposed is that I am not sure exactly what Professor Goldstein means by "contradiction." It is noted that the Moorean sentences are not *formal* contradictions, since they are not of the form "*p* and not *p*." But the question is whether there is a contradiction in the semantic sense: whether the contradiction is a feature of the content that would be expressed by the Moorean sentences. A sentence of the form "He knows that *p*, but not *p*" is not a *formal* contradiction, but it is still a semantic contradiction—a sentence whose literal use could expresses only a proposition that could not possibly be true. If Moorean sentences are contradictions in this sense, then we must deny that they express propositions that are the same as the propositions expressed by the nonMoorean analogues. On the other hand if they are contradictory only in some pragmatic sense (they are sentences with which a speaker using them would be "speaking against himself.") then there is no problem—no reason to deny that a common content is shared by Moorean sentences and their third person analogues.

If Professor Goldstein is using the term "contradiction" as a term that applies to speech acts, and not to propositional contents, then he has no need to answer the objection that derives from the Frege-Geach point—it is not an objection to this solution, but to a solution that rejects the sameness of content. And he has no need to deny that when I say what I believe, I am describing my own state of mind.

Perhaps Professor Goldstein thinks that the very idea of sameness or difference of propositional content derives from some phantasm picture of language, but I think that assumptions about the identity of content in abstraction from force—the assumption that underlies the Frege-Geach point is an assumption that is essential to an understanding of the actual use of language, and not just a point based on some phantasm. To understand actual reasoning (in speech or in thought) we may, for example, need to identify the content of a sentential clause that occurs unasserted embedded within an assertion with the content of another assertion. Suppose one were to reason as follows: "If I believe that it would be better for France if Jospin were to win, then I ought to give money to his campaign. I do believe that it would be better for France if Jospin were to win, so I ought to give money to his campaign." The argument seems reasonable because there does not seem to be any equivocation. It seems intuitively clear that what was supposed in the antecedent of the first premise was the same as what was said in the second premise. And it seems clear that the force of the argument, in context, depends on this fact.

One also needs to identify content across the speech acts of different people in order to give an adequate description and explanation of ordinary conversation. Suppose you say about me, "Bob believes that Balladur will win." I say "No I don't; I think it will be Chirac." I am contradicting you, since what you affirmed is what I am denying. You were attempting to describe my state of mind, and I say that you have got it wrong. So aren't I also describing my state of mind? This may not be all I am doing, but the fact that I am expressing an opinion about the political situation need not be a reason to deny that I am also reporting a fact about my state of mind. (Suppose a pollster asks for my opinion. "Who do you believe will win?" she asks. She is not asking because she wants to know who will win—she wants to know the state of public opinion, which she may regard as quite unreliable. She wants me to describe my state of mind, and I oblige: "I think it will be Chirac," I say. The fact that it is a description of my state of mind that is at issue would not make a Moorean sentence any less paradoxical. (I say to the pollster: "if you want a description of my state of mind, you should know that I believe that Chirac will win. But if you really want to know who will win, and not just what I think: it will be Balladur.")

Probably Professor Goldstein will agree with me that there is no contradiction in the content of what would be said with a Moorean sentence. It would be a contradiction only in the sense that the speaker would be speaking against himself. But this does not seem to be a solution to a problem, but only a description of the phenomenon that is supposed to be problematic. We begin with the fact that a speaker of a Moorean sentence would be speaking against himself. But why? Just what is it about what he says and does that makes it the case that it is some kind of absurd or self-defeating act? One explanation would be that the content of one conjunct contradicts the content of the other. But this requires us to deny that the content of my present self-ascriptions can be the same as past, future or conditional ascriptions, or ascriptions by others. So we need another explanation. It may not be hard to find one, but I think more needs to be said than that the speaker is speaking against himself, or that he is acting absurdly.

Professor Goldstein says that he is endorsing Wittgenstein's solution to the problem. What did Wittgenstein mean by "contradiction," and would he really have agreed that the Moorean sentences express contradictions? I am not sure, but the particular quotation that Professor Goldstein cites in favor of his interpretation seems to me to suggest the opposite: that Wittgenstein would deny that the Moorean sentences were contradictory. To repeat the quotation: "This just shows that logic isn't as simple as logicians think it is. In particular: that contradiction isn't the *unique* thing people think it is. It isn't the *only* logically inadmissible form." Wittgenstein is saying that Moore's paradox shows that there are logically inadmissible forms *other than* contradictions. As I read this, Wittgenstein is presupposing that the Moorean sentences are *not* contradictions. Rather, they are logically inadmissible forms of another kind. As the last sentence of the quotation makes clear, the claim that "contradiction isn't the unique think people think it is" means not that there are different kinds of contradictions, but that we shouldn't try to fit all logical inadmissibility into the category of contradiction. Now the difference of interpretation may be merely terminological, but on the face of it, it seems to me that Wittgenstein is pretty explicitly denying the thesis that Goldstein is approvingly attributing to him.

I have been suggesting that Moore's paradox does not give us reason to disagree with what not only philosophers caught the grip of a phantasm, but also ordinary speakers would say: that when you say of me "He believes that Chirac will win," you say the same thing of me that I say of myself when I say "I believe that Chirac will win." We don't need to deny that a first person present tense belief attribution is a description of the speaker's state of mind. It's not just that I think we can solve the problem without denying that self-ascription is self-description: I also think that denying this does not solve the problem. One has to say more than that a certain English form of words—a sentence of the form "I believe that P"—is not in fact used to describe the speaker's state of mind—that might be simply a fact about the way certain words are used. But Moore's paradox is not about a curiosity of English usage: it is about belief itself, and a person's relation to his own beliefs. If denying that self-ascription is self-description were really to solve the problem, one would have to say that it is impossible for a speaker to describe his own present state of mind. For suppose there were some other expression—some form of words other than "I believe" with which one might describe one's beliefs in the way one describes those of others. Or even if there weren't words available in any language, suppose there were some way to think about—to form descriptive judgments about—one's beliefs. Moore's paradox would arise for this form of expression or thought as well. So if the original paradox gives us reason to deny that "I believe that P" can be used to describe one's state of mind, it as well will give us reason to deny that there could be a way to talk or think about one's state of mind—at least about one's own present beliefs. This would be somewhat ironic: it might seem that Moore's paradox arises because one's mind is so transparent to oneself: I cannot be wrong about what I believe. But if self-description, even in thought, is impossible, it seems that the mind is quite opaque. This line of thought leads to the conclusion that it is conceptually impossible to talk or think about what is presently going on within one's mind. And that seems to me more paradoxical than Moore's paradox itself.

Let me close with a second person analogue of Moore's paradox. Suppose you say to me something of the form "p, but you won't believe that p." There need be nothing paradoxical about this—perhaps you regard yourself as a shrewd political prognosticator, but know that I am skeptical of your abilities. You say, "Chirac will win, but you won't believe that he will." Your intention is not to convince me, but to put yourself on record, with the expectation of later saying "I told you so." But suppose the situation is not like this. Suppose instead that I am disposed to regard you as an authority, not only on French politics, but also on human psychology: I believe you always speak the truth, so I am initially disposed to believe whatever you tell me, either about politics, or about my state of mind. But despite my initial disposition, I cannot believe what you say when you say "Chirac will win, but you won't believe that he will." To believe what you say, I would have to be prepared to believe a Moorean sentence. I might believe one or the other parts of what you tell me, but suppose I have no reason to think that you are more reliable about politics than about my state of mind. My trust in you is undermined by the fact that you have told me something I cannot believe. So since I can't rely on your authority, and have no other reason to believe it, I don't come to believe that Chirac will win. But now, on reflection, I realize that you might well be correct. You have correctly predicted that I would not believe you— why should I not think that you have also correctly predicted the outcome of the election? On reflection, it seems that your authority is not undermined after all, so perhaps I should follow my initial inclination and believe you. But on further reflection, I realize again that I can't do that. So I don't, but I continue to harbor the nagging suspicion that it is partly because I cannot believe you that you are right.

ON WANTING TO BELIEVE

Michael Losonsky
Colorado State University

1. INTRODUCTION

A recent episode of Bill Waterson's syndicated cartoon "Calvin and Hobbes" has Calvin in a fractured setting. "Oh No! Everything has suddenly turned neo-cubist," he exclaims. The cartoon continues:

It all started when Calvin engaged his Dad in a minor debate! Soon Calvin could see both sides of the issue! The poor Calvin began to see both sides of *every*thing! The traditional single point of view has been abandoned! Perspective has been fractured! The multiple views provide too much information! It's impossible to move! Calvin quickly tries to eliminate all but one perspective.

The setting returns to normal and Calvin is exuberant: "It works! The World falls into a recognizable order!" He then marches to his father, who is writing at his desk, and proclaims, "You're still wrong, Dad."

As is often the case with Bill Waterson's cartoons, this episode illustrates an important point about human beings. Sometimes people lose confidence in their own views and begin to feel that arguments really cannot be resolved because 'there are two (equally valid) sides to every issue'. This state of irresolution and the resulting loss of conviction can inhibit our ability to act effectively, and when this happens, human beings sometimes, for better or worse, overcome this state of affairs by simply deciding to stick with a point of view. We

101

decide to ignore the other sides of an issue and believe what we want to believe.

The problem of multiple perspectives and how to maintain conviction in such a setting is not peculiar to a 'post-modern' milieu. Doubt, irresolution or vacillation of the mind, and how to guide our mental lives in the face of doubt were important themes in 17th-century philosophy. There are *Rules for the Direction of our Native Intelligence* (Descartes 1964, 10:359), guides *Of the Conduct of the Understanding* (Locke 1824, 2:323), and treatises *On the Emendation of the Intellect and On the Way by which it is Best Directed Toward the True Knowledge of Things* (Spinoza 1985, 1:3),[1] all of which tell us how we should conduct our thinking and maintain proper conviction. These guides assume that belief acquisition is sometimes a voluntary activity for which we are responsible just as we are responsible for our voluntary bodily interactions with our environment.

The view that sometimes belief fixation is a voluntary mental activity, and hence that there is such a thing as an ethics of belief and thinking,[2] has played an important role in recent philosophy. C. S. Peirce (1877) maintains that belief fixation is a product of method, and he argues for the superiority of the scientific method over reliance on tenacity, authority, or what in effect is reflective equilibrium. W. K. Clifford (1879, 1:185-6) and William James (1896) both appeal to the voluntary nature of belief to argue for contrary positions on religious belief. C. I. Lewis (1955) and Roderick Chisholm (1968) as well as H. H. Price (1954) defend the thesis that sometimes accepting a proposition in the sense of taking it to be true is a voluntary mental action. Recent defenses of this view, which has been labeled "volitionalism" (Pojman 1985), include Meiland (1980) and Naylor (1985). What ties these positions is the view that to believe a proposition, which involves assigning to it some chance of its being true, is a mental action that directly involves an act of will on the part of the believer. This does not mean that we can simply believe something at will without reason or motivation, but it does mean that we can believe a proposition because we have some inducements to believe it. That is, we can believe it because we have some practical reasons, such as that belief satisfies a certain desire, for believing it (Bennett 1990).

Recently, volitionalism has been subjected to a number of criticisms, and I wish to challenge three assumptions underlying these critiques. The first is that there is a sharp division between belief and the processes of belief-fixation such as inquiry or reasoning (Curley 1975; Bennett 1990; Cohen 1992). The second assumption, is that the conception of beliefs as maps by means of which we steer is incompatible with volitionalism (Pojman 1985). The third assumption is that belief, by nature, aims at truth (Williams 1973). The fourth assumption is that there is a distinction between belief and acceptance, and that cases that look like voluntary belief acquisition are actually cases of acceptance (Cohen 1992).

In response, I argue in section 2 that some lines of defense and development are opened up for volitionalism if belief is a proper part of the process of belief formation. In section 3 I maintain that beliefs can be maps by means of which we steer as well as insignias for the social status of the user, and this social information can be used to steer through a social terrain. I argue that in some cases the function of beliefs as insignias can trump their function as maps, and in these cases beliefs can be acquired at will. In sections 4 and 5 I describe situations in which it is rational to rely on volition and desire to determine belief, namely when one's belief-fixation mechanisms are dysfunctional due to irresolution or lack of confidence. Reliance on volition and desire to either direct belief-formation at truth or away from truth, depending on what are the causes of irresolution, can be a remedy for dysfunctional belief-formation mechanisms. Finally, in section 6 I address the distinction between belief and acceptance and argue that if the acceptance of a proposition can be motivated, then beliefs can also be motivated.

2. BELIEF AND BELIEF-FORMATION

The sharp division between beliefs, on the one hand, and inquiry and reflection, which are a means to belief, on the other is especially clear in Edwin Curley's critique of the ethics of belief. Curley (1975, 175) claims that it is a truth of "conceptual analysis" that belief (which, for the sake of convenience, includes the suspension of judgment) is a state one finds oneself in and not an action, and the distinction between inquiry and belief sustains this analysis. The fact that belief is always a consequence of inquiry shows that belief is a state one finds oneself in and not an action. He supports his analysis by appealing to the fact that Descartes insists on having some reasons for his doubt, and that in the First Meditation Descartes "urges his readers to reflect carefully and frequently on those grounds, treating the First Meditation as a kind of spiritual exercise." Curley adds: "We cannot just decide not to believe something we find highly probable, but we can bring it about that we no longer find it probable by attending to arguments which cut against the belief or against the grounds on which we hold it" (176).

Although beliefs are not actions, it is granted that inquiry and reflection can be voluntary, and it is this fact, according to Curley, that justifies an ethics of belief even though belief itself is not a voluntary action. "Though belief is not a voluntary action, we must allow that it is often connected with activities of reflection and inquiry which are or can be voluntary," he writes, and adds that the distinction between "acts we perform" and "states we produce in ourselves by an action" might not be morally significant. The fact that we can have an "indirect influence of the will on belief" and "produce belief in ourselves by our actions, or preserve it by our inactions" is sufficient to justify the moral appraisal of belief (183-4).

This distinction plays an important role in other critiques of volitionalism. For example, Pojman's (1985) target is the view that "some beliefs are obtained by acts of will directly upon being willed" (39) and he does not deny "that the will plays an indirect role in acquiring [some] beliefs" (43). Cohen maintains that beliefs are involuntary "feeling-dispositions" that can be controlled voluntarily only indirectly, e.g. by "acquainting ourselves with all the relevant evidence and evaluating it within a balanced perspective" (1992, 26).

Bennett (1990) sharpens the question about volitionalism as follows: "Can I immediately induce you to acquire a belief? Can I, without giving you evidence for the belief and just by offering convincing bribes or threats get you to acquire the belief 'just like that', immediately, without setting your thought on producing some intervening event that will lead to your getting the belief" (89). Although Bennett explicitly does not limit the intervening events to inquiry after truth because he wants to allow for belief formation processes besides the gathering of evidence, inquiry is still an example of such an intervening process. For Bennett, motivating someone with bribes or threats to engage in an inquiry that leads to a certain belief is not a case of a voluntary belief because the belief was not motivated immediately, but only mediately *via* the inquiry.

There is no doubt that there is a conceptual distinction between belief and inquiry, but it is not clear how to draw the real distinction between belief and belief-formation processes. It is especially difficult to see how belief itself will not be voluntary if it is allowed that the inquiry leading to belief is voluntary. Beliefs play a crucial role in any inquiry, and for example one of Locke's concerns is that the beliefs that play a role in inquiry are the products of volition and desire. For example, some of the beliefs involved in inquiry are about the entailment relations between propositions, and sometimes a strong desire to show the conclusion will motivate a person to accept that one proposition follows from another. I desire the conclusion, and for the sake of the conclusion I desire the entailment, and so 'insensibly and instantaneously' I accept this entailment simply as a result of my strong desire (Locke 1824, 2:382-3, also see 380 and 391).

The close interplay between belief and inquiry suggests a view more along the lines suggested by Peirce, James and Dewey. A belief, Peirce writes, is a proper part of the process of inquiry and reflection: "It is the demicadence which closes a musical phrase in the symphony of our intellectual life" (1878, 290). The belief is a state of equilibrium, which includes a settled set of dispositions or principles of action, and this unity or equilibrium completes an inquiry that began with a specific "irritation of doubt" (Peirce 1877, 1878), "inward trouble" (James 1907, 43-81), or "unsettled" and "indeterminate situation" (Dewey 1938, 101-119). Thus a belief is in part individuated by the doubt it alleviates and the inquiry that settles the doubt or determines the unsettled situation. On this conception of belief, it is strictly speaking false that inquiry is a means to attaining the belief in the same way that it is false that the symphony is a means to playing the coda. Playing the coda is a constitutive part of playing the symphony.[3]

The analogy between beliefs and musical cadences has severe limitations, but the relevant point of the analogy is that a belief is a structure that is part of the process of inquiry. We can find this idea in contemporary functional accounts of belief. If we think of a belief as a function or role in a network that has for its input sensory information, desires, as well as other beliefs, and for its output behavior and other beliefs, then it is hard to see how inquiry and reflection can be separated from the belief. The sensory information and other beliefs that were part of the inquiry will also play a role in the belief structure, for example as the inputs that in part define the function of belief.[4]

This model of belief is also helpful in clarifying how desires and other inducements can cause beliefs. The discussion of volitionalism often takes bodily actions such as lifting ones arm as paradigms of direct action, and then considers whether a belief can be like that. For example, one can then ask whether one can "acquire a belief, just like that, *simply* because he wanted, as though acquiring a belief were like raising one's arm" (Bennett 1990, 89-90); (Naylor 1985). This is misleading on several counts.

First, one needs to be clear what counts as the voluntary behavior in the case of raising one's arm. The raising of one's arm is an individual datable event, and there are several candidates for this.[5] Following Dretske (1990, 11-16) there are three candidates for the particular act of, say, my raising of my arm. The first two are:

(1) the movement of my arm's rising;
(2) the movement of my arm's rising, which is produced
    by some internal cause.

In both of these cases the behavior is identified with an event, namely the movement of my arm, except that in the second case it is a particular kind of event, namely one that has the right kind of cause. If either one of these is the paradigm for understanding voluntary action, then it will indeed be difficult to think about beliefs as actions for the simple reason that beliefs are not simple events such as my arm movement.

However, consider the third candidate that Dretske defends as the proper locus of voluntary behavior:

> (3) the movement's being produced by some internal cause.

Now voluntary behavior is identified with a complex event, namely a causal process of which the movement as well as the internal cause are parts. Behavior is not just a state or condition, but something that involves a change, namely the production of an external event (typically bodily movements, but it can include other effects) by an internal event. As in any other process, the product of this process, the internal event that causes this product, as well as the causal relation between the internal and external events are all part of the process. Moreover, the parts of the process are not causes of the whole, and consequently the internal cause of, say, the arm movement, is not the cause of behavior. It causes the movement, but the internal event's causing the movement is the voluntary behavior.

This model of voluntary external behavior, and similar ones that understand acts as complex entities involving inner endeavours as well as outer movements (Thalberg 1977; McGinn 1979), lends itself to understanding a belief as a voluntary mental action. As in the case of the raising of one's arm, we need to distinguish between the product, namely the belief, and the process, namely the acquisition or production of the belief. The belief is no more a voluntary act than is the movement of my arm when I raise it. The mental act of belief acquisition is a process that involves internal causes that include the believer's motivational states (such as desires and drives), a product, namely the belief structure, and the causal relation between the motivational states and the belief structure. Volitionalism can maintain that belief acquisition can be voluntary as much as is my raising of my arm properly understood, namely as the process of my arm's movement being produced by an appropriate internal event.

A second misleading feature of letting one's thinking about voluntary activity be guided by the example of the raising of one's arm is that it steers away from nested and extended voluntary activities, and these are better models for voluntary belief. Nobody can acquire home-baked bread 'just like that' because baked bread cannot be pulled out of the oven simply as a result of earnestly willing to have it. The desire for such bread sets an extended and nested process in motion, namely baking bread, and the result is a completed action, namely baking bread, and a product: baked bread. The fact that baking bread is an extended and nested action does not make it any less voluntary than the lifting of one's arm.

To see this, it helps to use the distinction between motivational immediacy and ontological immediacy (Bennett 1990). The lifting of my arm, say, in response to a sufficiently motivating reward for this act, is voluntary even though it is mediated by a causal chain of neural events, and one can argue that a belief is to the gesture as the inquiry is to the neural events (Naylor 1985). Inquiry and reflection mediate belief as the neural events mediate the gesture. Bennett (1990, 89) responds that the gesture is not ontologically immediate, but it nevertheless is motivationally immediate. He writes: "When I offer you a reward if you will raise your arm and you raise it 'just like that', you don't set yourself to do something which will lead to your arm's going up; so the offer of a reward does not relate in a *motivationally mediated* way to your arm's going up." For example, no motivating thought about the ontologically mediating neural events "intervenes in the practical syllogism that takes you from the reward premiss to the action conclusion."

An extended action can be as motivationally immediate as a quick action such as the raising of one's arm. For example, the practical syllogism that gets me to bake bread might go like this: I desire sourdough bread with a crust. I can satisfy this desire only if I bake bread myself. So bake bread. The desire relates in a motivationally immediate way to my baking of bread. Now, of course I will have to go about doing the things required for baking bread, and I will not have finished baking bread until several hours later when I pull the bread out of the oven, but doing the intermediate steps in bread-baking is not a case of setting oneself up to do something that will lead to baking bread. It is part of bread-baking. In the same way, belief acquisition may be motivated immediately by inducements even though it may be an extended activity that includes inquiry.

For example, the practical syllogism may run like this: I desire a promotion. I will satisfy this desire only if I acquire the belief that p. So acquire the belief that p. If I then attend to the right arguments and exclude the troublesome ones, my acquisition of a belief is as motivationally immediate as is my baking of bread or my lifting of my arm. That is, I acquire a belief *simply* because I wanted to, just as I baked bread, simply because I wanted to.

It seems that I could do this even while being aware that I am acquiring a belief just because I want to have it. Pojman (1986) maintains that it is incoherent to believe a proposition simply on the basis of wanting to believe it while being aware that this is the reason for believing it. He claims that the willed belief together with the awareness of this cannot be sustained in much the same way that G. E. Moore's (1912, 125) "It is raining, but I do not believe it is raining" cannot be sustained although strictly speaking it is not a contradiction. Pojman is right only insofar as my beliefs aim at truth and consequently look for beliefs with good evidence. When this is my aim, I cannot sustain believing that *p* simply because I want to believe that *p* while being aware that this is my reason for believing that p. However, as I will argue in sections 4 and 5, there are situations in which a person can give up aiming at truth and instead aim to have beliefs that satisfy other desires.

Finally, and most importantly, the example of the raising of one's arm leads one to look for the wrong kind of cause. The example assumes that volition and desire are causes that trigger the belief in the way that flipping a light-switch causes a light to go on or a rapid increase in atmospheric pressure causes a headache. These are triggering causes, and they are not the only kinds of causes. In addition to triggering causes there are structuring causes (Dretske 1991, 42-4). The heat that causes the bimetallic strip in a thermostat to bend is a triggering cause of the bending, while the engineers and workers that made the thermostat, specifically that made it such that the strip is calibrated to bend at certain temperatures and to close an electric circuit are structuring causes.

Volition and desire can be triggering causes, as they might be in the case of the raising of my arm.[6] However, volitionalism need not be committed to the claim that volition and desire trigger beliefs. Volition, desire and other conative states can operate as structuring causes. They can play a role in structuring the process of belief acquisition so that we have the desired belief structures. The motivating desire may be for true beliefs, but it can equally well be for other features of beliefs, such as coherence, prestige simplicity, and so forth. In other words, volition and desire can determine a belief structure in the way that an engineer's actions structures thermostats, rather than in the way my desire causes my arm to move. As long as we look for inducements as triggers for beliefs, we will have a hard time understanding the role of desire and volition in belief formation, and consequently we will be blind to the role of conation to cognition.

3. BELIEFS AND MAPS

The view that ideas are representations by means of which we steer through the world still has a place in contemporary theorizing about cognition. Ramsey (1931) suggested that beliefs are maps in the mind by which we steer and this has been elaborated in recent philosophy of mind (Armstrong 1973; Dretske 1991). For example, on Dretske's account, "beliefs are representational structures that acquire their meaning, their maplike quality, by actually using the information it is their function to carry in steering the system of which they are a part" (Dretske 1991, 81). Although it might seem that this conception of belief is incompatible with volitionalism (Pojman 1985), as a matter of fact, this model helps us understand the various ways volition and desire can play a role in belief formation.

The function of a map is to represent a certain terrain, and desires can play a role in determining what maps are available and what maps we use in navigation. For example, we will map those regions through which we might want to steer. In ordinary cases, one of those desires will be to have an accurate or true representation of the terrain, but this will not be the only desire we have even in ordinary cases. We seek accurate maps of regions where accuracy matters for other reasons. For example, we want an accurate map of a mountain pass because we have a desire to get safely across the pass.

Thus desires play a role in determining the terrain that is mapped. Conative states can also play a role in determining the amount of information and the degree of accuracy that is mapped and used for a given terrain. For example, two maps may represent the same terrain, but one abstracts from, say, elevation, while the other does not, although they are both equally accurate with respect to the features they represent. Nevertheless, our desire may be for the simpler map without elevation. Perhaps the simpler map is more prestigious or we desire simplicity for aesthetic reasons. Simplicity may even determine us to choose a less accurate map because the speed of use gained as a result of simplicity may significantly outweigh the advantages of accuracy.

So far we have considered maps in terms of their function to represent a geographical terrain and they can be used to steer through the mapped terrain. This is the paradigm case, as when I use a map of Iowa to steer across Iowa. If we cash out our analogy for beliefs, this is the ordinary case of using the representational structure of a belief, say, that Iowa City is east of Grinnell, which has the function or job of indicating that Iowa City is east of Grinnell, to steer across Iowa. Let us call this its *primary representative function* of a map or belief, and we can think of the truth of a map or belief as a function of how accurately it performs this function, that is, how accurately it represents the terrain.

Beliefs are not only maps of a terrain, but sometimes they are also insignias. An insignia is a badge, emblem or other distinguishing mark that represents status, authority and membership in a social group. Badges indicating military rank, coats of arms, heraldic emblems and some flags are all insignias. An insignia not only indicates rank and membership, but it also allows the bearer to steer through social terrains by means of the information carried by the insignia.[7] The insignia indicates rank and membership, which determines where the bearer can go, what the bearer can do, what expectations the bearer has of others and what demands the bearer will make. For example, a badge worn by the police indicates the sorts of rights and privileges they have in society.

Insignias and maps are not incompatible. Maps have many functions besides being maps of a terrain. They can simply be decorations on a wall, they can be primarily commodities used for financial gain, and they can be insignias or very much like insignias. Maps are used in badges, coats of arms and flags. A map may function much like an insignia even when it is not strictly speaking part of a badge, flag or coat of arms. For example, a world map with the Western Hemisphere at its center or a map with a certain kind of projection (e.g. the Peters Projection, which preserves the relative sizes of the continents) can indicate political allegiances. A map of the Spanish Empire was more than just a map of the extent of Spanish control, but in the Spanish court it represented the status of Spain as a world power. As such, a map can be accurate, but it can also misrepresent the present because of its function as an indicator of adherence to a geo-political cause, as was the case in maps of Greater Germany used by Hitler. A map can also function as a kind of badge in more innocuous cases, for example, when it is used to represent one's status as a world-traveller. For instance, a mountain climber can represent her mountain-climbing expertise with the display of a worn and marked-up map used during a major expedition.

In the above examples, the map's function as a social indicator depends on its primary representative function. The map represents social status in part because it represents a terrain involved in the social status. But this is not always the case. For instance, a rare map hanging on an office wall may have the function of indicating the owner's means, namely as someone who has sufficient influence to obtain and maintain such a map. The map as insignia can also be a means for steering through a social terrain. For example, it can help the owner maintain a certain edge during negotiations that occur in the office. The former mountain climber who now sells trips to tourists can use the map to sustain her business.

The function of a map as a social indicator can be tied to other information the map carries besides the information it has about the mapped terrain. For example, a map carries information about who made it, when and where it was made, how it was made, and out of what it was made, e.g. the ink and paper used in production. This information about the map's origins, which need not be indicated explicitly on the map but may be carried implicitly by certain facts of the map, e.g. the style of projection used, indicates something about the causal history of the map, including how it was acquired. This information about origins and acquisition can contribute to the map's role as social indicator. For instance, a map can function as an insignia of its owner's financial status only if it is an authentic 17th-century map, and not a copy, and it was acquired in an authentic financial transaction (e.g. not a robbery). Authenticity also plays a role in military insignias. Military insignias have to be made by the proper authorities using appropriate material, and they are awarded only under certain conditions. The badge indicates that the bearer has the appropriate qualities or experiences and that these are duly recognized by the appropriate authorities. Without these features, the badge is fraudulent.

Thus a map can come to have a dual representative function: to represent a terrain and to represent status. These functions can come apart in much the same way that a map can simply become a decoration. For instance, a rare map once functioned primarily as a map of a terrain, but hanging in an office this function can atrophy and the map can become primarily a symbol for social status used to steer through social interactions. The acquisition of a map can be motivated only by a desire to have it as an insignia rather than a map of a terrain. A map collector may buy a map simply because of its rarity and beauty, and use it to indicate his capacities as a collector of rare maps without any regard to the fact that it maps a specific terrain. Its accuracy as a map may be irrelevant as long as it has proper origins.

In sum, a conception of beliefs as maps that are used to steer through the mapped terrain is compatible with the view that beliefs are insignias used to steer through a social terrain. This is not to say that we steer through social terrains only by means of beliefs as insignias. We have beliefs about social facts, as we do about other facts, and use these beliefs to steer through the social terrains these beliefs represent.

For instance, an employee's belief that his employer does not like a certain sort of project, can be thought of as a complex map whose job is to indicate the employer's influence and the attitudes the employer has to certain kinds of projects. Here the information the map carries about the terrain is used to steer around the employer. However, often we are less direct, and this is where beliefs as insignias play a role. Beliefs are ordinarily acquired during a learning process in which external conditions as well as internal conditions, such as cognitive competencies and receptivity to certain rewards, were necessary part of learning. Thus in addition to the information a belief carries about external conditions, namely what the belief primarily represents, it also carries information about the believer, and this latter information can determine the role of the belief as a social indicator.

I think that there are beliefs whose primary function is not to be maps but to be insignias by means of which we steer through a social environment.[8] For instance, it seems to me that sometimes, if not always, religious and political beliefs are social indicators. Adherence to a certain set of beliefs are often used as indicators of one's membership and status in a group. For instance, adhering to a creed—the Nicene Creed or the Pledge of Allegiance—can be a simple affirmation of a set of propositions, but it can also function as an indicator of one's membership and status in a social organization.

Consider the belief that bread is literally changed, that is transubstantiated, into flesh during certain Orthodox or Roman Catholic rituals. This belief's primary representative function is to represent a state of affairs in which baked dough is changed into flesh, but this information is not used to steer through a divine terrain. The belief functions as an insignia that is used to navigate through a social terrain. It is not simply the verbal expression of the proposition that bread is literally changed into flesh that plays this role, but the inner conviction. The person believes this proposition, but it also happens that the representational structure of this belief also indicates something about the believer, and this is the belief's primary function. The believer primarily uses it to main her identity as a certain kind of religious believer, and it is used to steer through intricate social situations. One of the things people can do by means of this conviction is to place themselves in a certain social setting, for example amongst practicing Catholics.

The contradictory belief that there is no such thing as transubstantiation can also have a similar role. It can be used to distinguish oneself from Catholics. This is not to say that this is its only role or even that it always has that role. Sometimes we may just be denying the doctrine of transubstantiation. However, sometimes transubstantiation is not at issue, but marking oneself out as a certain kind of person who has been in certain kinds of learning situations. Political beliefs can also be of this sort. The belief that one's nation is morally superior to other nations can be a straightforward belief about morality and nationality, but this belief can also be a social indicator for the learning situations, in this case the degree and kind of socialization, the believer has undergone, and this can become one of its functions and be used to locate the believer in a social setting. Claims about sports have a similar function. For example, the belief that a certain team from some city is the best team in a league or conference can function in a straightforward manner, but it can also indicate something about the believer's social status, and this can be used to steer through the social environment.

If we grant that beliefs are representational structures that can have a dual function, it is not difficult to see that conative factors other than the desire for truth can play a role in determining our beliefs. Just as maps can be acquired for their social role rather than their role as maps of a terrain, so beliefs can be acquired and maintained because of what they indicate about us and how this can be used to steer through a social environment. If a person desires to avoid certain features of the social environment, and she can steer around them only be means of what a certain belief indicates about the believer, then the desire may be sufficiently strong to motivate the person to have this belief, that is, the desire might be sufficiently strong to create the appropriate belief structure.

Consider a king's belief in his divine right to rule over other people. This belief in the divine right of kings is a structure that represents the proposition that he has a God-given right to rule. But it can also function as an insignia indicating his status as a person with the level of training and degree of confidence necessary to be a successful king. Thus, someone who desires to be a successful ruler may be motivated to acquire this belief in order to attain or maintain his status as a ruler. The proposition that he has a God-given right to rule need not be true for the belief in that proposition to function as a social indicator and guide the king through his social environment. This is not always true and requires an appropriate social context; in some situations such a belief may indicate one's status as crank.

4. BELIEFS AND TRUTH

If sometimes beliefs function primarily as social indicators, it is not surprising that it is not always the case that truth is the aim of belief (*pace* Williams 1973).[9] Rather, the aim of belief can be to attain or maintain a certain social status just as the acquisition of a map can be motivated by its role as a social indicator. For example, suppose that certain beliefs in one's place of work are rewarded with raises and promotions, and that these beliefs are distinguishing features of people who have attained a certain status in the work place. Only low-level and temporary employees are skeptical about the superiority of the company's product. Skepticism are marks of an inferior status in the company, and optimism and confidence are the marks of a higher status in the company. In this situation, the pressure to maintain employment and succeed in the company can trump whatever desire for truth one had.

As Locke points out, often we assent to propositions out of "Passion or Interest" (E 4.20.17). Even "Men of Name and Learning in the World, and the Leaders of Parties" can have "secret motives" other than a desire for truth for its own sake for the "Doctrines they owned and maintained." Of course, often the overt profession of beliefs is motivated by one's desire to please or succeed, and this verbal behavior is not accompanied by an inner conviction that is required by real belief. In fact, Locke thinks that most people "stick to a Party, that Education or Interest has engaged them in; and there, like common Soldiers of an Army, shew their Courage and Warmth, as their Leaders direct" without really caring about the proposition itself. People can profess an opinion to "support ... the common cause, and thereby approve [themselves] to those, who can give [them] Credit, Preference, or Protection in that Society" without ever being convinced of the opinion or even having "it so much as floating in their Heads" (E 4.20.18).

Perhaps Locke overestimates people's capacity to separate overt profession of belief from inner conviction and underestimates the role of overt expression in building inner conviction, or perhaps he is right about the degree of cynicism human beings can sustain. In either case, he is right that at least sometimes inner conviction is driven by other desires besides the desire for truth. Certainly this is true of the religious and political convictions of children, whose first concern often is to 'approve themselves to those who can give them credit, preference and protection.' They seek this approval not just for their outward behavior, but for who they are, and this includes their inner preferences and convictions. This need to have belief structures of which other people approve is pronounced in children, but it continues into adulthood. In many situations adults seek acceptance by their peers or superiors, not only of their behavior but of their personalities, and the acquisition beliefs serves that end rather than the need for truth.[10]

This is especially true in situations in which people lack confidence in their own cognitive abilities. In general, people aim at truth in their beliefs when they believe that there is some reasonable chance at attaining it, and truth loses its attraction in a skeptical environment. Volitionalism is in part a recognition of the role of volition in belief formation in periods of wide-spread skepticism. Because skepticism and irresolution were important 17th-century concerns, these phenomena and the way people respond to them motivated 17th-century volitionalism. This is especially clear in Hobbes, who relies on political will, not truth, to settle intellectual disputes in morals and religion because of his moral and religious skepticism, and perhaps even in the natural sciences. In all matters of controversy, including those about "right, policy, and natural sciences", Hobbes writes in De Cive (1839, 2:268-9), it is up to the civil authorities to decide who is right according to what is politically expedient (Watkins 1973, 110 and

129-31; Tuck 1987, 1989; Popkin 1992, 9-49).[11] As Popkin has stressed on many occasions, 17th-century Europe was dealing with a very pervasive crisis of skepticism, and one way to handle the conviction that truth is beyond our ken is to rely on desire and volition for other things to guide our beliefs. After all, even when you doubt your capacity to have true beliefs, you have to have beliefs, and this holds for groups as well as individuals.

It is easy to see the role of political desire and volition in the case of what is officially accepted and denied by a society's institutions, but it might be thought that this is really about public pronouncements, not inner conviction. However, there are important parallels in the individual case. Consider a personal crisis of skepticism in which the pursuit of truth in important areas of concern repeatedly ends in irresolution. This can be true of religion and politics, but it can also happen to one's beliefs about matters pertaining to the social and natural sciences. In extreme cases, one may actually lose confidence in one's judgments about other people's states of mind, or even the reality of the external world. Whatever its extent, I am thinking of conditions of skepticism that are not just theoretical postures but crises of epistemic self-esteem. These are conditions in which a person simply cannot fix her beliefs as long as truth and evidence are her only guides. The person does not trust her mental capacities, including her reasoning skills. Even when a modicum of conviction is attained, it is short-lived because of subsequent self-doubt in the processes that led to conviction.[12] As a result of this kind of doubt, one's instincts and intuitions about right and wrong, true and false are dulled by an over-arching conviction in one's own incapacity for attaining truth.

For certain subjects such a crisis can be sustained as a cognitive achievement. In some areas it is not necessary to have settled beliefs and irresolution can be sustained personally and socially. For many, religion as well as physics may fall into this category. However, having settled beliefs on some important issues is necessary for personal happiness. Irresolution is debilitating, and it needs to be treated if it becomes pervasive. It dulls one's mental capacities, curtails one's activity, and where one nevertheless has to act, one acts without conviction. Moreover, as we will see in the next section, it makes our beliefs inconsistent and liable to be used against us.

One way of responding to such a crisis is to re-direct one's aims away from truth and pursue other goals, such as life, liberty, happiness, or personal integrity. This turning away from truth will itself be motivated by a desire to overcome the debilitating crisis and regain some control over the conduct of one's understanding. The pursuit of truth is believed to be part of the cause of the crisis, and the considered remedy is to find other apparently more constructive pursuits. In sum, if with respect to some subject matter you do not think truth is within your reach and, as far as you are concerned, the pursuit of truth will not produce conviction, but you nevertheless require conviction in this area, then other inducements will guide your belief fixation.

An example of such an inducement is the desire to conform to community standards. One may adopt beliefs because they are widely accepted and respected. Sometimes this practice may exhibit some degree of respect for truth because it is also guided by the belief that the community is a reliable authority for truth. However, if this belief in the authority of the community in matters of truth is not itself based on any evidence, but is driven by a passion to sustain the authority of the community in the face of any threats to it, then truth has ceased to be a goal. The goal is the preservation of authority, and truth is assigned to the authority not for the sake of truth, but for the sake of authority.

Volitionalism recognizes this strategy in the conduct of the human understanding. However, this strategy can also direct one's pursuits back to truth. A personal crisis of skepticism can also be one in which one comes to believe that one's beliefs are mostly driven by expediency, such as the desire to conform to community standards, without a role for truth. This crisis also involves irresolution, except this time it is irresolution due to the pursuit of agreement. When community has deep and divisive disagreements about an issue or the standards of truth change too often with changes in political authority, belief formation may also by stymied by irresolution. In this case it is the shifting grounds of authority that cause irresolution rather than one's lack of epistemic self-esteem. If the desire for communal approval leads to irresolution because of the unstable nature of this authority and this irresolution is sufficiently debilitating, then a search for other goals of belief fixation may ensue, and truth may step into the limelight.

5. AIMING FOR INTEGRITY

Van Fraassen (1984) argues that belief, understood as gradations of subjective probabilities, are voluntary. He describes a case of epistemic irresolution, highlights a debilitating feature of it, and shows how volition is a remedy for this case of irresolution. I will outline his case, and argue that the proposed remedy, namely to become committed to stand behind one's commitments, need not involve truth as a goal.

Consider a case of a person, perhaps someone struggling with heliocentrism in 17th-century Europe, who lacks confidence in the reliability of her beliefs and consequently is irresolute about her subjective probabilities. For example, she believes with a mild degree of subjective probability (say .4) that some time in the future she will believe with certainty (that is, a subjective probability of 1 or something very close to 1) that Earth orbits the sun. But she lacks confidence in the reliability of her beliefs: she also believes with some degree of subjective probability (say .3) that although some time in the future she believes with certainty that Earth orbits the sun, it is false that Earth orbits the sun. This entails that her present degree of conditional subjective probability for the Earth's orbiting the sun, on the supposition that in the future she will believe with certainty that Earth orbits the sun, is less than the degree of probability of this future opinion. Her present degree of belief about this subject, relative to the information that she has a certain opinion about it in the future, is less than her future opinion.

This low epistemic self-esteem is the source of a problem. Assuming she operates with a Bayesian, subjectivist conception of probability, given the beliefs she has, she will regard each bet in a series of bets as fair, even though these bets are such that she loses no matter what their outcome is. This is a Dutch book, and for the Bayesian consistent or rational individuals would not consider a bet fair that they will lose no matter what the outcome is.

According to van Fraassen, there are only two ways to avoid this Bayesian irrationality due to lack of confidence. One is not to have any beliefs about the reliability or lack of reliability of one's future beliefs. If this condition is satisfied, the person will simply not have a belief of any strength whatsoever that in the future she comes to believe with certainty that Earth orbits the sun, but this is not so. This condition is too restrictive and, it seems to me, difficult to sustain psychologically. Human beings are creatures that have beliefs about their own futures, and they are creatures that have varying degrees of confidence in themselves. Thus as a matter of contingent fact, they will have beliefs about how reliable they will be in the future. This condition could be satisfied only if a person willfully suspends judgments about the reliability of his own future beliefs.

The other condition also depends on willful action, namely to adopt as a matter of principle an exceptionally high opinion of the reliability of one's own future beliefs (Van Fraassen 1984, 243-4). Specifically, the person that lacks confidence violates the following principle: an individual's present subjective probability for a proposition p, on the supposition that in the future their subjective probability for p equals r, also equals r. Van Fraassen calls this principle "Reflection," but he suggests that is could be called "Self-confidence," and I will use this term because it highlights the role of this principle as a remedy to irresolution.

How can the person suffering from irresolution satisfy Self-confidence and avoid an irrational set of subjective probabilities? Van Fraassen argues that Self-confidence is a form of commitment to stand behind one's cognitive commitments, and it is by making this commitment that a person overcomes the Bayesian incoherence of irresolution. It is a mental action because it involves the intention to stand by one's epistemic commitments across time. This seems right, but it should be noticed that an important aspect of this remedy for irresolution is that, strictly speaking, incoherence is overcome not by aiming at truth, but by aiming at personal integrity. If given the information that I will promise tomorrow to do A, I still regard it today as unlikely that I will do A tomorrow, I undermine my own personal integrity. Personal integrity requires that I am now committed to stand behind my future commitments. By the same token, if relative to the information that in the future I will regard a proposition that p as likely, I still regard it presently as unlikely, I am not committed to my "cognitive engagements" and this undermines my integrity (van Fraassen 1984, 255). It is the goal to develop or maintain one's integrity, namely to be committed to one's own commitments, that remedies Bayesian incoherence due to lack of self-confidence, not a desire for truth.

A person can be committed to stand behind her own commitments without also having an interest in truth. Consider this possible state of affairs, which, according to the cynic, actually obtains. The strengths of beliefs people have in some domain (say, politics, religion or economics) are not driven by available evidence, but only by non-evidential prudential concerns. Perhaps people's interests in this domain would not be served by the truth. Even though people do not aim at truth in this domain and the degrees of confidence they have in the propositions about this domain are determined by non-evidential concerns, they can still aim to satisfy the principle of Self-confidence. That principle does not restrict the sources that determine the future degree of confidence I have in a proposition. A person can ensure that her present subjective probability for a proposition p, on the supposition that in the future his subjective probability for p equals r, will equal r, even if the future subjective probability for p is determined by the most ignoble disdain for truth.

The kind of situation I have been considering in which volition is seen as a remedy is well illustrated by Bill Waterson in his syndicated cartoon "Calvin and Hobbes."

6. BELIEF AND ACCEPTANCE

One can draw a distinction between belief and acceptance, and it may be argued that in the kinds of cases I am considering in which beliefs seem to be acquired voluntarily what is actually going on is that propositions are being accepted, but not believed. L. J. Cohen draws the distinction between belief and acceptance as follows: "belief is a disposition to feel, acceptance a policy for reasoning," and he adds that "'belief' carries no conceptual implications about reasoning, 'acceptance' carries none about feelings" (1992, 5). When you believe that p you have a disposition to "feel it true that p and false that not-p," (4) and he calls these feelings "credal feelings" or "belief-feelings" (8-12). To accept a proposition is "a mental act, or a pattern, system, or policy of mental action" (12), and the action involved is one "of including that proposition or rule among one's premises for deciding what to do or think in a particular context" (4).[13]

While beliefs are involuntary, acceptance is voluntary mental action. Cohen rests his case for the involuntariness of belief on his claim that it is a disposition to a feeling and that feelings in general and our dispositions to have them are involuntary. He writes that "no one can be said to decide to be disposed to feel one way or another" (1992, 21), and "feeling-dispositions themselves are certainly states of mind that we cannot switch on and off at will" (26). We may "induce or inhibit our dispositions to have feelings of belief, jealousy, alarm" by attending to the relevant evidence or "by discussing the problem with our friends, or maybe by prayer, meditation, exercise, or deep breathing. But that does not make our feeling-dispositions, whatever they may turn out in the end to be, any less involuntary when they actually arise" (26-7).

I am not sure I know what credal feelings are, and I do not see why beliefs should be identified with these feelings. This is not to deny that possibly beliefs come with phenomenological qualities and that in our own case we use these qualities to identify beliefs (Goldman 1993). But the nature of belief or commitment is not exhausted by the properties we use to identify them. Moreover, commitment and acceptance may come with phenomenal properties as well, and thus 'feeling' might not help us to distinguish belief and acceptance.[14] As far as I can tell, the only credal feelings I have for propositions are attitudes of acceptance that are marked by a phenomenal readiness to use these propositions in my reasoning and deliberation. My belief feeling is something like an urge or passion to use the proposition in my thought and action.

Cohen grants that it is difficult in fact to know whether a particular mental attitude towards a proposition is one of belief, of acceptance, or of both. (1992, 17). He agrees that there is a natural tendency to run them together and that belief and acceptance are linked together in everyday experience in a "combined state" (18). This natural tendency suggests that perhaps there are unified belief-acceptance states in which belief and acceptance are not simply conjoined as the arm of a chair is conjoined to its back, but they form a single unit in the way the way the matter and form are unified in a particular vase or statue. The fact that sometimes belief and acceptance are distinct or that there is a conceptual distinction between belief and acceptance does not show that belief and acceptance are always in fact distinct states. Our conceptual distinctions may be based on flawed or incomplete information about belief and acceptance, and Cohen admits he does not know what the neurological bases are for belief-feelings and acceptance, and what the relation is between these states and their neurological bases (67).

Perhaps particular feeling-dispositions and instances of acceptance are reducible to, or at least supervenient on, the same neurological bases. For example, certain dispositions to feel it true that p might supervene on the same physical structure as the acceptance of that proposition. These credal feelings would be constituted by a physical state that constitutes having a policy or pattern of using a proposition in reasoning and deliberation. In such cases, the acceptance of a proposition does not merely cause a belief-feeling, but constitutes the belief-feeling. Thus if the acceptance is voluntary, the belief is voluntary. The voluntary acceptance of a proposition in such a case constitutes the acquisition of a credal feeling for that proposition.

Finally, and most importantly, if it is easy to conflate belief and acceptance because in everyday experience they come in a combined state, then they can be easily conflated in our motivations. If I can decide, desire or want to accept a proposition for my deliberations and it is possible and even common to conflate acceptance and belief-feelings because they usually come together, then I can decide, desire or want to have certain belief-feelings towards that proposition. While one person uses the properties of acceptance to identify this combined state in her motivations, another person relies on the qualities of belief-feelings to identify that combined state. But now it is hard to see why someone's desire for credal feelings cannot be responsible for her credal feelings. Just as a person's decision to accept a proposition is responsible for the combined state of belief-acceptance, a person's decision to have a belief-feeling can be responsible for the combined belief-acceptance state. The motivational structure that involves representations of belief-feelings for a proposition can have the same power or role as the motivational structure that involves representations of acceptance. Thus if acceptance is voluntary in virtue of a certain motivational structure that is responsible for acceptance, it seems that belief can be voluntary in virtue of a motivational structure that differs from the structure for acceptance only in that it represents belief-feelings rather than acceptance.

Even if the desire for a belief-feeling is satisfied by way of an intervening causal processes, the belief can still be motivationally immediate. For example, it certainly is a possibility not ruled out by conceptual or even known empirical facts that sometimes a person simply wants to have a belief-feeling. Moreover, it is not ruled out that sometimes this motivation is so strong that it produces a process that yields the belief-feeling without any intervening conscious motivations.[15] The fact that belief is a feeling-disposition does not rule this out. It is not obvious to me that we cannot sometimes decide to be disposed to feel one way or another and that we cannot switch some feeling-dispositions on and off at will.

I certainly can want to be less despondent, angry or jealous (to use Cohen's examples), and it may be that this desire itself plays a role in bringing about a change in my dispositions. Even if the causal chain between my desire and the change in disposition is mediated ontologically by other states, it may still be that the change in disposition is motivationally immediate. We often want to change our dispositions, and sometimes it seems we can effect this change in virtue of having a sufficiently strong desire for change. For example, it seems to me that I inhibit my disposition to despondency or anger by forming an intention to avoid despondency or anger and feel greater peace of mind. My wish not to feel despair or anger and feel more tranquility itself, as far as appearances go, by itself and 'just like that' turns off my feelings of despondency or anger and turns on a greater sense of happiness. In much the same way, a strong enough motivation to believe in certain propositions can without any intermediate motivations trigger a process that yields a belief in this proposition as a product.

It should be kept in mind that usually only beliefs that make a difference between a life of despair and a life of contentment or at least hope for contentment can be objects of passions strong enough to succeed in making you believe what you want to believe. Propositions that make little difference to one's life, such as that it rained three hours ago on Jupiter, are usually not the sorts of propositions we can even imagine wanting to believe (Curley 1975, 178-9). Propositions about our present and future providence (for example, propositions about religious, political and economic matters) are much better candidates for propositions that people want to believe and for which belief is strongly motivated by prudential considerations.

7. CONCLUSION

I have defended volitionalism against four important criticisms. In the process of defending volitionalism, I have tried to give the outlines of an account of the role of volition and desire in human belief formation. I have maintained that human volition and desire are structuring causes that are responsible for belief-fixation processes, including the belief structure that is built by these processes. I have tried to show how our beliefs can have both a representative function and a role as social indicators, and that this social function of our beliefs makes them liable to be used to pursue other goals besides truth. Finally, I have suggested the role volition can play in conditions of deteriorating confidence in one's own capacities at belief formation. For example, the desires for cognitive integrity, communal agreement or even truth can be remedies for crises of confidence and establish better processes of belief fixation.

NOTES

[1] There is some debate whether in this early work Spinoza is committed to an ethics of belief. See Curley's editorial preface to the *Treatise* in Spinoza (1985).

[2] The phrase "ethics of belief" is due to Clifford (1879). "Ethics of thinking" is due to Ryle (1971).

[3] This does not preclude us from detaching the coda and playing it by itself, but its nature as a coda is determined by the symphony of which it is a detached part.

[4] An analogous point is made by Daniel Dennett about consciousness. Consciousness is not a state or subsystem, but a "spatiotemporal smearing" in the brain (Dennett 1990, 126). It is a "mode of action" of the brain that includes many functions, including perception, memory and the control of behavior (1990, 166).

[5] I intend "the raising of one's arm" to be a perfect nominal that names an event. On this and related issues see Bennett (1988).

[6] Perhaps my desire is also a structuring cause.

[7] Thus in an extended sense, clothing, cars and other property over which one disposes can be insignias insofar as they are not simply exemplars of one's status but are also used to signify one's status.

[8] In other words, I am claiming that using a belief as an insignia is not like using a dollar bill as a kleenex because being a kleenex is as a matter of fact not the primary function of a dollar bill. Beliefs as insignias are more like books some people use primarily to decorate the living rooms.

[9] It should be noted that even if Williams is right that beliefs always aim at truth, it does not exclude, as Bennett (1990) shows, cases in which desires motivate beliefs just like that.

[10] In fact, it is a live option that the primary function of the acquisition of belief is not to aim at truth but to aim at other things, for example social cohesion and other conditions that enhance reproduction and replication. For an extended critique of the view that truth is the primary aim of belief, see Stich (1990).

[11] On the central role of appetite in human reason according to Hobbes see Losonsky (1993).

[12] See Descartes's discussion of irresolution in the *Passions of the Soul* (1964-76, 11:459-60; 1985 1:390-1).

[13] This is not to be confused with hypothesizing or supposing that the proposition is true. Also it should be noted that Cohen's distinction between belief and acceptance is not the distinction often drawn between acceptance and a high degree of subjective

probability (de Sousa 1971; Maher 1981). For Cohen, a high subjective probability is a kind of acceptance, not a kind of belief (1992, 113-4).

[14] In fact, the beliefs Goldman (1993) suggests are represented by us in terms of their phenomenal properties are, on Cohen's account, species of acceptance. For James (1890, 2:283) belief is a kind of acquiescence or consent, which is a feeling or emotion.

[15] While teaching a section on philosophy of religion to an introductory class that contained many vocal Christian fundamentalists, I was admonished to want to believe. "You have to want to believe, and you will believe" they told me reporting on their own conversions and responding to my rational considerations for and against God's existence. They clearly were not talking about deliberation and reasoning, but of credal feelings they had once wanted and acquired, and they were recommending this course of action to me. My electrician also stated that his religious belief is a result of his "desire to believe".

BIBLIOGRAPHY

Armstrong, D. 1973. *Belief, Truth and Knowledge*. Cambridge, UK: Cambridge University Press.

Bennett, J. 1988. *Events and their Names*. Indianapolis: Hackett.

Bennett, J. 1990. "Why is Belief Involuntary?" *Analysis* 50:87-107.

Bennett, J. 1995. *The Act Itself.* Cambridge: Cambridge University Press

Chisholm, R. 1968. "Lewis's Ethics of Belief." In *The Philosophy of C. I. Lewis*. Ed. P. A. Schilpp. La Salle: Open Court.

Churchland, P. S., Ramachandran, V. S. and Sejnowski, T. J. 1994. "A Critique of Pure Vision." In *Large-Scale Neuronal Theories of the Brain*. Cambridge, MA: MIT Press. Forthcoming.

Clifford, W. K. 1879. *Lectures and Essays*. 2 Vols. Ed. L. Stephen and F. Pollock. London: Macmillan.

Cohen, J. L. 1992. *An Essay on Belief and Acceptance*. New York: Oxford University Press.

Curley, E. 1975. "Descartes, Spinoza and the Ethics of Belief." In *Spinoza: Essays in Interpretation*. Eds. E. Freeman and M. Mandelbaum. La Salle: Open Court, 159-89.

Dennett, D. 1991. *Consciousness Explained*. Boston: Little Brown.

Descartes, René. 1964-76. *Oeuvres de Descartes*. 12 vols. Eds. C. Adam and P. Tannery. Paris: J. Vrin.

Descartes, René. 1985. *The Philosophical Writings of Descartes*. Eds. J. Cottingham, R. Stoothoff and D. Murdoch. Cambridge: Cambridge University Press.

de Sousa, R. B. 1971. "How to Give a Piece of Your Mind: or, The Logic of Belief and Assent." *Review of Metaphysics* 25:52-79.

Dewey, J. 1931. "The Unit of Behavior." In *Philosophy and Civilization*. New York: Minton.

Dewey, J. 1938. *Logic: The Theory of Inquiry*. New York: Henry Holt and Company.

Dretske, F. 1991. *Explaining Behavior: Reason in a World of Causes*. Cambridge, MA: MIT Press.

Goldman, A. I. 1993. "The Psychology of Folk Psychology." *Behavioral and Brain Sciences*. 16:15-28.

Hampshire, S. 1959. *Thought and Action*. London: Chatto and Windus.

Hobbes, Thomas. 1839. *Opera Philosophica Quae Latine Scripsit Omnia*. Ed. W. Molesworth. London: John Bohn.

James, W. 1896. "The Will to Believe." In: *The Will to Believe and Other Essays in Popoular Philosophy*. New York: Longmans, Green and Company.

James, W. 1907. "What Pragmatism Means." *Pragmatism: A New Name for Some Old Ways of Thinking*. New York: Longmans, Green and Company.

Kaplan, M. 1981. "Rational Acceptance." *Philosophical Studies* 40:129-45.

Kenny, A. 1972. "Descartes on the Will." In *Cartesian Studies*. Ed. R. J. Butler. New York: Bobbs-Merrill.

Lewis, C. I. 1955. *The Grounds and Nature of the Right*. New York: Columbia University Press.

Locke, John. 1824. *The Works of John Locke*. 9 vols. London: Rivington.

Losonsky, M. 1993. "Passionate Thought: Computation, Thought and Action in Hobbes." *Pragmatics and Cognition* 2:245-266.

Meiland, J. 1980. "What Ought We to Believe or the Ethics of Belief Revisited." *American Philosophical Quarterly* 17:

Montmarquet, J. 1986. "The Voluntariness of Belief." *Analysis* 46:49-53.

Moore, G. E. 1912. *Ethics*. London: Williams and Norgate.

Naylor, M. B. 1985. "Voluntary Belief." *Philosophy and Phenomenological Research*. 45:427-436.

Passmore, J. A. 1986. "Locke and the Ethics of Belief." In *Rationalism, Empiricism, and Idealism: British Academy Lectures on the History of Philosophy*. Ed. A. Kenny. Oxford: Clarendon.

Peirce, C. S. 1877. "The Fixation of Belief." *Popular Science Monthly* 12:1-15.

Peirce, C. S. 1878. "How To Make Our Ideas Clear." *Popular Science Monthly* 12:286-302.

Pojman, L. P. 1985. "Believing and Willing." *Canadian Journal of Philosophy* 15:37-55.

Pojman, L. P. 1986. *Religious Belief and the Will*. London: Routledge & Kegan Paul.

Popkin, R. H. 1992. *The Third Force in Seventeenth-Century Thought*. Leiden: E. J. Brill.

Price, H. H. 1954. "Belief and Will." In *Proceedings of the Aristotelian Society* 28:126.

Ramsey, F. P. 1931. *The Foundations of Mathematics and Other Essays*. London: Routledge and Kegan Paul.

Rorty, A. 1986. ed. *Essays on Descartes' Meditations*, Berkeley: University of California Press.

Rosenthal, D. M. 1986. "Will and the Theory of Judgment." In Rorty 1986, 405-434.

Ryle, G. 1971. "John Locke." In *Collected Papers*. London.

Stich, S. 1990. *The Fragmentation of Reason*. Cambridge, MA: MIT Press.

Thalberg, I. 1977. *Perception, Emotion and Action*. Oxford: Basil Blackwell.

Tuck, R. 1987. "The 'Modern' Theory of Natural Law." In: *The Language of Political Theory in Early Modern Europe*. Ed. A. Pagden. Cambridge: Cambridge University Press.

Tuck, R. 1989a. *Hobbes*. Oxford: Oxford University Press.

Tuck, R. 1989b. "Hobbes and Scepticism." In: *Hobbes Studies*. Ed. G. A. J. Rogers. Oxford: Oxford University Press.

van Fraassen, B. 1984. "Belief and the Will." *Journal of Philosophy* 81:235-56.

Watkins, J. 1965. *Hobbes's System of Ideas*. London: Hutchinson.

Williams, B. 1973. "Deciding to Believe." In *Problems of the Self*. Cambridge UK: Cambridge University Press, 136-51.

CHOOSING TO INTEND, DECIDING TO BELIEVE

Jean Pierre Dupuy
CREA, Ecole Polytechnique and CNRS

1. INTRODUCTION

According to a number of distinguished authors, prominent among them Jonathan Cohen (1992), it would be useful or even necessary, if one is to clear up a series of puzzles in philosophy of mind, to draw a radical distinction between two kinds of mental states: belief and acceptance. The former would be involuntary, the latter voluntary or intentional. Belief would aim at truth, acceptance at success or utility. Belief would be passive, because shaped by evidence; acceptance, active and one could, for the sake of pragmatic concerns, accept something even if one doesn't believe it. Belief would be context-independent; acceptance, context-dependent. Belief would be a matter of degrees, acceptance an all-or-nothing matter.

Maybe due to an innate taste for monsters, I always look for miscigenated creatures when I run into such a neat typology. That's what I am going to do here, drawing on the literature on the paradoxes of rationality. My aim is purely one of deconstruction, and I shall make no efforts at this stage to propose alternative accounts. My own view would be that we are dealing with a continuum of cases rather than with clear cut, radical distinctions—and I think that some of the confusion in the discussion of the subject matter stems from the fact that our natural languages divide up this continuum into discrete boxes in ways that are idiosyncratic to the languages in question.

2. WILLING AND DESIRING

According to Cohen, belief is involuntary whereas acceptance occurs at will. Michael Losonsky, in his contribution to this conference, questions this opposition for being too sharp .

Losonsky's critique is obscured, I submit, by the fact that, alongside with many authors in this debate, he systematically pairs volition and desire, writing in a single stroke of pen things like: "the role of desire and volition in belief formation..."; "I can decide, desire or want to accept a proposition", etc.

This association seems to me highly problematic. Actually I would have thought volition to be a notion held in high suspicion by any philosophy of mind which attempts to "naturalize intentionality". After all, wasn't one of the first moves made by Cybernetics, the ancestor of cognitive science, an attempt at demystifying the classical distinction between voluntary action and reflex thanks to the notion of feedback loop? As for desire and volition, a history of practical philosophy could be written on the basis of their varying relationship. At one end one would find Aristotle and his notion of prudence; at the other, Kant who sets them at odds. What about analytic philosophy?

One can surmise that if there is a room for the will in analytic philosophy, it has to do with decision making and the forming of intentions—which themselves are related to desires (and beliefs) via the practical syllogism. Cohen makes precisely this point in his section 21: "Do Intentions imply Beliefs?", claiming that intentions are volitional or voluntary, as opposed to beliefs. He writes: "Contrary to what many authors contend, an intention to do act A cannot entail belief that, unless prevented, act A will occur, since the formation of an intention is in principle under the intender's own direct control while the formation of a belief is in principle not under the believer's direct control" (Cohen, 1992, p. 126-28).

Unfortunately, this theoretical position is not tenable, as the following case shows. It is a case in which an intention has autonomous effects, distinct from the effects of the action itself. As a consequence, forming the intention may be desirable in itself and come into conflict with the desirability of the act.

I am referring to Gregory Kavka's celebrated "*toxin puzzle*". A billionaire, who has made his fortune in cognitive science, comes to you and proposes the following exchange. "You see this vial," he says, "it contains a toxin which, if you swallow it, will make you as sick as a dog for two days but will not kill you and will leave no after-effects. If you swallow the contents of this vial, I will pay you a million dollars." You are already rejoicing over this unexpected deal because you consider that the physical discomfort will be greatly dwarfed by the fortune you have been offered, when your eccentric acquaintance adds: "I am not even interested in whether or not you actually drink the toxin. I will be satisfied if you form the intention to do so. I have brought along this machine I have invented which is able to detect intentions precisely. You will attach it to your brain tonight at midnight and it will then record whether or not you have the intention to drink the toxin tomorrow at noon. And, since I am generous, I won't even wait for you to drink it to give you your reward. If the machine detects a positive intention, you will find the million dollars in your bank account first thing tomorrow morning." On this, the billionaire leaves you to your bitter thoughts because, as a well-informed philosopher of mind, you have quickly understood that the pot of gold which appeared to be at your fingertips, or rather your lips, has slipped away forever.

This is how Kavka (1983) analyses this problem. Tomorrow at noon, whether or not you have found the million dollars in your account, you have no reason to drink the toxin, and you have a very good reason not to drink it. The past is what it is, and your decision will not change it. There is a dominant strategy, not to drink the toxin, and it is the rational strategy. You know this from now on, and thus also tonight at midnight. Since, Kavka claims, *you cannot will yourself to form an intention*, it is impossible for you to form the intention to do X if you know that when the time comes it will be unreasonable for you to do X. It is thus impossible, tonight at midnight, to form the intention to drink the toxin tomorrow at noon. The true poison is not that in the vial, as you thought, but indeed the billionaire's generosity.

It is clear here that, possibly in spite of itself, analytic philosophy of mind is led to distinguish sharply between desire and volition. As we said, we are dealing here with a case in which an intention has autonomous effects, distinct from the effects of the action itself. If I *could* it would be rational for me to form the intention. I *wish* I could form it. Forming the intention is a *desire* I have. What would be required for me to fulfill it? An act of the *will*. This discussion clearly assumes that willing and wanting, volition and desire, are distinct. Kavka claims that the lesson of his puzzle is that reasons (based on desires and beliefs) are stronger than the will.

Kavka's lesson flatly contradicts Cohen's contention that intentions are volitional or voluntary. He writes: "If intentions were simply decisions, and decisions were volitions fully under the agent's control, there would be no problem. But intentions are better viewed as dispositions to act which are based on reasons to act (...) This puzzle reveals that intentions are only partly volitional. One cannot intend whatever one wants to intend any more than one can believe whatever one wants to believe. As our beliefs are constrained by our evidence, so our intentions are constrained by our reasons for action."

To be sure, Kavka's interpretation is not beyond questioning. There are authors who, like David Gauthier (1988) and Edward McClennen (1989), contend that it is possible and rational to form the (1-million-dollars-worth) intention in the toxin puzzle. Their argument is that the agent has a good *reason* to drink the toxin when the time comes, and therefore *can* form the intention to so act. I believe the argument to be unsuccessful (Dupuy, forthcoming). I shall not review it here, but I want to point that the name these authors give to their central notion: *resolute choice* , betrays that the notion appeals more to the will than to reason.

It therefore seems clear that analytic philosophy of mind and action cannot do without a concept of the will that is wholly distinct from those of desire, intention and decision, but remains so far deprived of any firm grounding. Witness the uncertainty on the fundamental question whether intentions are acts of the will or not. The distinction between belief and acceptance along the voluntary/involuntary line seems to be hanging in the air.

3. THE CASE OF RELIGIOUS BELIEFS

Cohen writes (p. 22): "Acceptance, in contrast with belief, occurs *at will*, whether by an immediate *decision* or through a gradually formed *intention*. This is because at bottom it *executes a choice*."(my emphasis)—and here again we find the idea that the formation of intentions is more voluntary than the formation of beliefs. I want to offer a case study which is meant to show that belief (in Cohen's sense), too, can be said to execute a choice. *Deciding to believe*, as it were. The case study has to do with *religious belief*—presumably the origin of our notion of belief.

Given Prof. Cohen's classification, a question arises: where are religious beliefs to be ranked? By two traits at least they seem to belong with Cohenite beliefs: they are context-independent (I cannot bring myself to believe that God exists when I am sick and that He does not exist when I am in perfect health); and religious belief is belief inasmuch as it is faith, aiming at truth, not at utility or success: people accept to be tortured for their faith, they kill other people in the name of their faith—i.e. in the name of Truth, of the only true God, etc. However, religious belief can be claimed to be, at least to a certain extent, voluntary.

My case study is about Calvin—the real Calvin rather than Hobbes's companion referred to by Losonsky. It is an illustration of the latter's point about "optimism and confidence [being] the marks of a higher status in the company" (p. 20 of "Wanting to believe"). I could make a similar point about Pascal and the Jesuitism/Jansenism quarrel.

It is a reading of Max Weber's paradox about the correlation between protestant ethics and the "spirit of capitalism (Weber, 1985). *Choosing one's predestination*, as it might be labeled.

I examine only the logical structure of Weber's argument, not its empirical validity. In virtue of a divine decision taken for all eternity, each person belongs either to the camp of the elect or to that of the damned, without knowing which. No one can do anything about this decree, and there is nothing anyone can do to earn or merit salvation. However, divine grace manifests itself through signs. What is important is that these signs cannot be observed through introspection: *they are acquired through action.* The principal sign is success obtained through testing one's faith in a worldly profession (*Beruf*). This test is costly. It requires one work continually, methodically, without ever resting secure in, without even enjoying, one's wealth.

The "logical consequence" of this practical problem, Weber points out, should "obviously" have been "fatalism." Here fatalism means the the choice of the "dominant" strategy, as it is known in game theory: whatever the state of the world - here, whether I am one of the elect or not—it is better for me to lead a lazy life. However, Weber's whole book attempts, as we know, to explain why and how "the broad mass of ordinary men" made the opposite choice—known, in the discussion on the foundations of rational choice theory and the class of problems called Newcomb problems (J. M. Fischer, 1989), as the *evidentialist* choice.

The popular Calvinist doctrine held it "to be an absolute duty to consider oneself chosen, and to combat all doubts as temptations of the devil, since lack of self-confidence is the result of insufficient faith, hence of imperfect grace."(Weber, 1985, p.111) "Intense worldly activity" was what allowed one to obtain this self-confidence, the means to assure oneself of one's state of grace.

I have shown elsewhere (Dupuy, 1996) that Calvinist faith strangely resembles what Sartre calls "the faith of bad faith"in *Being and Nothingness* (1966). The fact that bad faith is faith, in other words, belief, he asserts, is precisely what distinguishes it from lying. "How can we believe by bad faith in the concepts which we forge expressly to persuade ourselves?" he asks. His answer: "the project of bad faith must itself be in bad faith." With respect to the "disposition" I take to persuade myself—and here one obviously thinks of the Calvinist *action*, performed in order to believe—he specifies: "For me to have represented it to myself as bad faith would have been cynicism; to believe it sincerely would have been in good faith." Sartre is looking for an intermediary position, of which the choice of the Calvinist, who believes himself to be neither entirely foreign to his election nor totally responsible for it, perfectly illustrates the coherence. The mere existence of this intermediary position is enough to make one seriously doubt that the contrast between involuntary belief and voluntary acceptance makes any sense at all.

"Faith is decision", Sartre writes. "It must decide and *will what it is*." Again, regarding these affinities between two human beings which are said to be determined by *choice*, "I believe that my friend Peter feels friendship for me (...) I *believe it*; that is, (...) *I decide to believe in it*, and to maintain myself in this decision; I conduct myself, finally, as if I were certain of it..." Calvinist faith could not be better defined.

4. THE CASE OF SELF-DECEIT

Professor Cohen contends that the belief/acceptance distinction provides a solution to the nagging paradox of self-deception. It turns out that the evidentialist (i.e. calvinistic) choice, in a Common Cause Newcomb Problem, is generally viewed as a case of self-deception or bad faith. The argument, applied to Max Weber's problem, can be put in the following terms. Propositions (1) and (2) are both true:

(1) The Calvinists believe that they have placed themselves among the elect by choosing to acquire the signs of grace;

(2) The Calvinists believe that they have not placed themselves among the elect.

(1) and (2) express contradictory beliefs. Furthermore, one could think that:

* The Calvinists find a way to hide (1) from themselves

* Because they *want to believe* they were chosen by God.

If we further postulate that the first belief is the *cause* of the second, without, obviously, constituting a reason for it, we obtain a pure case of self-deception as described by Donald Davidson.

There is no denying that this is an acceptable interpretation of the Calvinist choice. The cognitive psychologist Amos Tversky has performed an impressive series of experiments at Stanford in which he places subjects in situations which have the structure of Weber's paradox. The remarkable result is that not only does the great majority of subjects make the Calvinist choice, they deny (to the experimenter, but also in all likelihood to themselves) having *intentionally* made this choice, in order to be able to make a favourable judgment about themselves.

If we are to follow Jonathan Cohen in his account of self-deception, we are led to say that the first belief is a passive belief, shaped by evidence (can the subject ignore that she has proclaimed herself a saint?, as Weber puts it), whereas the second belief is actually an acceptance: she accepts that she was chosen by God in the sense, to paraphrase Cohen, that she adopts the "policy of deeming, positing, or postulating that" such is the case, she includes that proposition among her "premisses for deciding what to do or think in a particular context, whether or not (she) feels it to be true that" she was chosen by God (Cohen, 1992, p. 4). Is that a plausible account of religious faith? We can seriously doubt that such is the case, all the more so since acceptance, being in principle a voluntary, conscious, reflexive attitude normally implies that the subject is aware of the motivation that caused her to accept what she accepts: she wants to hide from herself the fact that she manipulated her election.

Following Alvin Plantinga (1986), I have proposed another interpretation which reveals the *rationality* of the evidentialist choice —and, therefore, the rationality of self-deception in this particular case (Dupuy, 1992).

This other interpretation attributes the Calvinists with the two following beliefs, which are not (necessarily) incompatible:

(3) The Calvinists believe they have not placed themselves among the elect because they believe God has chosen them;

(4) The Calvinists believe they were free to make the
    opposite choice when they chose.

Under the first (orthodox) interpretation, the irrationality is found
in proposition (2): the Calvinists set themselves on the belief that they
did not place themselves among the elect because "at the bottom of
their hearts," they know very well that they have acted to give
themselves the signs of their election and that they want to hide this
truth from themselves. According to the second (heterodox)
interpretation, the Calvinists believe that they have not proclaimed
themselves saints simply because they take seriously the givens of the
problem as they were submitted to them, or as they have internalized
them: God has proclaimed them to be as they are. This is their faith.
Nonetheless, they must face a serious problem: they must consider it
not incoherent to believe at once that God has chosen for them
(proposition (3)) and that they were free to choose (proposition (4)).
In other words, in order for them and us to be able to take Max Weber's
problem seriously, they must first convince themselves that it is
reasonable to be a "*compatibilist*": to believe in the compatibility of
(here, causal) determinism and free will.

I am obliged here to pass directly to the conclusion of a complex
analysis. Being a compatibilist implies reasoning thus. Just as "when
Adam took the apple it would have been *possible* for him not to take it"
(Sartre, *Being and Nothingness*, p. 602), when the Calvinist makes the
Calvinist choice, it would have been possible for him to make the
opposite choice. Just as there would then have been another Adam,
there would have been another Calvinist: instead of being chosen, he
would have been damned. The example of Adam and the apple is, as
we recall, the one that Sartre takes in order to distinguish his position
from that of Leibniz. According to the latter, Adam's essence is not
chosen by Adam, but by God. His freedom is thus only illusory.
According to Sartre, to the contrary, Adam's existence precedes his
essence. Free Adam chooses himself: his existence determines his
essence, "henceforth what makes his *person* known to him is the future
and not the past; he chooses to learn what he is by means of ends
toward which he projects himself." (B and N, p. 603) Under the

heterodox interpretation of the Calvinist choice, the free Calvinist follows Leibniz and Sartre at the same time. His essence determines his existence, but, since he is free to choose his existence, he can determine his essence. He has, literally, the power to choose his predestination. However, as Plantinga insists, this power is not causal —which would make it inconceivable since causality would then fly counter to the arrow of time. It is a "*counterfactual* power over the past." The nature of this power appears in the linking of the reasons which lead to the rational choice.

The subject, knowing himself to be free, reasons thus. If I make this choice, rather than the opposite choice, this action would be the *sign* that I am in a certain world, with its past, its determinism, my essence specific to this world. If I choose to act differently, I will be in another world and my essence will be different. It is not that my action causally determines my world: it *reveals* it. However, since I am free *and* rational, my choice must satisfy an extremal principle: it must maximize my utility, pleasure, happiness—whichever here, for one readily accepts that the Calvinist prefers eternal salvation to damnation, even if this salvation is acquired at the price of a life of labour. I thus choose to acquire the signs of my salvation—without, however, considering that I thus *cause* my salvation by buying it.

On this alternative interpretation, the belief that expresses the Calvinist faith—(3), which has the same content as (2) in the first interpretation—is a belief proper, not an acceptance. My conjecture is that the Calvinist faith oscillates between the two readings, hence its fragility, elusiveness, "evanescence", as Sartre puts it. Are we prepared to say that it is sometimes a belief proper, sometimes an acceptance? I would rather conclude that it is neither one nor the other. The two categories define each other through their opposition, and this opposition is too radical to have any chance of being pertinent.

BIBLIOGRAPHY

Jonathan Cohen, *An Essay on Belief and Acceptance*, Oxford University Press, 1992.

Donald Davidson, "Deception and Division," in Jon Elster (Ed.), *The Multiple Self*, Cambridge University Press, 1986.

Jean-Pierre Dupuy, "Two Temporalities, Two Rationalities: A New Look at Newcomb's Paradox", *Economics and Cognitive Science*, Eds. P. Bourgine and B. Walliser, Pergamon Press, 1992.

Jean-Pierre Dupuy, "Not to know what one knows: some paradoxes of self-deception" in J. Schlanger (ed.), "What Do We Not Know?", *Diogenes*, 169, vol. 43/1, 1995, p. 53-68.

Jean-Pierre Dupuy, "Rationality and Self-Deception", in *Perspectives on Self-Deception*, J.-P. Dupuy (ed.), forthcoming.

John Martin Fischer, ed. , *God, Foreknowledge, and Freedom*, Stanford, Stanford University Press, 1989.

David Gauthier, "In the Neighbourhood of the Newcomb-Predictor (Reflections on Rationality)", *Proceedings of the Aristotelian Society*, Vol. 89, Part 3, 1988/89.

Gregory Kavka, "The Toxin Puzzle", *Analysis*, Vol. 43, 1, Jan. 1983.

Edward McClennen, *Rationality and Dynamic Choice: Foundational Explorations*, Cambridge University Press, 1989.

Alvin Plantinga, "On Ockham's Way Out," in *Faith and Philosophy*, 3, 1986.

Jean-Paul Sartre, *Being and Nothingness*, trad. Hazel Barnes, Simon and Schuster, Pocket Books, 1966.

Max Weber, *The Protestant Ethic and the Spirit of Capitalism*, Trans. Talcott Parsons, Allen & Unwin Inc., 1985.

TRANSFORMATIONS OF BELIEF

Richard Jeffrey
Princeton University

1. EARLY MODERN DOGMATISM, SKEPTICISM, AND PROBABILISM

Today, religious and secular belief are commonly set apart, but it was not so when modern epistemology was taking shape in Europe; by offering new, life-threatening religious choices, the Reformation gave a new sort of practical importance to *"Credo, "*and, with it, to meaning and truth (a propos of *"Hoc est corpus meum").* Here is a famous 16th century statement of the problem and its skeptical solution:

> How many quarrels, and how important, have been produced in the world by doubt of the meaning of that syllable *Hoc!*
>
> Let us take the question that logic itself offers us as the clearest. If you say "It is fine weather," and you are speaking the truth, then it is fine weather. Isn't that a sure way of speaking? Still it will deceive us. To show this let us continue the example. If you say "I lie," and if you are speaking the truth, then you lie. The art, the reason, the force of the conclusion of this one are the same as in the other; yet there we are stuck in the mud.
>
> I can see why the Pyrrhonian philosophers cannot express their general conception in any manner of speaking; for they would need a new language. Ours is wholly formed of

affirmative propositions, which to them are entirely repugnant; so that when they say "I doubt," immediately you have them by the throat to make them admit that at least they know and are sure of this fact, that they doubt. Thus they have been constrained to take refuge in this comparison from medicine, without which their attitude would be inexplicable: when they declare "I do not know" or "I doubt," they say that this proposition carries itself away with the rest, no more nor less than rhubarb, which expels evil humors and carries itself off with them.

This idea is more firmly grasped in the form of interrogation: "What do I know"the words I bear as a motto, inscribed over a pair of scales. (Montaigne, "Apology for Raymond Seybond")

Montaigne allied himself with the Pyrrhonian skeptics.

Descartes, treating belief as voluntary, reintroduced the Stoic *criterion* (clarity, distinctness) as a curb on the will to ensure truth of dogmatic judgment. (Here I mean "dogma" in the ancient sense of *belief* In that sense, *dogmatism* is simply a matter of taking belief and disbelief as the right judgmental attitudes—e.g., instead of skeptical suspense.) Pascal, a subtler voluntarist, saw the belief that would lead to salvation as an end to be sought through lesser acts of the will, "taking the holy water, having masses said, etc." *(Pensées,* 233). His famous Wager was meant to be a probabilistic, decision-theoretic bridge to dogmatic belief.

Four years after Descartes' s death, Pascal and Fermat offered a resolution of the clash between skepticism and dogmatism—in effect, by adapting Montaigne's scales to represent a continuum of probabilistic states of mind. Montaigne's scales were an equal-arm balance, registering acceptance or rejection (or suspense) by tipping one way or the other (or exactly balancing). The scales under his motto were shown in exact balance, indicating the recommended suspense. The probabilists let the arms have different lengths, and used exact balance to signal *judgment* (Fig. 1).

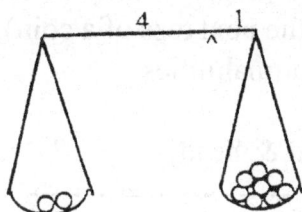

Fig. 1. The ratio 1:4 of lengths measures preference for truth over falsity.
The ratio 8:2 of weights measures odds on truth against falsity.
The scales balance when those ratios are inverse.

Where do probabilistic judgments come from? An important source is statistical data—interpreted in the light of certain stable qualitative probabilistic judgments. Here is the relevant theorem of the elementary probability calculus:[1]

(1) *The Law of little numbers.* In a finite sequence of equiprobable propositions, if the probability is 1 that the relative frequency of truths is p, then the probability of each is p.

In judgmental terms: if, judging a sequence of propositions to be equiprobable, you learn the relative frequency of truths in a way that does not change that judgment, your probability for each proposition will agree with the relative frequency. Note that turning statistics into probabilities in this way requires neither conditioning nor Bayes's theorem, nor does it require you to have a particular probability for the propositions prior to learning the relative frequency.

2. ANSWERING HARMAN

It is a commonly but erroneously supposed that probabilistic judgment must be a matter of assigning definite numerical probabilities to propositions. But as we have seen in applying (1) to turn statistics into probabilities, probabilistic judgment may well attribute bare equiprobability to propositions, with no particular probability being specified. And as we all know, probabilistic judgment may determine conditional probabilities (e.g., for head on the next toss of a coin), and thereby determine ratios of indeterminate probabilities:

$$\mathbf{pr}[\text{head} \,/\, \text{tossed}] = 1/2 = \frac{\mathbf{pr}[\text{tossed \& head}]}{\mathbf{pr}[\text{tossed}]} = \frac{?}{?}$$

Another class of examples arises from the scheme for updating probabilities by generalized conditioning when new information leaves you uncertain about which members of some sequence of incompatible, exhaustive data sentences is true but does lead you to adopt probabilities d_1, d_1,... for them. If you have definite conditional probabilities c_1, c_1,... for a hypothesis given the successive data sentences, then if *the c's are unchanged by the observation,* your posterior probability for the hypothesis will be

(2) $c_1 d_1 + c_2 d_2 + \dots$

To compute posterior probabilities in this way, no priors are needed apart from the invariant c's; in particular, the probabilites whose ratios the c's determine can be quite indeterminate, as can be the priors corresponding to the posterior d's.

The foregoing paragraph is my rebuttal of the charge that, generalized or not, conditioning is generally unfeasible because of the dreaded combinatorial explosion.[2] The rest of this section deprecates a proposed correction to the present way of treating probabilistic judgment which is related to Harman's view; but as I am not sure how closely, I call its proponent "X".

X sees probabilistic judgments as a species of dogmatic judgments; e.g., X represents my odds of 1:1 on head objectively, as (3) below, whereas I would represent them judgmentally, as (4).

(3) The (real) probability of head is 1/2.
(4) My (judgmental) probability for head is 1/2.

Note the asymmetry: In saying (3) I imply (4), but by saying (4) I do not imply (3). That is not because I doubt that the objective notion makes sense in such contexts. I do, but even if I did not, my probability for head might be 1/2 because I am sure the coin has either two heads or two tails, and my odds on the two possibilities are 1:1. Here my judgmental probability would be 1/2, while I am sure that the objective probability is either 1 or 0.

So I reject (3) as a rendition of my 1:1 odds on head.

X thinks that, when reasonable, (4) will be forthcoming from (3), and that (3) will follow from non-probabilistic beliefs of mine by a process called "inference to the best explanation." If so, X thinks, I may add (3) to my body of beliefs if that would be useful for my purposes. X thinks I have no need of its consequence (4), and that (3) itself is what I should use to compute expected utilities of gambles.

But where are we to stick the label "best explanation"? In the case of statistical explanations, the best seems to be the one maximizing probability of the explanandum. (A ball, drawn at random from an urn bears the number seven. What was the composition of the urn? "All sevens" is the "maximum likelihood" answer, relative to which the outcome is most probable.)

But I know when I find that sort of inference acceptable, i.e., when the competing hypotheses are equiprobable.[3] In this, as in other cases, I prefer to use my full probabilistic judgment guided by maxims and techniques I understand.

3. OVERCOMING HOLISM

Quine, often credited with overthrowing logical empiricism, remains a positivist stalwart. This is evident from chapter 1 of his *Pursuit of Truth*[4] where observation sentences appear early as "occasion" sentences "on which speakers of the language can agree outright on witnessing the occasion" (p. 3). These give his dogmatic epistemology its firm experiential foundation. Quine's account of theory-testing is like Descartes's *(Principles...,* Book 4, §205), i.e., hypothetico-deductivism relieved by a gesture toward probability.

> [O]ne continually reasons not only in refutation of hypotheses but in support of them. This, however, is a matter of arguing logically or probabilistically from other beliefs already held. [...] Pure observation lends only negative evidence, by refuting an observation categorical that a proposed theory implies.
>
> (Quine, *Pursuit of Truth* p. 13)

This sets us up for the Duhem move:

> [T]he falsity of the observation categorical does not conclusively refute the hypothesis. What it refutes is the conjunction of sentences that was needed to imply the observation categorical. In order to retract that conjunction we do not have to retract the hypothesis in question; we could retract some other sentence of the conjunction instead. This is the important insight called *holism*. Duhem made much of it early in this century, but not too much.
>
> (Quine, *op. Cit.*, pp. 13-14)

Quine sees this holism as discrediting sentence-meaning and other dogmas of empiricism (but not the empiricist dogma itself—anyway, not by name). And perhaps holism would be credible if the hypothetico-deductivism on which it stands were all we had in the way of a methodology. But as Jon Dorling has shown, probabilistic considerations can let us focus the effect of experience more sharply than on the whole set of premises that contradict an observation sentence. An illustration is provided by the following treatment of the confirmation of Einstein's general theory of relativity in 1919. (Direct quotations are from Dorling's unpublished 1983 manuscript.[5])

"In the solar eclipse experiments of 1919, the telescopic observations were made in two locations, but only in one location was the weather good enough to obtain easily interpretable results. Here, at Sobral, there were two telescopes: one, the one we hear about, confirmed Einstein; the other, in fact the slightly larger one, confirmed Newton. Conclusion: Einstein was vindicated, and the result with the larger telescope were rejected." (P. 19)

Dorling sets the scene:

(New theory)   General Relativistic light-bending effect of the sun
(Old theory)   No light-bending effect of the sun
(Auxiliary)   Both telescopes are working correctly
(Observation)   The actual, conflicting data from both telescopes

The auxiliary hypothesis is independent of each theory. Then as the conditional probability is 0 for the observation given joint truth of the auxiliary and either theory, the likelihood ratio (left) for truth of new against old theories can be expressed as at the right:

$$(3) \quad \frac{\text{pr[observation} \mid \text{new true]}}{\text{pr[observation} \mid \text{old true]}} = \frac{\text{pr[observation} \mid \text{new true, auxiliary false]}}{\text{pr[observation} \mid \text{old true, auxiliary false]}}$$

"Now the experimenters argued that one way in which the auxiliary hypothesis might easily be false was if the mirror of one or the other of the telescopes had distorted in the heat, and this was much more likely to have happened with the larger mirror belonging to the telescope which confirmed the old theory than with the smaller mirror belonging to the telescope which confirmed the new theory. Now the effect of mirror distortion of the kind envisaged would be to shift the recorded images of the stars from the positions predicted by the new theory to or beyond those predicted by the old. Hence the numerator [on the r.h.s. of (3)] was regarded as having an appreciable value, while, since it was very hard to think of any similar effect which could have shifted the positions of the stars in the other telescope from those predicted by the old theory to those predicted by the new, the denominator was regarded as negligibly small, hence the result as overall a decisive confirmation of the new theory and refutation of the old...." (p. 19)

Thus the likelihood ratio (3) is considerably greater than 1, from which it follows by Bayes's theorem that, conditionally on the observation, the new theory is considerably more probable than the old. In such ways, probabilistic analysis can yield principled resolution of conflict—in this case, rejecting the auxiliary hypothesis and identifying one of the competing theories as confirmed by the ambiguous data.

4. PRAGMATICS

Judgmental probabilities belong to the branch of the theory of signs called "pragmatics," which puts users up front. There is a real connection with pragmatism, the philosophical attitude that puts choosing and doing up front and sees practical reason as prior to the theoretical kind. Decision theory places practical reason in the framework of a logic of practical preference, i.e., in my book,[6] preference for truth of one sentence over another when all is said and done, even if truth of the second is preferred in certain respects. Ethan Bolker's axioms for preference imply the existence of probability and "utility" functions which jointly represent the relation, in this sense:[7]

Owners of those preferences prefer truth of A to truth of B *iff* expectations of utility are greater conditionally on A than on B.

The probabilities entering into these conditional expectations are also meant to serve their owners' theoretical purposes.

There is also a pragmatics of ordinary assertion. Probabilistic pragmatics may help here, e.g., as a way of understanding the conditions under which indicative conditional sentences are thought to be properly assertable. To set the scene, consider *modus ponens* on a truth-functional reading of "if" as *or not:*

> A
> C if A (i.e., $C \lor \neg A$)
> -----------------------
> ∴ C

Suppose you believe C *if* A only because you disbelieve A. Then coming to believe A will remove your ground for belief in C *if* A, and, with it, the ground that validity of *modus ponens* might give for belief in C. The problem is that in such a case, **pr[C if A]** falls as **pr[A]** rises.

So stability of pr[conditional] as pr[antecedent] changes would seem to be a normal condition for assertability of the truth functional conditional. Now note that, since $C \lor \neg A = \neg A \lor (A \& C)$, the probability of that truth functional conditional is a weighted average (4) of 1 and **pr[C | A]**:

$$(4) \ \mathbf{pr[C \lor \neg A] = 1.pr[\neg A] + pr[C \mid A].\, pr[A]}.$$

It follows that stability of the probability of the truth functional conditional as the probability of its antecedent varies comes to the same thing as stability of the conditional probability at the value 1 (so that the downward-sloping line in Fig. 2 moves to the dashed horizontal position).

pr[¬A ∨ C]

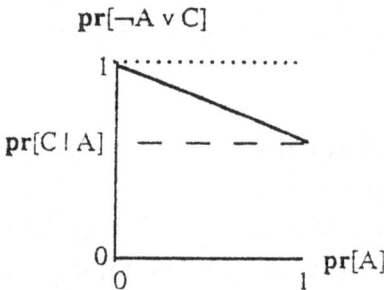

Fig. 2. The probability of the conditional is a weighted average of I and the conditional probability, with respective weights pr[¬A], pr[A]. Then as pr[A] varies, pr[¬A ∨ C] is constant iff pr[C | A] is constant at and = 1

One hundred percent is a very large probability; the corresponding odds are infinite. Then usually, when a conditional probability is constant as probability of the condition varies, the probability of the corresponding truth functional conditional will also vary. But constancy of conditional probability as probability of the condition varies is an interesting property even when the conditional probability is not 1, for that constancy seems to be the active ingredient in judgments of probabilistic causality. This strikes me as the key to "Newcomb" problems, in which you see your choices as ineffectual symptoms of states of affairs that you would promote or prevent if you could. The thought is that these are not properly described as decision problems.[8]

In any decision problem in which the outcome is not clear from the beginning, probabilities of possible acts will vary during deliberation, for finally an act will be chosen, and have probability near 1, a probability no act had initially. Newcomb problems seem ill posed as *decision* problems because too much information is given about conditional probabilities—i.e., enough to fix the unconditional probabilities of the acts! We are told that there is an association between acts (making A true or false) and states (truth or falsity of S) which makes acts strong predictors of states, and states of acts, in the sense that the conditional probabilities of S given A and of A given S are large relative to those of S given ¬A and of A given ¬S. But these four values (in fact, the first three) are enough to fix the agent's probablity for A, or odds on A:[9]

$$\frac{pr[A| S] \cdot pr[S | \neg A]}{pr[S| A] \cdot pr[\neg A| S]} = \frac{pr[A]}{pr[\neg A]}$$

Example:The Similar prisoners' dilemma. Two prisoners—Ann and Sam—think they think pretty much alike. Their problem: if one confesses and the other does not, the one goes free and the other serves a long prison term; if neither confesses, both serve short terms; and if both confess, both serve intermediate terms. From Alma's point of view, Sam's possible actions (S, confess; $\neg S$, don't) are states of nature. She sees herself as facing a Newcomb problem; she thinks her choices (A, confess; $\neg A$, don't) are pretty good predictors of his, and vice versa, even though neither's choices influence the other's. Numerically, suppose that $pr[A | S] = pr[S | A] = .8$ and $pr[S | \neg A] = .1$. Then Ann's odds on A are $(.8)(.1)/(.8)(.2) = 1:2$, so her $pr[A] = 1/3$. If this is her view of the problem, Ann sees herself as unlikely to confess. And if her four conditional probabilities are stable, so are her probabilities for her confessing and for Sam's confessing; both are 1/3. Then Ann sees it, she has no decision to make; her strategy is already determined, i.e., confess or not, with probabilities 1/3 and 2/3, respectively.

5. BAYESIAN BUMBLEBEES
(Abstract)

Q. How is it that bumblebees evolved so that their foraging behavior is describable in the same, utility-maximizing, terms that apply to the behavior of more complicated organisms like bankers?[10]

A. Because since adaptively important frequencies were targets of Darwinian adaptation, imputed pr can be expected to track such frequencies, given that imputed utilities match Darwinian fitness.[11]

Our language and conscious deliberation don't substitute for that; they build on it. In us as in other animals, domain-specific sensitivities to once (and still?) evolutionarily important frequencies combine with evolutionarily crafted tastes to guide spontaneous action in such a way that behavior is explicable in the framework of Bayesian decision theory. I take that sort of explicability to be a necessary background for our conscious deliberation and interpretation of behavior, and for selfconscious strategic thinking. That is explicability of actual behavior in Bayesian terms, e.g., in view of actual tastes—with no adaptive account needed of how current tastes were shaped by the exigencies of life in the Pleistocene era.

NOTES

[1] See "Probabilism and induction," *Topoi* 5(1986)51-58, especially sec. 2, or *Probability and the Art of Judgment* (Cambridge, 1992), p. 59-64.

[2] As in Gilbert Harman's *Change in View* (Cambridge, Mass.: MIT Press, 1986), pp. 25-27.

[3] The "likelihood" of a hypothesis relative to data is the conditional probability of the data given the hypothesis. By Bayes's theorem, equiprobability of the hypotheses is necessary and sufficient for the ratio of their likelihoods relative to data to equal their conditional odds given the data.

[4] 2nd edition (1992), Harvard University Press.

[5] Reproduced here with small alterations in notation. His published paper on this topic is "Bayesian personalism, the methodology of research programmes, and Duhem's problem" *Studies in History and Philosophy of Science* 10(1979)177-187. He elaborates in an unpublished paper of ca. 1983, "Further illustrations of the Bayesian solution of Duhem's problem," (29 pp., photocopied, undated: Centrale Interfaculteit, Universiteit van Amsterdam, Grimburgwal 10, Amsterdam). See also Colin Howson and Peter Urbach, *Scientific Reasoning: the Bayesian approach* (Open Court: La Salle, Illinois, 2nd ed., 1993), pp. 136-142, and Richard Jeffrey, "Take back the day! Jon Dorling's Bayesian solution to the Duhem problem", *Science and Knowledge*, ed. Enrique Villanueva, Ridgeview (1993) 197-207.

[6] *The Logic of Decision* (2nd ed., University of Chicago Press: Chicago, 1983, 1990).

[7] Ethan Bolker, "A simultaneous Axiomatization of Utility and Subjective Probability," *Philosophy of Science* 34(1967), pp. 333-340. Further references are given there. See also my *Logic of Decision* (2nd ed., University of Chiucago Press: Chicago, corrected, paperback edition, 1990), pp. 142-149.

[8] See "Causality in the Logic of Decision," *Philosophical Topics* 21(1993), pp. 139-151. Elsewhere I had accepted Newcomb problems as decision problems, and accepted "2-box" solutions as correct. In the 1983 version of *The Logic of Decision* (sec. 1.7 and 1.8) I proposed a new criterion for acceptability of an act — "ratifiability"—which proved to break down in certain cases (see p. 20 of the 1990 version). In "How to probabilize a Newcomb problem" and "Probability Dynamics and Causality" *(PSA* 92, vol. 2: Philosophy of Science Association, E. Lansing, Michigan, 1993), ratifiability was recast in terms more like the present ones —but still treating Newcomb problems as decision problems.

[9] I.e., by Bayes's theorem in the form $pr[G \mid H]/pr[H \mid G] = .pr[G]/pr[H]$.

[10] Leslie A. Real, "Animal Choice Behavior and the Evolution of Cognitive Architecture," *Science 253* (1991), pp. 980-986.

[11] This is an application of Ethan Bolker's representation theorem (see *The Logic of Decision*, chapter 9) in view of Brian Skyrms's "Darwin Meets *The Logic of Decision*": *Philosophy of Science* 61(1994)503-528.

BELIEF AND ACCEPTANCE: A LOGICAL POINT OF VIEW

Jacques Dubucs
Institut d Histoire des Sciences et des Techniques,
CNRS/ Université de Paris I

The concept of belief seems to crystallise most of the vexed issues of contemporary philosophy, and the numerous and seemingly unrelated debates around this notion give today the impression of an ubiquitous brownian motion rather than of an even modest progression in some definite direction. Perhaps this feeling simply results of not standing at the right distance, perhaps after the time will have accomplished its cruel work of decantation, it will be possible to get some clearer perspective, and eventually to grasp the genuine *problem* to which so many solutions had been proposed. But perhaps not so. Perhaps most of the current debate rests on a fundamental equivocation, and there is simply no minimally coherent concept able to play so many roles as today attributed to "belief": to underly sincere utterances in public languages, to be entertainable by animals and infra-linguals too, to represent, when true or justified, the final aim of science, to be also responsible for overt behavior, articulated with desire according to some pragmatic formula, and so on. If inconsistency is the case, the best thing to do is to divide this unmanageable empire of beliefehood into separate provinces: on one hand belief *stricto sensu* (if one dare say), and various non-credal attitudes on the other hand.

Cohen is of this persuasion, and he puts forward a new notion of acceptance, intended to replace the current notion of belief in some functions it usurpatorilly deserves. Such an attempt calls for meticulous evaluation. For one thing is to solve enigmas, so to speak, by the mere mechanical effect of having at one's disposal a supplementary degree of freedom in explanation, another is to draw the frontier in a sensible, natural and fruitful way. In this respect, Cohen's way of dividing up things appears to the newcomer as idiosyncratic if not stipulatory, for it is orthogonal to most of the distinctions that the average reader has in mind, as between attitudes related to a "propositional content" (definable up to provable equivalence) and attitudes sensible to hyper-intensional differences between expressions with the same content. But a further reflexion shows—this is in any case what I shall argue in the first part of this article—that Cohen's demarcation is exactly what it was needed: I eventually came to the conviction that, apart from a certain point about which I shall discuss, Cohen's *Essay on Belief and Acceptance* decisively contributes to the conceptual clarity in philosophy of science (in this paper I leave completely aside issues that have to do with the philosophy of mind). As examples of the kind of clarification that one can expect from his distinction, I will also sketchily propose, in the two last parts of my paper, Cohen-style solutions for two major difficulties, namely the paradox of logical omniscience and Kyburg's lottery paradox.

1. REFLECTIONS ON COHEN'S ESSAY

Cohen's book appears as representative of a general tendency (Van Fraassen is arguing in the same way) to try to change the general image of scientific activity which is supposed to be widely dominant today. Against any routinizing conception, according to which scientists are causally—if not automatically—driven to truth, Cohen emphasizes the rôle of human will and decision in the making of science: his distinction between acceptance and belief, respectively echoing active intellectual prophyllaxy and uncontrolled prejudice (e.g. pp 88, 98), clearly expresses an *axiological* preference for the first attitude. Such a train of thoughts is hardly objectionable. Even philosophers of bayesian persuasion, who seem much in view[1], could subscribe to this position in arguing with some appearance of right that their own conception of collecting evidence is far away from the picture of a whale passively bolting plankton while swimming haphazardly, but involves deliberate reflexion, balanced judgment, and planned experiments.

Yet a central question is whether Cohen's contrast between belief and acceptance is a mere difference "in the head", or whether it is able to be publically manifested, in some other form, of course, than from vague and debatable imputations of "conservativism" or "revolutionarism", presumed to attest the respective predominance of the passive or of the active components in the cognitive repertoire of the subjects. Two ways are traditionally proposed for registering such public manifestations: linguistic utterances, and overt behavior (or better, as it is here question of doxastic states which may concern such objects as quarks or neutrinos, which are infrequently involved in overt behavior: betting behavior accomoded to the ramseyan well-known mood). In view of the fact that neither belief nor acceptance, in Cohen's acception, are regularly publicizable by these ways, one risks to find oneself once again in situation of attributing to the distinction between belief and acceptance the status of a merely *private* distinction.

Let me give another example of this problem of publicization, which has also to do with acceptance of theoretical claims. It concerns the debate (to which Cohen alas never alludes) in the sixties on "acceptance rules" (the word "acceptance" had at the time a different (however not unrelated) sense than in Cohen's book. It appeared (e.g in Lakatos) that this notion was not only polysemic, but also by no means robust. Minor deviations in its characterization are able to provoke catastrophic changes of view: the same philosophers who reject acceptance$_i$ as a vile attitude, namely who declare *never* to accept$_i$ *any* theoretical claim, may also consider acceptance$_j$ as a stance which is basically the right one, and declare themselves prepared to accept$_j$ *whatever* theoretical claim. But the fine-grained distinctions which were supposed to justify such extreme differences of view seem often to rest on the mere *purpose* in which theoretical claims are accepted (e.g. 'accepting$_i$' may be like 'accepting with the firm and sincere intention of submitting the claim to severe tests'). Clearly, nothing really objectivable emerges from such a mention of a secondary attitude, accompanying, so to speak, the main attitude that is to be a matter to publicize: there are few activities more similar to the activity of testing in *hoping* failure than the activity of testing in *fearing* failure [2].

Thus the central problem is to show how exactly the difference between belief and acceptance becomes manifest in the *actual* practice of science (what is obviously very distinct from the question is how it appears in the representation the scientists themselves may have of this activity).

Let us begin in a non Cohenian way, by stating a principle that may be considered as hardly objectionable, for it immediately results from rejection of *regressio ad infinitum*:

Recognizability Principle(RP): The conditions C' to which we recognize that such and such conditions C are realized have themselves to be recognizable when they are realized.

In this principle, we can think the conditions C' as consisting in the existence of some public or publicizable entity playing the rôle of witness for the satisfaction of C, like a mathematical construction, a string of formulas in some formal language, a sequence of chemical reactions, and so on. The definition of such an entity Π is, of course, constrained by a

Correctness Requirement: The existence of Π has to imply the satisfaction of C.

But (RP) insists upon another condition, namely a

Feasability Requirement (FR): If there is at all such Π, then we have to be able, on the ground of our own cognitive or physical capacities, to place ourselves in a position permitting to recognize its existence by producing or designing a replicatum of it.

To speak strictly, (RP) and (FR) are *schematic* requirements, from which genuine constraints only arise when the floating "we" is precised by delineating some typical class of recognitional abilities. For the relevant witnesses Π are of course distinct, according as it is a question of beings as ourselves, lucidely conceived as equipped with strongly limited capacities, or of hypothetical beings whose capacities would arbitrarily extend ours: in the limit, (FR) becomes here empty and no distinction between the conditions C and the conditions to which we recognize their realization is no more necessary.

We are now very near to Cohen's territory. Rationality may be estimated from two different point of view:

(i) substantively, by reference to something like the "belief-box" of the subject: the subject is reputed as more rational as this box contains more truths and less falsities, i.e. so to speak by the brute result of the exercice of his cognitive abilities.

(ii) procedurally, by reference to the way the subject uses his cognitive abilities.

Cohen clearly advocates the second viewpoint: the hypothetical *Übermenschen* to which I alluded above are not at all, according to this conception, to be considered as more *rational* than ourselves. In other words, what is capable to be said rational is not belief (which has to do *directly* to truth), but "acceptance" (which is not so).

Moreover, Cohen defends the thesis he calls "the attainability of rationality norms", according to which all the norms we can stipulate about the rationality of the subjects (i.e. the way he deals with his cognitive capacities, by using them in order to write proofs, to design experiments, a.s.o.) have to be such that the subject is able to satisfy them. This thesis may be suspected (and it has not failed to be actually so) to imply the rationality of any subject, for, briefly stated, it has a certain air of obliging the subjects only to what they do: is not rationality equated with mere reality ?

Instead of discussing and vindicating Cohen (supposed of course he needs some help from myself) in some abstract way, I propose to treat the point by reference to a particular problem (that Cohen, in my view, completely misses in the relevant chapter of his *Essay*).

2. A COHENIAN WAY OF SOLVING
THE PARADOX OF LOGICAL OMNISCIENCE

This paradox has been so much discussed since Carnap's *Meaning and Necessity*, that it is hardly necessary to restate it in pedantic detail. Let me however very briefly recall how the story goes. When one defines belief in the possible-worlds framework (as one has rather convincing reasons to do), belief appears unaffected by too many logical transformations: e.g. if you believe that φ, then you are committed to believe that ψ as soon that ψ is a logical consequence of φ. One can of course retreat from Kripke semantics, in which this phenomen is attested, to Scott-Montague semantics, and limit this "omniscience" to the following: believing that φ is equivalent to believing that ψ for any ψ logically equivalent to φ. But that clearly remains too much, and despite innumerable attempts nobody is today able (*pace* Hintikka, *pace* Cresswell, *pace* so many) to do better without logical oddities.

From a conceptual point of view, the paradox of logical omniscience invariably arises from the confrontation between beliefs ascribed on the ground of overt behavior (there is no possible *behavioral* evidence that you do not believe some theorem, for the reality itself cannot be illogical) and beliefs ascribed on the ground of utterances (there may be a lot of *linguistic* evidence that you do not believe a certain theorem). Whence various manoeuvres to by-pass the contradiction, which rest most of the time on a distinction between "implicit beliefs", and "explicit beliefs", that are respectively said to be "objectively deductively closed", and "subjectively deductively closed".

The notion of acceptance gives rise to a similar difficulty, for there is some tension between the committing aspect of acceptance and its voluntariness. On one hand, you *ought* to accept the consequences of whatever you accept, on the other hand, you cannot accept something without *willing* and *knowing* that: both features together seem to imply logical omniscience. But Cohen is in better position than possible-worlds theorists, for acceptance is the internalized assent of some *linguistic* entity, while they conceive belief as relative to a *propositional* content. Taking this difference into account, it should be possible to do better than Cohen, and to eliminate the unfortunate mixture of logic and psychology he resigns himself to when he invokes in his turn "perceived implications" (p 27) and "subjective deductive closure" (p 28). What are the specifications of a solution to that variant of the problem of logical omniscience ?

(i) We have to replace "subjectively deducible" by such a *logical* term, say "$_c$deducible", that one who accepts φ may be reasonably considered as committed to accept (and therefore, to recognize) also any sentence which would be $_c$deducible from φ. $_c$Deducibility is to be conceived widely enough to make this commitment somewhat substantive ("$_c$deducible from φ" cannot reduce, for extreme example, to "type-identical to φ"), but it has to be also strictly enough conceived to avoid to oblige the subject to an impossible task.

(ii) As regards the voluntariness issue, we have hardly to worry about that. For the logical rules in terms of which $_c$deducibility will be inductively defined, as logical rules in general, are *permissive* rules that wholly differ from *compulsory* rules as bayesian conditionalization. Thus they have not to be conceived as necessarily reflecting the way the subject himself *ought to proceed*, or even *actually proceeds*, in order to improve his knowledge, but rather as furnishing, considered in the totality of their effects, a standard by which could be evaluated the extent of the epistemic obligations of anyone who accepts a given sentence.

(iii) If the above point into account, we have, in defining $_c$deducibility, to look for rules which, so to speak, transmit to their conclusion the *executability* of their premises: while our rules may very well not exactly correspond to the channels the subject goes through, we have however to be sure that if he is able to get the premisses of the rule by expending some cognitive effort, then he is also able to get its conclusion at a similar price. For example we should think of a rule which allows to conclude "(φ and ψ) implies ξ" from "φ implies ξ" as an unacceptable licence, as y may contain concepts which are not at disposal of the subject who has obtained "φ implies ξ". (NB: do not forget the direction of rotation of the gears-wheels: given that we have to do with *permissive* rules, the less they are constrained, the more the acceptance of φ is for you constraining, as you are committed to accept, and therefore to recognize as such, sentences which may be obtained from φ by a richer array of inferential moves).

Now let us proceed. Acceptance has not *directly* to do with truth, but *indirectly*, via "witnesses". Similarly, it has not directly to do with semantical consequence, but indirectly, via proofs. Things should therefore be going smoothly for, once again, logical omniscience is not as deeply entrenched in proof-theoretical notions as it is involved in semantical notions. Proofs are of course committed to transmit truth. But it does not suffice to define them. Else it would be enough to write "H" under "Γ" to have a proof, in the case where H is semantical consequence of Γ, which is absurd. Proofs are also constrained by some feasibility requirement (or, if you prefer, by some norm of rationality). Therefore if we succeed in defining some *attainable* norm in that domain, the so-called paradox will be resolved. Thus our objective is to get some logically rigourous notion of proof in terms of which human beings *could be* considered as perfect reasoners.

If we consider the tradition of modern logic, the feasibility requirement has been massively interpreted as recommending a kind of proof canonized, for example, in Church's *Introduction to Mathematical Logic* (1944). Accordingly, a proof has simply to be *effective*, i.e. able to be carried out in a finite number of elementary steps: a deduction of H from Γ is a finite sequence of type-formulas whose last one is H and among which any is either a member of Γ or immediately results from a previous member of the sequence by virtue of an inference rule, these rules being themselves in a finite number. This effectivity condition is clearly necessary to communicate acceptance of theoretical claims in the scientific collectivity: one needs some mechanical procedure, requiring no hermeneutical gift, to decide with plain certainty if a pretended deduction from given premisses is genuinely correct.

Whether this condition is *sufficient* is however highly dubious. Consider for example the process of *finding* a proof of H from Γ in propositional logic, or, equivalently, of testing the satisfiability of $\Gamma \cup \{ \neg H \}$. It is an exponential process which may, in the case Γ and H contain more than 100 distinct propositional variables, require more than the time since the origin of the universe, even if each step is done in the time required by the light to pass through a proton ! It makes no sense to ground the commitments arising from acceptance on such a notion of proof.

We are therefore confronted to the following dilemma:

—Either we admit that a subject may manifest his capacity to recognize the deductive relationship only in an *inchoative* way, by merely *engaging* himself in a process that he will never bring to a successful conclusion if he is not helped by *luck* to immediately find the most appropriate inferential moves (but the recognizability principle becomes satisfied in a very weak sense)

—Or we renounce to any idealization, and we engage ourselves in detailed considerations about our own cognitive working, in order to formulate rules intended to *describe* this working to the nearest point (but that is no longer genuine logic)

The way out consists in trying to conceive a system of rules that would be constrained enough to avoid the transcendance of the deducibility conditions, but in the same time general enough not to reduce to the *codification* of our particular way of proceeding. As an acceptable arrangement, we could be satisfied with taking into account the *most general* constraints able to limit the cognitive abilities of any *physically possible being*, in other words in admitting as legitimate some deductions that we could not execute, except if we had cognitive abilities greater than our actual ones, but in subordinating this admission to the condition that this hypothetical excess of resources may be attributed without radically altering the most fundamental physical laws (e.g. the principles of thermodynamics)[3].

Effectivity in principle clearly exceeds this notion of physical feasibility. It is however difficult to *localize* anything to modify in the classical rules: as they stand, they appear as crystal-clearly simple and easily executable, and the whole problem arises from the iterated *application* of them. That means that the only possible revision does not concern the rules themselves, but the way of applying them. A compelling suggestion is to adjoin to the logical rules something like *application decrets*, assumed that such decrets consist in the only following clause: don't apply the rule if you actually cannot apply it ! Let us call *explicitly effectuable* such rules, which expressely define the limits in which they are to be applied [4]. What is objectionable is not that these rules put the "ought" nearer to the "can"—for that is precisely the objective one tries to obtain,—but that they do *only* that: they are mere *legalizations* of the way of proceeding of the agents. One would much prefer dispositions which achieve their effect in the form of the *generality*, i.e. without to take expressely in account the characteristics of the subjects to whom they apply, in other words *implicitly effectuable* rules to which the subjects could obey whitout this obedience being stipulated in the rule: that would be the correct background to define $_c$deducibility.

The design of such implicitely effectuable rules is a substantive and difficult issue, for the traditional notion of proof *à la Church* is much too coarse-grained for such subtleties: it does even not permit, for example, to distinguish between the inference from A&A to A which keeps the left instance of "A" and the inference which keeps its right instance. To define $_c$deducibility, we have therefore to move towards other formats of logic. One of them is "natural deduction", which provide enough information to make visible possible choices between *different ways of applying* a given logical rule.

Consider for example the →-introduction rule of Gentzen's system NJ for intuitionistic natural deduction:

$$[A]$$
$$\vdots$$
$$B$$

$$\overline{\quad A \to B \quad}$$

It keeps room for different ways of discharging active instances of an hypothesis: one may wonder, for example, if all the active instances are to be discharged together. Whitout any supplementary instruction, one gets the full intuitionistic logic, which is a logic of effectivity. But one can also specify more rigidly the licit inferential moves, by never authorizing them in any situation where it would be *cognitively* or *physically* aberrant for an agent to do them systematically. The main objective is to warrant that the resources, either cognitive or physical, that have allowed the subject to conquer the premisses are also sufficient in any case to conquer the conclusion. Let us give some examples of this way of making intuitionistic logic genuinely feasible, therefore presumably appropriate to the definition of $_c$deducibility.

(i) The instruction of *compulsory* discharge prohibits "vacuous discharge", as for ψ in the following deduction:

$$\varphi_1$$

$$\frac{}{\psi \rightarrow \varphi}$$

$$\frac{}{\varphi \rightarrow (\psi \rightarrow \varphi)} 1$$

Or, in the format of Gentzen's Sequenz-Kalkulus (where Γ is supposed to contain the occurrences which are still active at the current node):

$$\frac{\begin{array}{c}\Gamma = x{:}\varphi \\ \Gamma \vdash \varphi\end{array}}{\Gamma, \psi \vdash \varphi} \, (*)$$

$$\frac{}{\Gamma \vdash \psi \rightarrow \varphi}$$

$$\frac{}{\Gamma \vdash \varphi \rightarrow (\psi \rightarrow \varphi)}$$

(*) is an application of the "substructural" rule of weakening

$$\frac{\Gamma \vdash \Delta}{\Gamma, \varphi \vdash \Delta}$$

If we adopt this instruction (or, equivalently, if we renounce the weakening rule), we are no longer able to conclude "irrelevantly" from A to B → A (as we have argued above, it is very questionable to consider that someone who accepts A is also committed to accept that B → A).

(ii) in the same way, the instruction of *unique* discharge prohibits from discharging at once more than an active instance, as for φ in the following deduction:

$$\frac{\varphi_1 \qquad\qquad \varphi \to (\varphi \to \psi)_2}{\varphi_3 \qquad\qquad\qquad \varphi \to \psi}$$

$$\frac{\qquad\qquad\qquad\qquad \varphi \qquad\qquad\qquad\qquad}{\varphi \to \psi}\ 1,3$$

$$\frac{}{[\ \varphi \to (\varphi \to \psi)\ ] \to (\varphi \to \psi)}\ 2$$

Or, in the sequential format:

$$\Gamma = x{:}\varphi\ ,\ y{:}\varphi \to (\varphi \to \psi)\ ,\ z{:}\varphi$$

$$\frac{\Gamma \vdash \varphi \qquad\qquad \Gamma \vdash \varphi \to (\varphi \to \psi)}{}$$

$$\frac{\Gamma \vdash \varphi \qquad\qquad \Gamma \vdash \varphi \to \psi}{}$$

$$\frac{\Gamma \vdash \psi}{}$$

$$\frac{}{x{:}\ \varphi,\ \psi{:}\varphi \to (\varphi \to \psi) \vdash \psi}\ (**)$$

$$\frac{}{\psi{:}\varphi(\varphi \to \psi) \vdash \varphi \to \psi}$$

$$\frac{}{\vdash [\varphi\ (\varphi \to \psi] \to (\varphi \to \psi)}$$

(**) is an application of the substructural rule of contraction

$$\frac{\Gamma,\ \varphi,\ \varphi \vdash \Delta}{\Gamma,\ \varphi \vdash \Delta}$$

If we adopt this instruction (or, equivalently, if we renounce to the contraction rule), we are no longer able to derive A → B from [(A & A) → B]. That removal has nothing to do with the requirement of a *conceptual* connexion between the premisses and the conclusion of an inference (for if A & A is conceptually related to B, then A too), but with the requirement of a *causal* balance between premisses and conclusion (from the viewpoint of the physical executability of rules, we have no reason to suppose that the effect which can be achieved by two tokens of the same type can be also achieved by only one token)[5].

To sum up, it is possible, by adopting very restricted ways of applying logical rules (or by much restraining the so-called "structural rules"), to obtain a notion of deducibility which approaches very nearly the requirements of our pre-systematical notion of $_c$deducibility. So far as the deductive abilities of the human beings are concerned, the problem of the attainability of norms seems therefore to be solvable. So much for the "paradox" of logical omniscience in Cohen's setting.

3. KYBURG'S LOTTERY PARADOX

It is tempting to propose a solution in the same vein to lottery's paradox.

3.1. Let us begin by a remark. As it is well-known, the paradox of the lottery arises when one tries to articulate belief and acceptance by considering the second attitude as the limit of the first one: belief comes by degree, and acceptance could be considered as compulsory when the degree of belief becomes very high, namely nearly to one. Of course, that is by no way the conception Cohen favours. One may however make sense of this paradox in the setting of his own distinction between acceptance and belief:

(i) The main objection he raises (p 111) against the significance of the posterior probability of a theory in determining whether or not it should be accepted has merely to do with the current conception according which probability measures the strength of the *belief that the theory is true*. But the paradox of lottery may be reproduced if we replace degree of belief by degree of "acceptance-worthiness".

(ii) Cohen is mainly concerned by acceptance of *theoretical* claims, and he argues at length that belief is neither necessary nor sufficient for this kind of acceptance. But *evidential* reports which constitute the "empirical basis" of the science are certainly not accepted in the same way, while they have also to do with the activity of "premissing with". It is clearly a case where you accept under pressure of beliefs that may be conceived as causally resulting from sensorial stimulations. To be sure, acceptance remains in that domain a matter of voluntary decision, but when it occurs, it is always *accompanied by* and *grounded on* high degree of belief. Contrary to theoretical claims, that you may, according to Cohen's leitmotiv, accept without believing them, the only space for will consists here in *refraining* himself from accepting what one believes. For acceptance of an evidential report without belief in it would inescapably mean the reduction of science to a matter of mere decision. In sum, the relevant notion of acceptance for evidential reports is *acceptance-cum-belief*, quite different, as such, from the notion of *acceptance-sine-belief* that Cohen analyses at length. Now *that* notion is typically vulnerable to the paradox of lottery.

Let me briefly restate the paradox itself. If you accept a sentence on the only basis of its high degree of probability, say if you accept φ as soon as $\Pr(\varphi) \geq (n-1)/n$, with n very high, you will come to the following difficulty. In a fair lottery of n tickets among which only one wins, you should accept for any ticket that it does not win. Thus if acceptance is deductively closed, you should accept that no ticket wins. But you are supposed to have accepted that one ticket wins. Thus you accept contradictory sentences: you are very irrational. Moreover, as Skyrms noticed, the paradox may be reproduced with full belief (of probability 1) instead of "ordinary" belief, if you think to an infinite lottery [6.]

3.2. I will not discuss the numerous solutions which have been proposed, and I will go directly to the Cohen-style solution I perceive.

Not unexpectedingly, the leading feature of this solution consists in putting acceptance in the forefront, and refusing to uncritically follow the pressure of belief: the rule of acceptance on the mere basis of high probability will be rejected.

A preliminary remark is in order. While some logical devices we have used in the previous section may be expected to be used again, the present situation is different. Here comes the empirical world and, no miracle, in that domain our correctness requirement does no longer fit our nice recognizability principle. Look lucidously at our epistemic situation: by contrast with the problem of deduction, we cannot here dream of an universal device permitting us to conclusively recognize if some sentence is actually satisfied. That is the main point. So, what can we reject. (RP) ? Not serious, it's nearly a truism. Thus we have to weaken the correctness requirement. What matters, after truth? Consistency, certainly, does. And completeness, in the same bargain, if possible. Such are our minimal norms of rationality in the domain: consistency, and completeness.

We accept sometimes sentences of which we are not *sure* that they are true. We accept them, say, by provision, on the light of the available evidence. Of course, there are also norms of rationality in collecting available evidence, in designing and planning experiments, in assessing the acceptance-worthiness of sentences [7]. But it is not my present point. Available evidence is not enough to certify many sentences conclusively, but we can decide to stop here, not to inquire further. We don't have eternity for us, and we jump to the conclusions. Of course we keep, as implicit *Hintergedanke*, that we have no strict warrant of it, but we go forward. Now back to logic, once again.

Consider the theory of feasible proofs ($_c$deducibility) that we have conconcted above. We have removed the so-called left-weakening rule

$$\Gamma, \Delta \vdash \Lambda$$

$$\overline{\Gamma, A, \Delta \vdash \Lambda}$$

It continues to be excluded, but for more dramatic reasons. It had been rejected on light of considerations about cognitive abilities. It is now to be rejected in order to avoid inconsistency. For when you accept Λ on the light of Γ and Δ, don't forget that you assume also some implicit hypothesis which could eventually be contradicted by the sentence A you introduce in your conclusion. Therefore we have to limit ourselves to the following way of weakening:

$$\frac{\Gamma, \Delta \vdash \Lambda \quad \Gamma, \Delta \vdash \Xi}{\Gamma, L, \Delta \vdash \Xi}$$

In following this attenuated version of the weakening rule, one avoids a major source of inconsistency (that is old wine in new bottles: the beverage has been sensibly concocted twenty years ago by E.W. Adams in his seminal *Logic of Conditionals*). It is not perfectly clear at what extent this way of solving the paradox actually implies the removal of the rule of high probability. For one can think of this solution as the result of a manner of tutoring the rule of high probability by a vigilant policy of acceptance. The explanation is as follows. We may accept sentences on the only ground of their high probability in the light of available evidence, but not in a collective and undistinguished manner. Once we have accepted, on the basis of the (accepted) evidence Γ of the design of the lottery, say, the sentence A_i which affirms that the i-th ticket does not win, we have to assess the acceptance-worthiness of the corresponding sentence A_j on the light of the *whole* class of the sentences which are currently accepted, namely by reference to $\Gamma \cup \{ A_i \}$. Now $Pr(A_j / \Gamma \cup \{ A_i \})$ is certainly less than $Pr(A_j / \Gamma) = (n-1)/n$. Thus it may be argued that the rule suggesting to accept any sentence with probability greater or equal to that amount is not actually *violated*, but simply *no longer applicable* in that situation (this solution, in terms of a *sequentialization* of acceptance acts, runs very similarly to the most intuitive solution to the well-known Sorites paradox).

3.3. Kyburg's paradox is an interesting example of the risks of in-consistency we are exposed to when we accept sentences on the light of a subconclusive evidence. Let me formulate, in guise of conclusion, a last logical remark about that. Among the rules we have to renounce or to restrict in order to avoid this risk, the more significant is the cut rule

$$\frac{\Gamma \vdash \Delta, A \quad A, \Gamma' \vdash \Delta'}{\Gamma, \Gamma' \vdash \Delta, \Delta'}$$

which permits to freely fusion the evidential contexts in which some sen-tence is accepted. E.g. the effect of the inference

$$\frac{\Gamma \vdash A \quad A, \Gamma' \vdash B}{\Gamma, \Gamma' \vdash B}$$

can be represented by the diagram

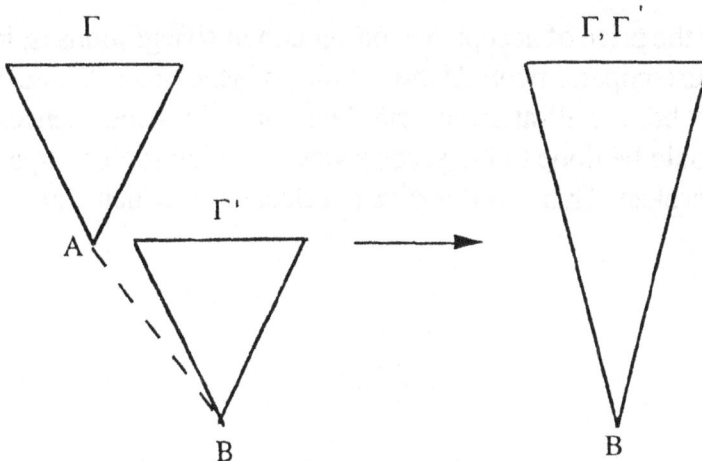

By contrast, acceptance (on subconclusive grounds) is clearly context-sensitive. For the only safe (i.e.: eliminable) cut rule for this notion is the following:

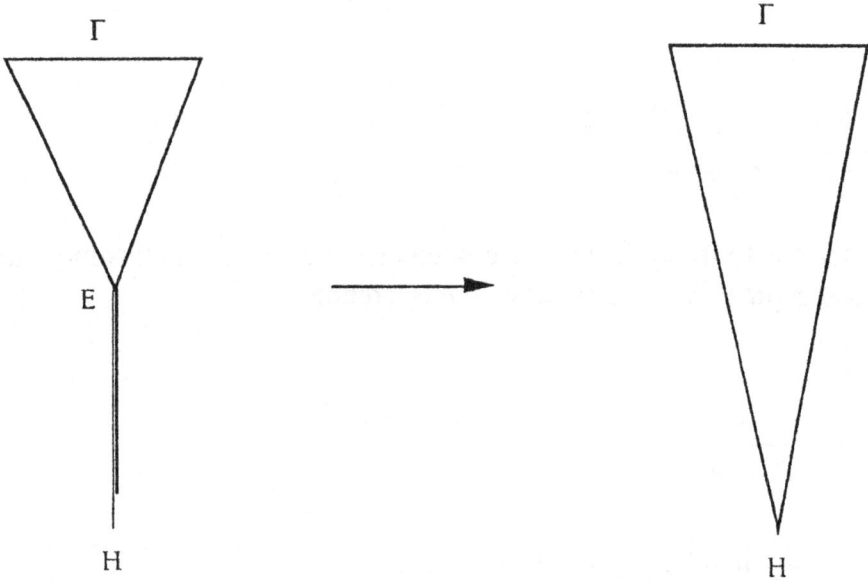

Γ   Γ

E

H   H

Thus the price of acceptance on subconclusive grounds is, in a certain sense, the compartementalization of the doxastic states. While the phenomenon is both well-attested and legitimate in some sense, much attention should be done to the precise way in which such compartments come to be broken. That is, *inter alia*, a reflection to which Cohen's book invites.

NOTES

[1] Actually, Cohen's *Essay* may be better viewed as a destructive attack against the kind of position illustrated by Goldman's "reliabilism", according to which science is explainable by the working of a cognitive process spontaneously tending to producing true beliefs.

[2] In *both* cases, investigation of the more improbable consequences of the hypothesis is recommandable. It is obvious in the first case. With regard to the second, i.e. if you wish to collect data which confer a great support to H, you should address to such consequences E of H that Pr(E) is low: for if E implies H, then Pr(H/E) = Pr(H)/Pr(E), which takes greatest value for lowest Pr(E). To sum up, what you wish does not matter to what you have to do.

[3] C. Wright discusses a similar suggestion in his paper on *Strict Finitism*, reprinted in *Realism, Meaning, and Truth*, Blackwell, 1987, p 124.

[4] There are many instances of such rules in the literature on automata theory. For example one has tried to make stricter the notion of Turing calculability by stipulating some supplementary condition in this following style: the ALB-calculable functions are Turing-calculable functions which may be computed whitout occuping *too much* place on the tape (precisely: if the computation of the value menaces to take greater place than the argument itself, then stop and return some arbitrary value a).

[5] *Computer Science*, 5 Cf J.Y. Girard, *Linear Logic*, *Theoretical* 0 (1987), pp 1-102.

[6] *Causal Necessity*, Yale U.P., 1980, pp. 152-153.

[7] That point is a very serious issue. And perhaps one can disagree with Cohen, who *seems* now to grade acceptance-worthiness by reference of classical probability calculus (I'm not sure about this point, but I wonder how he can reconcile the viewpoint he defends in this book with the theses he defended some times ago about *non-additive* probability).

SCIENTIFIC OBJECTIVITY
AND THE AIMS OF BELIEF[1]

Peter Railton
The University of Michigan, Ann Arbor

I

Science aims at knowledge. Knowledge involves belief. And belief aims at truth. Or so it is said. And so, therefore, it may also be said: science aims truth. These claims might be seen as belonging to a set of truisms or near-truisms that the philosopher of science denies at his peril. Realist and anti-realist, empiricist and pragmatist—all alike must be able to capture them, or re-explain them.

Although these claims invoke centrally the notion of truth, they pose a serious challenge even for the realist. For this short list of platitudes can be used to generate a good deal of internal tension. Scientific theories are vastly stronger and more informative than our evidence for them, which covers at most a relatively small patchwork of space and time. If scientific belief is aimed at truth, how can it be so ambitious?[2] Moreover, recent work in the history and sociology of science presses us to recognize that the dynamics of the scientific community—including the evolution of belief—are the result of a number of competing influences, not all of which bear any obvious relation to truth.

How severe are these tensions? To what extent can they be reconciled within a coherent picture of scientific practice? To begin to answer such questions, we will need both a fuller account of what it is for belief to "aim at" truth and a clearer conception of the purported relevance of the recent history and sociology of science. In this paper, we will try to make some progress on these two fronts. First, we will observe that, although truth may indeed play a goal-like role in cognition in general, the regulative role of truth with respect to belief

179

in particular is *constitutive* (to use a term of David Velleman's) rather than instrumental.[3] Second, we will consider a *reconciliationist* argument meant to show how the objectivity and reliability of scientific inquiry might be sustained—even partly explained—by radical revisionist accounts of the history and sociology of science. But third, we will see that the reconciliationist argument and the constitutive claim seem to be in direct tension with one another, since the one pulls us in the direction of seeing scientific belief as "aiming at" truth instrumentally and collectively, and the other, constitutively and individually.

Is there a higher-order reconciliationist argument, one capable of showing that these tensions can themselves be resolved? This question takes us beyond the scope of the present paper, into broad questions about the psychology of belief and acceptance, and the prospect for epistemic vs. "pragmatic" vindications of inductive practices. Nonetheless, as we will note in concluding, a curious fact about the relation of motivation to belief may help us (in the spirit of Hume?) to glimpse how a real-world epistemology might be possible.

II

First, the platitudes about belief. We take up various attitudes toward propositions: for example, we can *imagine* that *p*, *pretend* that *p*, *believe* that *p*.[4] What distinguishes belief from the others? A lot, really. Beliefs typically have a different role from imaginings in shaping decisions and choice; beliefs typically are less under voluntary control than pretendings; expressions of belief typically have different interpersonal functions from expressions of imagination or make-believe; and so on. One feature that has often been remarked upon, but the exact nature and implications of which are not well understood, is the special relation of belief to truth, as reflected in "Moore's paradox". G.E. Moore drew attention to the oddness of assertions like:

(1) *p*, but I believe otherwise.

By contrast, there is no special difficulty about:

(2) p, but I pretend otherwise.

or

(3) p, but I'm imagining otherwise.

Indeed, some of the peculiar linguistic and social functions of talk of imagining or pretending depend upon this talk drawing attention to states of affairs we know not to obtain. Of course, the difficulty with (1) is not the difficulty of failing to believe something true or of believing something false. That isn't hard. There is nothing odd about:

(4) p, but I didn't believe it at the time.

or

(5) p, but John doesn't believe it.

What seems odd is full-fledged, occurrent recognition on my part that p, conjoined with full-fledged, occurrent failure to believe that p or believing otherwise than that p, when there is no difference in "mode of presentation" or awareness to explain the discrepancy.

This idea is sometimes put by saying that belief—unlike imagining or pretending—"aims at" truth. But this way of putting it misleadingly suggests an image of belief as a form of goal-directed action: truth is the end, belief is the means. This image is problematic in various ways.

First, belief is not an action but (crudely) a state. Even *coming to have a belief* is not typically a form of deliberate action. Thus it is sometimes argued that belief is not subject to the will. Sometimes one can, by a deliberate act, initiate a course of action that will have the effect of bringing it about that one has a certain belief, but this typically would take the form of seeking experiences that tend to produce particular beliefs rather than making a direct or transparent application of will to belief.

Second, the sort of "aiming at" truth involved in belief not merely instrumental. Pretending that p will not *ipso facto* come closer to believing that p simply upon discovery that this pretense tends to promote truth in the long run. And one might well recognize that certain beliefs would, if held, enable one to increase overall knowledge without thereby thinking this in itself an argument for their credibility. Perhaps I am exploring strategies of proof, and I wrongly believe *that a certain theorem T has been proven*—call this proposition q—and this gives me the confidence to persist through some severe difficulties in developing a procedure that turns out to be highly fruitful in producing new proofs. Now as it turns out, not only has T not been proven, but I am mistaken in thinking that either T or its provability has the relevance I have supposed to the procedure in question. Nonetheless, my belief that q was crucial to my success—had I believed instead that no such theorem had been proven, I would have given up pursuing the procedure as hopeless. Then it would seem that if my goal were to maximize net balance of truth in my beliefs, I had an instrumental reason to believe the falsehood, q.

But the instrumentality of q in promoting further true beliefs does not give me a reason to believe that q in virtue of giving me *evidence* for q. Nor does the instrumental reason tend to "bring me to believe that q" in anything like the way that evidence for a proposition normally does. Is this reason for believing that q, then, a case of a *purely* practical reason? Perhaps not. For this reason for believing that q is in one sense epistemic: the goal of possessing true beliefs is a recognizably epistemic one. It might be better to say that this is a case in which an epistemic value, truth, is being treated in purely practical way—as if the point of belief were solely long-run goal-attainment.

What we can say is that the instrumental argument supplies me with "a reason for being a believer-that-q", to the extent that my overall goal is net truth in belief. Call this *a [net-truth-as-goal] rationale for being a q-believer*. Since this rationale for being a q-believer would *not* tend to carry me toward belief "in the normal way", we must, if we are to follow the rationale, find some nonstandard way of bringing me to believe that q. Perhaps a regime of mental conditioning along with some chemically-induced forgetfulness would do the job. Something like forgetfulness—or some other failure to see connections—might even *typically* be essential to success in the enterprise of cultivating "useful belief".

By contrast, even though imagining and pretending both involve a kind of relation to *truth*—to imagine or pretend that p is to imagine or pretend that p is true—there is no in-principle barrier to my imagining or pretending that q while seeing that the rationale for this is solely the usefulness (for whatever goal) of so doing.

It is, then, distinctive and *constitutive* of belief not only that it represents its content as true, but that it takes itself to be correct only if that particular content really is true. This constitutive involvement of belief with truth is "internal" to belief as a propositional attitude, but also gives belief an "external" orientation. It is part of the "job description" of belief as a distinctive propositional attitude that beliefs are correct or incorrect depending upon the state of the world in ways that some other propositional attitudes—wishing, pretending, etc.—are not. To be sure, one can successfully believe without getting things right—belief differs as well from such "success condition" propositional attitudes as remembering or recognizing. But getting things right is what a belief presents itself as doing. This feature of belief, in turn, helps explain its distinctive role, alongside desire, in shaping action. One might think of this feature as exhibiting the *price of admission* to the belief state regarding a given proposition.

So: if belief is to be said to "aim at" truth, then this would appear not to be "aiming at" in the familiar, teleological sense in which a goal is regulative of action.

Now, it is important to add that we might as cognizers *also* be thought of as aiming at truth in a goal-directed sense. It is a function of cognition in general, we might say, to be a faculty that represents things as they are, corrects errors, etc. Moreover, we do value truth—perhaps not just for the benefits that come from possession of truth, but also because we value knowledge intrinsically—and we seek to find and follow methods that are reliable. So in these various ways we can think of truth as a regulative goal in the familiar sense for cognition "in the large". Put in more evolutionary terms, we might also think of truth as a "design target" for various of our cognitive faculties. It is quite unlikely that truth is the only goal or "target". Evolution almost certainly selected our cognitive faculties to do more than represent accurately, and we certainly value, even value *epistemically*, more than truth: we also care about whether our beliefs are justified, coherent, manageable, applicable, informative, confident, explanatory, fruitful, etc. Perhaps some of these values can be understood as merely instrumental toward the maximizing of true-minus-false belief. Do we value fruitfulness only when we assume it will in the end contribute more to truth than falsity?—Even in this case one suspects that the argument is more complex, and involves trade-offs between truth and other epistemic desiderata.

Saying that "belief aims at truth" does not tell us how to balance these various goals as cognizers. Indeed, speaking of these goals as relating to *belief*-formation already assumes that we are able to identify the distinctive propositional attitude of belief. The contribution of "belief aims at truth" is to this latter task: helping us identify the sort of thing a belief is—or represents itself to the believer as being—such that we can then go on to ask questions like "What norms we should have for belief-formation?" Thus an injunction like "Don't believe everything you read in the newspaper", which no doubt can justified by reference to such cognitive goals as reliability, gets its point partly from the fact that believing something is holding it true, and everything that comes with that.

All of this must be taken with a grain of salt. I have been speaking of a folk notion, belief. It is always safe to say that folk notions are unlikely to be perfectly clear, coherent, or determinate. At best, perhaps, we can delineate more or less basic elements of central cases of belief and believing, while providing some commentary on more marginal cases. Moreover, nothing in what has been said constitutes a justification for saying that the folk notion of belief has been or will be vindicated by a scientific psychology—or, for that matter, that it even is hostage to scientific psychology. In what follows I will simply assume this notion of belief to be something that applies to our cognitive faculties and operates in our actions in roughly the way we commonsensically imagine. So this paper can be read in a hypothetical mode. (Indeed, it will be multiply hypothetical by the time we reach the end.)

III

Let me now turn to my second subject: objectivity in science. Elsewhere I have suggested a "revisionist" approach to objectivity as a possible philosophical response to radical historical and sociological challenges to orthodox conceptions of scientific objectivity.[5] I will briefly review the strategy of such a rethinking of objectivity.

Although 'objectivity' has been an important term in both philosophical and non-philosophical discussions of the status of science, there is (to my knowledge) no "orthodox" philosophical theory of objectivity akin, say, to Hempel's theory of explanation. It does seem to me, however, that at least three elements figure in claims about objectivity that are common in (what was once) orthodox logical empiricist philosophy of science:[6]

(i) objective inquiry is value free and disinterested;

(ii) objective inquiry is based upon evidence and not biased by factual or theoretical preconceptions—e.g., it is based upon theory-neutral evidence and does not adopt a theory until the evidence is rationally compelling;

(iii) objective inquiry uses procedures that are public, intersubjective, and independent of particular individuals or circumstances—e.g., its experiments are in principle reproducible.

To these we might want to add a fourth, if it is not already somehow contained in what has gone before:

(iv) objective inquiry is such that all rational participants
     will, as evidence becomes complete, tend to
     converge on determinate, true conclusions (on all
     non-vague, unambiguous questions).[7] Once all the
     evidence is in, there will be no room for variable or
     "subjective" determination of conclusions among
     rational participants.

Has anyone actually held, or articulated, all of (i)-(iv)? That is an
exegetical question. Setting aside (iv) for now, all that is needed is that
many of the key elements of (i)-(iii) would at some point have been
accepted by most "orthodox" logical empiricist philosophers of science.
      The past three decades have witnessed an increasingly widespread
challenge to the idea that scientific practice is, or could be, objective in
senses (i)-(iii). Historians and sociologists of science, in particular,
have drawn upon such diverse sources as archival research, cognitive
psychology, ethnographic observation, and interpretive theory to throw
into question the idea that scientific inquiry is free of values, interests,
or substantive biases, or the notion that scientific change can be
explained in terms of a rationally required response to mounting
evidence.
      These purported conclusions are certainly not without echo in
philosophy itself. Many philosophers now would insist that
epistemology is normative, and that any systematic mode of inquiry
therefore cannot be wholly "value free". Moreover, most philosophers
would concede that learning from experience requires that one bring to
experience definite expectations about similarities and uniformities.
And comforting Bayesian thoughts about the influence of prior
probabilities washing out in the long run require not only a very long
run, but also a short run full of many more alternative hypotheses and
much more active conditionalization than anything we actually see in
scientific practice. Further, at least since Carnap, it has become
increasingly difficult for philosophers to convince themselves that the
strong theoretical conclusions scientists draw from their rather narrow
evidential base are "rationally required". Finally, many philosophers
have adopted more or less strongly naturalistic positions in

epistemology, with the result that the *actual* historical processes by which science has arrived, or is arriving, at its theories have become directly relevant to the epistemic status of those theories.

So it seems that the challenge of "radical" historians and sociologists of science cannot be ignored, or turned aside with the blanket label: 'irrationalism'. Much of what they deny in (i)-(iii) has already been denied by mainstream philosophers. Moreover, although some of these historical and sociological accounts have taken exaggerated forms—forms from which some of the most influential researchers (Kuhn, Bloor, Latour, etc.) have since distanced themselves—and although some of this work is more aprioristic than genuinely historical, psychological, or sociological, it has, I think, become evident that there is a great deal to be learned from the best of it.

Philosophers of science therefore need to ask whether a "revisionist" conception of objectivity might be found that would be compatible with these "revisionist" theories of the practice of science. This should not be a merely apologetic enterprise. Instead, philosophers of science should attempt to identify the fundamental concerns to which earlier conceptions of objectivity addressed themselves, and ask whether a conception of objective inquiry different from (i)-(iii) would enable us to meet those concerns. Such a revised conception would not set up an unattainable (even, "unapproximatible") ideal of objective inquiry, but rather enable us to differentiate *among* value-based, interest-driven, presupposition-laden, etc. modes of inquiry those that do better (or promise to do better) at meeting some (or most) of the original concerns.[8]

Let us proceed as follows. First, we will introduce in a caricatured way a few of the images of scientific practice that have figured in recent revisionist history and sociology of science, images that raise problems for seeing scientific inquiry as objective. Then we will ask whether an alternative conception of objectivity might enable us to see how these practices might actually form part of an overall activity that to a substantial degree meets the concerns that have underlain discourse about objectivity.

Here is a caricature:

Modern Science.   Modern science is not a disinterested, contemplative mode of inquiry but a large-scale industry, well integrated into the overall division of labor in advanced capitalist societies.   As an indirect reflection of the cultural and social changes effected by the pervasive expansion of market relations into every area of modern life, and a direct reflection of career incentives, modern scientists have largely adopted an instrumental attitude toward the natural world, seeing it as a potential locus for prediction and control—in a word, domination—rather than disinterested appreciation. The unprecedented growth of "research and development" and university-based science under capitalism depends at bottom upon the capacity of science to produce novel, usable forms of manipulation of natural phenomena. Scientists moreover are not by and large individual inquirers, but members of teams and laboratories.   These groups are hierarchical, non-democratic, industrialized enterprises led by dominant principal investigators—usually male—who are overcommitted to their research program, just as scientific disciplines as wholes are overcommitted to paradigms. High-level participation in the lab presupposes similar allegiance to the project, and serious alternatives to the project are not explored, nor are results unfavorable to it sought out.   Labs regularly, and without independent testing, ignore the implications of work that conflicts with their own while seizing upon work that supports it. In return for their contribution and allegiance, graduate students and postdocs are able to benefit from the prestige and grant-getting power of principal investigators, to support their own training, and to launch their own careers with the prospect of sharing in discoveries or inventions of visible novelty that would be well beyond their means working alone. Laboratories and research groups are not engaged in a co-operative enterprise of trying to enlarge our common understanding of nature, but rather in an intensely competitive commercial or quasi-commercial arena in which discoveries and inventions are property, and research appointments, awards, postdocs, prestige, and grants are capital. Individual scientific labs select projects and approaches with an eye toward funding, impact, and payoff in the relentless competition for novelty.

Well, enough caricature. But suppose that, like many caricatures, this picture of modern science in its very exaggerations affords a useful antidote to naive, traditional ways of looking at things, and throws into relief some important truths. Even when heavily discounted, this picture does not bode well for resuscitating storybook ideas of the objectivity of scientific inquiry. Indeed, those engaged seriously in the history or sociology of science often look on with something like condescending disbelief at philosophical discussions of the epistemology of science.

That smugness can prompt a curt, even dismissive response from philosophers, a charge of incoherence on the part of the historian or sociologist of science: the notorious reflection argument. How, after all, are we to understand the critique being offered of the cultural "privileging" of science? Is it this?—Science is held by many to have special epistemic authority because it is viewed as objective and able to get at "the facts"; but careful historical, sociological, psychological, and anthropological research shows that science isn't *really* the way it has been portrayed as being. But then, are history, sociology, psychology, and anthropology able to get at "the facts" behind mere narratives or ideology in a way that natural science itself cannot? What would insulate these disciplines from the very same critique, and the very same purported loss of credibility? Radical historians and sociologists of science have struggled with this argument, though without notable success. Latour and Woolgar, for example, ask that their account of "the construction of scientific facts" not be exempted from reflexive scrutiny and decry the tendency of Marxist sociology of science to cling to prospect of "real science", saying:

> instead of using this argument [from reflexivity] ironically, as a way of characterizing the work of *others* ..., we should accept the universal applicability of fallibility and find ways of coming to

terms with it. ... Our concerns for reflexivity would perhaps have begun to succeed where the text suggests to the reader that he ask himself whether or not the observations [described in this book] really took place, whether or not Jonas Salk really wrote [this book's] introduction, and so on.[9]

But of course the idea of fallibility, and of what "really took place", are—unless further explained—invocations of the old idea of truth as "fitting the facts", not radical challenges to it.

There might therefore be some satisfaction for philosophers in the curt response. But it would be unfortunate to rest matters there. For *if* "careful historical, sociological, psychological, and even anthropological research" calls into question orthodox ideas about objectivity in natural science, then it is little comfort that it also calls into question orthodox ideas about objectivity in social science. Perhaps—unless we can identify something wrong with these social-scientific studies *as* empirical studies—we have discovered that the methodological and substantive structure of modern natural-cum-social science is simply not self-supporting.

Now, as philosophers, we have no special expertise in empirical matters. Where we might make a contribution to this debate would be in asking whether the historical and sociological results are really so damaging to the special epistemic status of science after all. How could they not be? Well, given what has been argued in the philosophical literature about such criteria of objective inquiry as (i)-(iii), philosophers already have grounds for rethinking ideas about what makes an inquiry objective. Might such a revised conception also enable us to understand how science, even if characterized in something like the terms found in contemporary history and sociology of science, could nonetheless appropriately claim special epistemic status?

The way I propose to think about objectivity begins very simply, with a picture that I think is ultimately best accommodated in a realist metaphysics, but which I think no sound irrealist or anti-realist would want to deny.

There is a world that is not just made by us. For a start, it was here long before Homo sapiens arrived on the scene. Homo sapiens are situated somewhere in this world, smallish subjectivities with a lot to learn. The world they confront is in a number of ways surprisingly resistant to mere suggestion: Homo sapiens cannot count on even their strongest and most widespread wishes to make things so. They worry: "We form representations of this larger world, which form the basis for our actions in it. But these are *our* representations, from our point of view, using our senses, our conceptual resources, etc. Our senses and minds—our subjectivities—evolved in the Late Pleistocene era, when capacity to understand the fine-grained microstructure or global macrostructure of the world was hardly an active locus of selection pressure. So: How well are we able, in our subjective way, to represent that larger world? How might we find out whether our representations are adequate to the world? One idea suggests itself: introduce some 'selection pressure' deliberately applied to our own most ambitious representations, through the creation of conditions in which success or failure would be linked to the adequacy of our ideas of (say) fine-grained microstructure. We should attempt, that is, to set up trial and error situations in which some outcome we care about is tied to success at predicting or controlling small-scale or large-scale natural phenomena."

This idea of trying to develop mechanisms for "feedback" pressure on our subjective representations can be thought of in a broadly *externalist* way: what forms of interaction with the world might selectively reward reliability in belief-formation, and thereby tend over time to enhance it?[10] Strikingly, an economically disinterested, contemplative, appreciative mode of inquiry would not appear a promising candidate to fill this bill. Given its lack of emphasis upon undertaking entirely novel projects for "domination" of nature, a contemplative and appreciative mode of inquiry can too easily remain essentially *projective* in character—finding resonances in our own subjectivities and then reading them into nature. Equally strikingly, an interested, instrumental, manipulative, ambitious, competitive mode of inquiry might better fill the bill of producing novel forms of feedback that can frustrate subjective projection—at least, up to a point. Let us, then, reconsider in this light some of the seemingly troubling features of the practice of science discussed earlier. Within the confines of this paper, our reconsideration must be entirely cursory.

The incessant demand in science for novelty of a practically useable kind, characteristic—according to historical and sociological accounts—since the industrial revolution, exerts a strong pressure to investigate new areas, create and explore new substances, experiment with untried methods and ever more extreme values for parameters—smaller, cheaper, faster, higher energy, lower temperature, etc. After all, well-known features of well-known substances and methods provide no competitive edge in the various marketplaces for or in science. The incentives for novelty, as well as the pressure on labs to operate as "export-oriented economies" by producing results that will win them visibility or income by gaining application in other research projects or commercial ventures, create strong pressure to produce results that can be replicated—results that will perform as advertised when put into a new laboratory or industrial setting, results that can patented and licensed, and so on. One effect of this is a vast, though certainly not uniform, proliferation of research activity in many areas and at all many scales. A notable consequence, intended or not, of this incentive-driven activity is to dramatically enlarge the scope for feedback in trial and error.

In a similar way, the reward structure of individual labs and of competition among labs has various "selectionist" effects. Academic fame and fortune depend, like commercial fame and fortune, upon the production of novel results, and especially results that others wish to utilize to generate their own novel results. This circumstance results in a possible reward for scientists who look for promising but unoccupied niches and competitive advantages, but who also are under great pressure to extend existing results in reproducible ways. If we stand back and look at this from the perspective of the field as a whole, we can even see benefits arising from (what we might call) the *epistemic overcommitment* of individual scientists and their labs, mentioned earlier. Just as an *investment portfolio* can reduce overall risk by adding risky investments whose upside and downside potentials would be realized in different circumstances, rather than placing all eggs in one relatively "unrisky" basket that then is entirely vulnerable or entirely stodgy in certain conditions, so, too, a community of inquirers can sometimes make more headway at trial and error if groups stake out significantly different, risky positions and pursue them competitively for all they're worth. Similarly, in evolution, species that lack internal variation (or ecological systems that lack species variation) are especially vulnerable to certain kinds of risk from disease, micro-organisms, novel exogenous competitors, etc. A mechanism for the regular endogenous production of variability, such as sexual reproduction (or multicropping, in commercial agriculture), may therefore be adaptive even though most of the individual changes thereby introduced are movements away from local optima.[11]

The idea here is that objectivity arises not so much at the level of the individual investigator as at the social level, a perhaps unintended consequence of competition for funds, glory, and other scarce resources in a circumstance in which innovation that enhances prediction and control is rewarded. Individual researchers or research teams may seem too incentive-driven and overcommitted to their own views—and too oblivious to contrary evidence—to be epistemically ideal, but it may be that the motivation to forge ahead and develop a hypothesis, without waiting for compelling evidence to emerge, is necessary to building up a competitive field. If individual researchers or laboratories adopted more "reasonable" epistemic probabilities, in order to converge on "the state of the total evidence in the field, on balance" rather than to promote ambitious individual ends, there would in consequence be less variability in feedback. "Reasonable" epistemic probabilities can be thought of as an emergent phenomenon, appearing at the social level, much as the *betting line* on a sports event emerges from the disparate odds individual bettors are willing to make or take. These more "reasonable" social probabilities would not necessarily be embodied in the mind of any particular inquirers. Rather, they would be embodied functionally in the state and structure of the field—e.g., through grant-review processes, peer-refereeing of publications, commercial investments, tenure decisions, postdoc allocations, patent assignments, etc. as spread unevenly across the competitive domain.

We have, then, the prospect of an *"invisible mind" argument* akin to the "invisible hand" argument of classical economics: individuals and corporate units motivated by the prospect of their own gain in a competitive situation are led to act in ways that contribute, whether intentionally or not, to the realization of a desirable overall goal. To be sure, the "invisible hand" argument itself is hardly entirely satisfactory, ignoring as it does many imperfections and having more to do with wealth-generation than welfare-maximization (the latter would depend also upon distribution). The "invisible mind" argument is, if anything, less compelling. There is extensive "collusion" or guild-like "restraint of trade" in the actual practice of science, and start-up costs are high. Moreover, given the total range of possible scientific hypotheses, the limited number of actual, serious research teams, the significant effects of individual sponsors of research, the restricted range of interests in prediction and control, the limited amount of data, and so on, there is no reason for easy confidence that this sort of social process will yield correct scientific beliefs, or an equilibrium in which an appropriate range of competing hypotheses is under an appropriate intensity of investigation at a given time to "maximize net truth" given potentially available resources. And consumers of manufactured products are better at assessing their own welfare gains than consumers of scientific "products" are at assessing their own knowledge gains.

But perhaps the relevant question is much less ambitious. In comparison with more disinterested, contemplative modes of inquiry in which each individual inquirer seeks to represent the total available evidence and avoid commitment to a research program before the weight of evidence becomes rationally compelling, would a competitive, interest-driven mode of inquiry of the kind described (things would obviously be different if different interests, such as those in religious orthodoxy or state security, were at the center) plausibly possess a greater prospect for informative feedback that would move the "center of gravity" of scientific opinion in a more objective direction?

If we assume there to be some accuracy in the caricature of modern science, then we can also see that the costs of this competitive, instrumental approach to nature would be great. Certain kinds of insights could be expected to be slow in coming—if they arrive at all. I certainly am not seeking an all-purpose defense of the current state of "institutional science" or scientific funding, etc. against reform. Rather, I seek, for example, some explanation of how an incentive-driven, instrumental scientific enterprise might yield the successes of modern science despite its great epistemic "impurity". In a world in which wishing will not in general make things so, we need to explain how the sorts of practices scientists actually engage in could have produced the unprecedented predictive and technological accomplishments of modern science.

IV

Let us, for the sake of argument, assume that there is something to the above revisionist, non-idealized conception of science and revisionist, feedback conception of objectivity. Indeed, let us assume that we will need to rely to some degree on some such *social emergence* account of scientific objectivity if we are to have any hope of locating a relevant sense in which scientific inquiry really is objective. Let us now note some serious problems for such an approach.

First, the approach is "instrumental" in its conception of rationality in belief, and "shamelessly *externalist*" in its epistemology.[12]

Externalism brings with it a familiar set of concerns. For example, without some internally-accessible sign of actual rather than merely apparent success in reducing subjectivity and increasing objectivity, what regulative role can this "revisionist" conception of objectivity have in scientific practice? Presumably part of the hope one could have for "social emergence" accounts is that they might be able to point to structural factors to help explain (indirectly, of course) the idea of "regulative role". But thus far this idea—like the general issue of how externalist accounts in epistemology might be given some suitable "internal side"—is simply too underdeveloped to assess seriously. One feature of externalism is that we might simply have to accept that it is an open question whether condition (iv) on "objective inquiry"—the inevitability of rational consensus—will be met by a form of inquiry as seemingly objective (in the revisionist sense of section III, but also in the eyes of common sense) as natural science. The potentially unsettling implications of this possibility must be passed over here.[13]

Instrumentalism brings a related but additional set of concerns. In particular: How is the agent to see himself? In the space that remains I will explore briefly some of the issues that arise in this connection. One might worry, for example, that a "socially emergent" account produces a conflict within reason itself over the regulation of belief, and that this shows an inherent defect in any such strategy for reconciling scientific objectivity with the actual practice of science.

Consider the individual scientist wondering what to believe. He has his strong commitments to a specific research program, but now has taken the dangerous step of looking into the mirror of self-awareness. The mirror in this case is held up by historians and sociologists of science, and although our individual scientist senses that much is exaggerated in the features he there observes, he also recognizes much that strikes home as all-too-familiar from his observations of his fellow scientists in his more cynical moments: an instrumental attitude toward nature; research agendas set by externally-generated demands and funding; scientific labs strongly committed to their own research program ignoring contrary findings on the part of other labs; hierarchically structured scientific training and labs, where questioning of certain methods or premises is discouraged, etc. He then wonders: "Am I not, myself, a *part* of this? What really motivates me? How much do I set my own research agenda? How much do I seek out contrary evidence?" He begins to worry that he is just one more instrumental, overcommitted, dominant male, and begins to think that he ought to scale back his confidence that he is on the right track in his research program. This loss of confidence of course becomes reflected in his work, his refereeing, his teaching, etc.

Next this same scientist comes across the "invisible mind" argument of section III. He sees the point. If he loses confidence in his own research program, he is in danger of failing to play his distinctive role in the grand scheme by which science makes progress in becoming objective. What to do? Or, more to the point, What to think?[14] Should he try to crank his confidence in his own research project back up to former levels? But (many philosophers would argue) belief is not so voluntary as that: one cannot simply decide to believe something more or less strongly. So wouldn't the only effective methods for restoring belief be in some measure self-deceptive?

One suggestion that might naturally arise at this point would be to take this dialectic of levels of self-awareness as counting in favor of seeing the fundamental propositional attitude of scientists as *acceptance* rather than belief. After all, there is no conceptual incompatibility in accepting a hypothesis *h*—where this might mean something like treating it *as if* true in all scientific contexts—even while recognizing that *h* is unlikely to be true and finding oneself unable really to *believe* it. No Moorean paradox haunts 'not-*h*, but I'll set my scientific agenda as if *h* were true'. The difficulty with this seems not conceptual (what state of mind *is* this?) but rather practical (isn't one irrationally courting disaster by committing oneself to acting as if *h* were true in all scientific contexts, given that it is not?).

Another way to put the difficulty is to engage in a fiction in which individual scientists receive their role in the grand scientific enterprise by assignment. It is not nearly so difficult to imagine someone accepting the assignment "Although as you know, the evidence is running strongly against *h*, your lab is to work as if it were true—that's the best way for us to extend our technical virtuosity, maintain the interest of our funding sources, and, not incidentally, see what *h* might have going for it", in contrast to the assignment "Although as you know, the evidence is running strongly against *h*, you are to wholeheartedly believe it—that's the best way for us to extend our technical virtuosity, maintain the interest of our funding sources, and, not incidentally, see what *h* might have going for it". The former role is akin to the familiar "devil's advocate"—maybe not one's first choice as a role to play in the drama of science, but not a threat to one's integrity, either; the latter looks more like a recipe for self-deception. The problem here is not that one cannot imagine some regime of psychological conditioning that would induce in one a belief that *h*; the problem is that one has not been given a reason to believe that *h*, but only (to use a figure of speech from section I) a rationale for being an *h*-believer.

It might be worth noting that this invocation of acceptance in the place of belief would be more radical than the suggestion of Bas van Fraassen that scientists accept their theories as wholes, while reserving belief only for their theories' empirical adequacy.[15] For the proposal we are now considering might well involve acceptance (and nothing stronger) even for claims of empirical adequacy. After all, claims of empirical adequacy are extremely strong, applying to all possible observations at all places and times. If the mechanism of section III requires that research groups commit strongly to certain hypotheses even on rather weak evidence, and not wait until the evidence becomes "rationally compelling", this would *a fortiori* include hypotheses about which theories are empirically adequate.

It might also be worth noting that the structure of this concern about self-deception or the internal instability of certain attitudes reflects a well-known debate in ethical theory. There the question has arisen whether attempting to base moral rights and prohibitions on utilitarian (instrumental) foundations results either in an unstable system—because, aware of utilitarian rationales, individuals would not take rights and prohibitions sufficiently seriously—or in the need for an "esoteric morality" in which *hoi polloi* are taught a strict, deontological moral code and never trusted to see its consequentialist foundation. Indeed, the underlying consequentialist theory might recommend that it not be accepted even by the experts—that it "usher itself altogether from the scene".[16] Either of these two possibilities—instability in practice or "self-effacement"—is thought to be very damaging to consequentialist moral theory.

The argument against consequentialism draws on several thoughts. First, there is the idea that the *motivational effectiveness* of moral principles will depend upon how people view them. If rights or prohibitions or permissions are viewed as merely instrumental to some further end, the argument runs, then conscientious and self-serving moral agents alike will tend to refer their actions to this underlying standard, undermining the effectiveness of the norms and defeating the moral theory's own recommendations. Second, there is the meta-normative thought that morality is the sort of thing that simply should not be esoteric—it should in principle be possible for all rational adults within an ethical community to know, and be able to discuss and accept, the fundamental justification of that community's norms. This is sometimes called a *publicity condition*.[17]

Are there similar worries about motivational effectiveness, self-defeat, or violation of a publicity condition in epistemology? If the psychological state of acceptance were sufficient for the mechanism in section III to work (roughly) as it currently does, then perhaps no self-defeat or violation of publicity need occur. But such sufficiency is an empirical question. (How well would it work for a coach to motivate his a team by saying: "I don't really believe we can win, but I'm going to act as if I did, and urge you to do likewise"?) We should ask what we would say if the *only* way for individual scientists or research groups to sustain enough commitment and energy to their research program to permit the mechanism to do its job were for them actually to *believe* the hypotheses with which they work (or, somewhat more weakly, actually assign to these hypotheses epistemic probabilities much higher than the total evidence would seem to warrant). This would then create just the tension that was a concern above between reasons for belief that h and rationales for being an h-believer. Would the result be a circumstance in which the epistemically best practice (as measured by reliability in producing net truth in belief overall) could not be fully transparent to those who participate in it?

The "invisible mind" argument may be significantly different from the "invisible hand" argument in this respect. There is nothing logically or psychologically problematic, as far as I can see (except perhaps in some degenerate cases), about being a self-interested entrepreneurial individual and recognizing that, in playing this role, one is contributing to total social wealth. Self-interest can remain a motivationally effective ground of action for individuals even after grasping the invisible hand argument. Actual entrepreneurs indeed typically embrace the invisible hand argument enthusiastically—they may not themselves be moved by considerations of total social wealth, but the argument gives them something to say to anyone who does take social welfare seriously and who criticizes the self-interestedness of entrepreneurs on that basis. Actual *believers*, by contrast, cannot happily see themselves as indifferent to truth-in-belief "in the small", while keeping in reserve the invisible mind argument in case someone else were to raise the issue of truth-in-belief "in the large".

Let us therefore consider the question "What happens when reasons for being an h-believer and reasons for believing that h come apart?", by looking at two kinds of cases, before asking how the section III model might resemble them.

Case I. The chief of your Neighborhood Bayesian Committee drops in and asks how your personal probabilities are doing today. You say that they're fine, though lately you haven't been paying close attention to most of them. He replies that you are leaving yourself vulnerable to a clever rascal who's been going around town making Dutch Book arguments. By not being a conscientious Bayesian in your personal probabilities, you are putting yourself at risk of losing a significant amount of money to this rascal. For example, he points out, scrutinizing your personal probability assignment, you have assigned probability q to winning a gamble described as G, and have also assigned probability $p < q$ to winning a gamble described as F—but G and F pick out probabilistically equivalent gambles.

Now, your neighborhood Bayesian chief has just given you two kinds of reason in one sentence! (1) An evidential reason for believing that

(r) prob(win, F) = prob(win, G),

namely, that F and G describe equivalent gambles, and (2) a prudential reason for being an r-believer, since otherwise you stand to lose some money to the clever Dutch-Book Maker. Happily, these two reasons seem to stand in no tension with one another.

Case II. Everything is just like Case I, except that the clever Dutch-Book maker is replaced by an avenging anti-Bayesian minor deity. This deity reads minds and punishes those who carry out certain Bayesian inferences. He is, however, a somewhat whimsical and inconstant god, which is why he's never been promoted. He only seeks vengeance from time to time, and often for trivial matters. His pet peeve this week is Bayesians who equate prob(win, F) with prob(win, G), and he will spare only those who deny this equation. Your local

Bayesian Wardboss drops by to warn you of this, pointing out that, although gamble F is equivalent to gamble G, you must believe not-r for the next week or so, for fear of dreadful consequences. He has given you a prudential reason for being a not-r-believer, but this is certainly no evidential reason to believe that not-r. Indeed, the reason he has given you stands in tension with your recognizing the evidential reason to *dis*believe not-r. Fortunately, therefore, the Bayesian Wardboss has some Reverend Thomas' Elixir that will rid you of any awareness that F and G describe the same gamble, induce in you the belief that not-r, and immunize you against changing this belief for at least the next fourteen days. Happily, the elixir also destroys any memory of the Wardboss' visit.

Case II helps us to see how a rationale for being a p-believer could plainly come apart from reasons to believe that p, and may make it easier to see how the familiar Dutch Book argument could be an example of the former rather than latter sort of reason. Since the goals seemingly involved are quite different—on the evidential (or theoretical) side, truth, and on the prudential (or practical) side, avoiding loss of money or some other grievous harm—there is no temptation to describe the conflict in Case II as a tension "within" epistemology.

But now return to the case of the self-aware scientist. He has learned that, if he will do his part and believe that h, his efforts can be a component of a larger scheme the result of which will be to best promote the growth of knowledge. If normative epistemology simply were a matter of identifying that system of norms, strategies, etc. which would best promote the growth of knowledge, then a justification *from an epistemic point of view*—not from a merely practical point of view—has been given for his being an h-believer. At the same time, the justification is instrumental, and it appears that no direct reason has been given for him to believe that h. Surely that thought, too, is part of normative epistemology. We may thus have a parallel with (at least one aspect of) the moral case: conflict here appears to be *within* epistemology, at least if that enterprise is conceived as wholly or partly "goal-directed" with respect to truth.

However, notice an important disanalogy with Case I. There two kinds of reasons are being offered with respect to r, one evidential and the other prudential, yet the second makes use of the first. The two kinds of reason, therefore, can be fully in view of one another, and fully before the mind of the believer. Indeed, they might be thought to be mutually supportive—the first reason "explaining" the second, and the second enhancing our interest in the first. We see how the "machinery" behind the Dutch Book argument draws directly, transparently upon the machinery behind reasons for belief.

By contrast, the newly-self-aware scientist discussed above has discovered a rationale for being an h-believer *regardless* of whether there is a reason to believe h—regardless of its truth or falsity, and in spite of the strong evidence against it. The rationale for being an h-believer is connected to the goal of truth only via complex mediating psychological mechanisms and social institutions. And as we saw in section I, the distinctive attitude of belief involves "holding true" constitutively, not instrumentally or teleologically. Thus, even if the rationale for being an h-believer is a reason in the service of truth "in the large", it does not appear to warrant belief that h "in the small".

V

It is tempting to leave matters at this point, with a conundrum about the status or force of section III-like defenses of the objectivity of science and the rationality of the overall enterprise of scientific belief-formation. *Is* there, for example, a compelling motivation for a publicity requirement in epistemology? The caricature *Modern Science* is certainly far from the truth about modern science, but what if it is not far enough? Would we be reduced to hoping that the scientific enterprise will never become sufficiently self-aware to collapse under its own scrutiny, and put an untimely end to its splendid record of success? Or should we hope that an attitude of acceptance (in the absence of belief) might be surprisingly feasible on the part of scientists, and also nearly as effective as belief in motivating the sort of engagement that yields high-quality research? This might permit scientists to achieve full self-awareness without undermining the scientific enterprise. Or perhaps our best hope would be that attention to an expanded psychological palette, beyond the dichotomous color scheme of belief vs. acceptance, would reveal hues of propositional attitude already widespread in the scientific community that are compatible with self-awareness yet better suited to the task of sustaining motivation in the absence of full-fledged belief. No doubt, the present discussion is entirely too crude from a psychological standpoint.

This last observation deserves a final comment. Recent work in "cold" cognitive psychology has shown that humans regularly form beliefs (or belief-like propositional attitudes) on the basis of such "heuristics" as salience and a bias toward positive instances. Recent work at the borderline between "hot" and "cold" cognition has shown that self-esteem and a sense of one's identity can play a significant role in the operation of these heuristics. What the historians and sociologists of science have observed by way of "tribalization" of competing laboratories and associated epistemic overcommitment on the part of individual scientists and laboratories may be strongly linked to these mechanisms of self-esteem and identity-formation. In general, for example, people "spontaneously" come to think that there is something special about where they live, *wherever* they live. Some element of location—neighborhood, town, region, country, etc.—typically, perhaps inexorably, becomes part of one's identity and self-image, and this helps to underwrite psychically the operation of salience ("Ever notice how many important people come from Ohio?", urges the Ohioan) and over-attentiveness to positive instances. And "location" is more than place of living. It can extend to the school one attends, the "school of thought" one is trained in, the social and personal roles one is—for whatever reason—led to take up. Even when subjects in a psychological experiment were asked to present debating positions they had drawn from a hat, they became, in the course of playing their role in the debate, more convinced of the merits of whatever position they drew.[18] Scientific training and early research experiences might, that is, suffice to generate strong loyalties and motivations on behalf of particular research projects even in the face of a recognition at some level on the part of the scientist that these projects are not "highly confirmed".

These mechanisms work in surprising ways. In one experiment, individuals were queried in order to compare their own image of how others view them with what others actually would say about them. Revealingly, the group of individuals whose images of what other people would say about their social skills best corresponded on the whole to what others in the experiment actually *did* say of them were the depressives.[19] It would appear to be part of the normal, healthy operation of one's self-image that one overrate oneself, discounting negative evidence and defying the odds. (Don't we almost all rate our own driving as "above average"?)

A "healthy skepticism" about theory or evidence might, therefore, not be so healthy after all. It might indeed be, so to speak, cognitively depressing. To invest in developing novel theory in the face of established opinion, or to commit a substantial portion of one's career to the pursuit of long-term experimental programs testing controversial hypotheses or untried apparatus, may be psychologically incompatible with an estimate of the epistemic situation that is fully in tune with the total evidence. The net result of a situation in which individual scientists were professionally trained and personally disposed to be fully responsive to the force of all current evidence, and to develop a "realistic" estimate of the chances of success for novel or different hypotheses and techniques, might be a much more static, uninformative scientific world.

Rather than think it would be appropriate for individual scientists to *internalize* the strictest epistemic standards and the fullest awareness of all evidence—negative, positive, and equivocal—we might think that "full scrutiny" works much better if it is the result of a competitive, social process. As we have suggested, epistemic overcommitment, asymmetric attentiveness to positive vs. negative evidence, and tendentious readings of equivocal evidence might be conditions for a scientific community that is both vibrant and objective. What therefore appeared to be discouraging evidence from cognitive psychology now looks more upbeat: we do seem fairly well equipped with the cognitive dispositions necessary generate and sustain such individual overcommitment. The other side of the coin of overcommitment to one's own program is of course a tendency toward epistemic *undercommitment* to competing hypotheses. The community of inquirers would thus not be without skeptics. But the skepticisms would be as selective as the enthusiasms, and could provide countervailing forces at the social level without dampening out interests or enthusiasms at the individual level.

Let us, not without some irony, put our own "optimistic" hypothesis. As long as scientists are not clinically depressed, it may not in the end be crucial whether they accept or believe the hypotheses they are initially drawn (for whatever reason) to explore: if they begin with acceptance, they typically will come via familiar psychic mechanisms to be intellectually and motivationally engaged advocates; if they begin with belief, and discover that the total evidence is hardly univocal, they typically will be more likely—unless they then *do* become depressed!—to redouble their efforts than to take a skeptical distance.

Indeed, we may need to look no further than our own discipline. We philosophers would, I think, often be at something of a loss to identify whether we believe or accept or ... the philosophical positions we find ourselves vigorously exploring, developing, and, even, defending. And we would be equally hard-pressed to defend our enthusiasm for the views we do develop—or the energy we are prepared to commit to them—as reflecting a well-balanced appraisal of the philosophical record to date. What we do presumably say to ourselves—and what inquirers across the disciplines presumably say to themselves as well—is not, "I have no business doing this" but more likely, "I think there's more to be said for this view than others have noticed." We will expand, "I think this view is on to something that needs to be taken into account. Moreover, I think there are greater difficulties than usually recognized for competing views." Most of us will be right to some degree in saying this. Some of us will be dramatically right. And all of us can see a certain epistemic respectability in the way in which these selective over- and under-commitments keep the process of philosophical inquiry alive and honest. This way of understanding ourselves and our discipline does not strike me as incoherent or debilitating.

Self-awareness, then, might be less of a threat than it would appear. As Hume noted long ago, it may only take engaging in the human interplay of actual life—including (we might add) contests in the study or lab as well as those in the streets—for doubts we cannot refute to lose their power to stymie our engagement in belief and the world.

NOTES

[1] An earlier version of this paper was presented to the Sociedad Filosófica Ibero Americana. It has subsequently appeared as "Truth, Reason, and the Regulation of Belief" in *Philosophical Issues* 5 (1994): 71-94. In the present version, section I has been rewritten and section V enlarged. I am grateful to Allan Gibbard, Mario Garcia Torrente, and David Velleman for comments on earlier versions, and to Daniel Schulthess and other participants in the conference on Belief and Acceptance at the University of Caen, April 1995. Special thanks to the organizers of the conferences, Enrique Villanueva, Ernest Sosa, Lourdes Valdivia, and Pascal Engel.

[2] A similar problem arises even for the more modest claim that scientific belief takes as its object not the truth of theories such as quantum mechanics or general relativity, but their *empirical adequacy*. For a claim that quantum mechanics (e.g.) fits all observations is a claim whose scope extends to a potentially infinite number of unobserved observables, indefinitely exceeding our finite evidential base. For discussion of the "more modest" object of scientific belief, see Bas van Fraassen, *The Scientific Image* (Oxford: Clarendon Press, 1980).

[3] See David Velleman, "The Guise of the Good," *Noûs* 26 (1992): 3-26 and "On the Possibility of Practical Reason," *Ethics* 106 (1996): 694-726. I am indebted to Velleman for helpful discussion and for his comments on earlier papers. I do not mean to suggest that he would agree with my use of this notion.

[4] I have benefited here from conversations with Allan Gibbard and David Velleman.

[5] P. Railton, "Marx and the Objectivity of Science", *PSA 1984*, Vol. 2, ed. P. Asquith and P. Kitcher (East Lansing, Mich.: Philosophy of Science Association), pp. 813-825. Reprinted in R. Boyd, P. Gasper, and J.D. Trout, *The Philosophy of Science* (Cambridge, Mass.: MIT Press, 1991). This section also draws upon material presented at the Philosophy Departments at Duke University and Harvard University, the Department of History and Philosophy of Science at the University of Pittsburgh, and the Collegiate Institute for Values and Science and the Society of Fellows at the University of Michigan. I am grateful to those who attended these talks—especially

a number of practicing scientists—for much lively and informative discussion. A related strategy has been discussed by Philip Kitcher, "The Division of Cognitive Labor", *Journal of Philosophy* 87 (1990): pp. 5-22. The critical concerns I will express later in this paper about externalist, instrumentalist approaches of this general kind are meant to apply specifically to views I have discussed, however, and might not apply to Kitcher's proposal.

[6] For further discussion of criteria (i)-(iii), see Railton, "Objectivity".

[7] Note that this way of putting things does not presuppose a realist conception of things. Various non-(or non-metaphysical)-realists might accept or even insist upon (iv) because it is partly constitutive of the idea of truth.

[8] One might, to borrow some terminology from Rawls, distinguish the *concept* of objectivity, and what issues it engages, from various *conceptions* of objectivity.

[9] Bruno Latour and Steve Woolgar, *Laboratory Life* (Princeton: Princeton University Press: 1986), Postscript, pp. 283-284.

[10] Reliability can of course exist at various levels and in various domains: reliability of expectations about experimental outcomes, about underlying explanations of these outcomes, etc.

[11] For some discussion of epistemic overcommitments, see P. Railton, "Explanation and Metaphysical Controversy", in P. Kitcher and W.C. Salmon (eds.), *Scientific Explanation* (University of Minnesota Press, 1989). Compare also Kitcher's (1990) discussion of the "cognitive division of labor".

Somewhat playfully, one might suggest the following response to the charge that there is much less real diversity in scientific research than would answer to the needs of the "diversification" rationale: just as variability will help a species reduce its vulnerability to disease only if the diverse individuals can successfully mate with one another, so variability in scientific hypotheses can produce fruitful feedback only if the diverse hypotheses can be integrated into the largish theoretical schemes and laboratory practices that make hypothesis testing possible.

[12] See Railton, "Objectivity", p. 819.

[13] Except that I will comment briefly on Simon Blackburn's view that:

> ... the best use to make of [the inevitability of rational] convergence is not as a phenomenon of which a realist has a superior explanation but rather as one in which he alone has faith. ... [I]f it is decided that even in the long run opinion need not converge, then to many people this is a powerful argument—perhaps *the* powerful argument—for denying that there is a reality which that opinion is purporting to describe. (Blackburn, "Truth, Realism, and the Regulation of Theory", p. 369)

I would speculate instead that this possibility—that ultimate rational convergence is not inevitable—is in fact more unsettling to various irrealist ("truth as ideally stable convergent belief") conceptions of reality than to realism.

[14] I am indebted here to Allan Gibbard for suggesting, in a response to an earlier paper, that the latter phrase is the appropriately flavorless way of posing the question.

[15] See his *Scientific Image*.

[16] For a classic statement of the criticism, see B. Williams, "A Critique of Utilitarianism", in J.J.C. Smart and B. Williams, *Utilitarianism: For and Against* (Cambridge: Cambridge University Press, 1973). For responses, see P. Railton, "Alienation, Consequentialism, and the Demands of Morality", *Philosophy and Public Affairs* 13 (1984), pp. 134-171; D. Parfit, *Reasons and Persons* (Oxford: Oxford University Press, 1984); and S. Scheffler, *The Rejection of Consequentialism* (Oxford: Oxford University Press, 1991).

[17] This is just one way of stating a "publicity" constraint. See J. Rawls, *A Theory of Justice* (Cambridge, Mass.: Harvard University Press, 1971).

[18] For discussion of experiments in cognitive psychology that bear on the examples used in this paragraph, see R. Nisbett and L. Ross, *Human Inference: Strategies and Shortcomings of Social Judgment* (Englewood Cliffs, N.J.: Prentice-Hall, 1980).

[19] P.M. Lewinsohn, et al., "Social Competence and Depression: The Role of Illusory Self-Perceptions", *Journal of Abnormal Psychology* (1980). Cited in Nisbett and Ross (1980), p. 198.

ACCEPTANCE AND BELIEF REVISITED

Keith Lehrer

This paper represents my attempt to clarify the distinction that I introduced earlier between belief, a first-order doxastic state, and acceptance, a metamental state ordinarily based on positive evaluation of belief. I shall indicate the way in which I would now revise my earlier views on the matter and explain how the notions should be characterized.[1] My thesis is that both belief and acceptance are functional states, though states of different systems. A consequence of my views concerning these two levels or kinds of states is that there are different levels of cognition that correspond to belief and acceptance, information at the first level, and knowledge at the second. The confusion between these two levels of mentality has resulted in disputes about the nature of knowledge which, though illuminating in the arguments and reflections they elicited, nevertheless obscure the nature of human cognition.

I start with a fundamental assumption concerning knowledge, namely, that it supplies us with premises of reasoning, justification and evaluation of the conclusions of human thought.[2] Though some reasoning may occur below the level of consciousness, reasoning is characteristically a process of conscious reflection in which the steps of reasoning are subject to reflective evaluation and criticism. Reasoning is, consequently, a metamental process. Evaluation and criticism involve reflection upon stages of reasoning. This notion of human reasoning must be distinguished from first-level inference or processing of information. Thus, I contrast first-level belief from metalevel acceptance and first-level inference from metalevel reasoning. The distinction between reasoning and acceptance, on the one hand, and inference and belief, on the other, is a distinction based on the distinction between information of the first-level mind and having any second-level idea whether the information is correct information. You mention a name of someone and ask me if I know the person's telephone number. A number occurs to me, and I tell you the number. You ask me whether the number is correct, and I have no idea. The number just occurred to me when you mentioned the name. Now if the number is correct, I possess the information, though I do not know that I do. I possess, for example, the information that the telephone number of David Armstrong is 9660 1345, for that is the number that occurred to me when you mentioned David Armstrong. I do not know that the number that has occurred to me is the number of David Armstrong, even if I believe that it is. I just cannot tell whether it is his number or not, and I do not have any idea why I believe that it is. I do not have the feeling of remembering the number.

The example is controversial. Some would allege that I know that the telephone number of David Armstrong is 9660 1345 though I do not know that I know this. I do not know that I know it, surely, though I possess the information. Is it knowledge? I have argued that I do not know because I do not know that 9660 1345 is the correct number of David Armstrong. This claim is made most plausible when the explanation for why I believe this is something like a hypnotic suggestion made by a person who was himself not sure that this was the correct number of David Armstrong. But my reason for saying that I do not know is that I do not have the sort of knowledge that I could use in reasoning. Suppose I know that David Armstrong lives in Sydney and find out that 9660 is a prefix for telephone numbers of those in Sydney who live in Glebe. I am not in a position to reason that David Armstrong lives in Glebe, though I know that if his telephone number begins with 9660, then he lives in Glebe, because I do not have the knowledge, the additional premise, that his number has the prefix 9660.

This sort of reflection led me to distinguish between acceptance and belief. I believe that Armstrong's number is 9660 1345, but I am not in a position to evaluate that belief positively, and, thus, to accept what I believe. Notice the problem is not that I lack knowledge of the origin of the belief. Rather, the problem is that I am not in a position to evaluate the correctness of the belief. To say that I am not in a position to evaluate the correctness of the belief is not equivalent to saying that I am not in a position to produce the original evidence I had to support the belief. I often forget the evidence that I originally had for a belief but have the evidence of memory for the belief, nonetheless. The evidence of memory is not the evidence I originally had, for that I have forgotten, but the evidence that I clearly remember. When, as in the case of Armstrong's telephone number, I do not clearly remember what I believe, then I am not in a position to evaluate the belief positively on the basis of memory. I lack the certification of memory. The certification of memory can supply me with evidence for a belief, the evidence that I clearly remember what I believe, without supplying me any information about the origins of the belief. But in the Armstrong example, all such certification and evidence is missing. The belief is not positively evaluated, consequently, not accepted and, therefore, not something I can use as a premise in reasoning.

When I originally thought about the distinction between acceptance and belief, I was influenced by Fodor's work on the modularity of mind. Belief, I was inclined to think, was the automatic output of encapsulated input systems, while acceptance, using the resources of memory for evaluation, was the plastic output of the central system. One could draw a similar distinction between inference and reasoning. Inference would be the output of some input-output module that was encapsulated and did not draw on the resources of memory to access background information. Reasoning would be plastic and would use the resources of memory to access background information to use for evaluation. At the level of belief and inference, the output is obtained automatically, while at the level of acceptance and reasoning, results are obtained by means of the plasticity of central system evaluation. That is the Fodorian version of the distinction between mind and metamind.

I am no longer inclined to attach the distinction between belief and acceptance or between mind and metamind to the distinction between input systems and central systems; though, assuming the Fodorian model, there may be a rough correspondence. My reason is simply that I am not willing to commit myself to an encapsulation theory of the first-order mind. There may be habits of first-order processing that arise from experience and become automatic-response mechanisms, but they are not unalterable. Similarly, there are some higher-order evaluations that are habitual, and, perhaps, even some that are automatic. Perhaps we cannot help but evaluate *modus tollens* positively no matter what arguments might be raised against it. Thus, I do not think that there is an exact fit between the distinctions of Fodor and those I wish to draw, but I do wish to acknowledge the influence of Fodor's theory of the modularity of mind on my own thinking about belief and acceptance, about mind and metamind.

One strong motivation for the distinction between belief and acceptance as well as between inference and reasoning is the literature in psychology generated by Kahneman and Tversky indicating that people infer conclusions in ways that, from standard models of reasoning, appear irrational. The literature is now robust, and many explanations are offered for the apparently unreasonable inferences and beliefs reported. Whatever the explanation for the inferences and beliefs in question, the fact that they are appreciated as unreasonable indicates that people reading the results of the inquiry evaluated the beliefs and inferences negatively even if, as may well be the case, they would have had the same beliefs and made the same inferences had they been the experimental subjects. I conclude that there is a conflict between such first-level beliefs and inferences and the negative evaluations of them, that is, a conflict between what we believe and infer on the one hand and what we accept and how we reason on the other. Aside from such sophisticated studies, there are cases in which one receives information one knows to be trustworthy but one finds that one cannot, in fact, believe what one is told. Information about the death of someone one has just seen a few minutes ago are sad instances in which one evaluates the information positively because the source of the sad news is impeccable, and hence, one accepts the sad news even though belief may lag behind.

I now think it important to introduce a similar distinction between desire and preference. There are desires that arise in one unbidden and often against one's will. One evaluates the satisfaction of them negatively and one does not prefer to satisfy them. Those desires that one evaluates positively, on the contrary, are ones that one prefers to satisfy. So, there are first-level desires, beliefs and inferences and metalevel preferences, acceptances and reasonings. The latter are often the result of positive evaluation of the former, acceptances resulting from the positive evaluation of beliefs, reasonings resulting from the positive evaluation of inferences, and preferences resulting from the positive evaluation of desires. However, this is not always the case. Sometimes acceptances arise from the positive evaluation of things we simply consider but do not yet believe, reasonings arise from the positive consideration of things we simply consider but do not yet infer, and preferences from things we consider and do not yet desire.

The case of preference and desire is, perhaps, the clearest. I may not have any desire to keep a promise I have made, but I prefer to do so because reason dictates that I must. I may have a limited choice between two awful alternatives and have no desire for the alternative I prefer. Similarly, belief may not conform to evidence, though acceptance does, and inference may not conform to logic, though reasoning does. The metamind is guided by the positive evaluations of reason in acceptance, reasoning and preference, while belief, inference and desire may exist without such guidance.

It is important to distinguish the states of acceptance, reasoning and preference from the positive evaluations that give rise to them. These states are attitudinal and functional states and should not be confused with episodes that cause or express them. There is much mischief in philosophy of mind and epistemology resulting from the confusion of functional states with expressions of them even at the first level of belief. Some are inclined to distinguish between occurrent beliefs and dispositional beliefs, for example, and to equate the former with some state of thought that is presently occurring to me. The thoughts that presently occur to me, though they may express some belief I have, are not the belief itself, for the belief may have existed before the thought occurred to me and will, in all probability, continue to exist when thought does not. Thoughts are evanescent things, coming and going, while beliefs are more stable states that drive the engine of thought. When I reflect on a subject, some historical topic, for example, various thoughts will occur to me revealing the beliefs that I have about the matter. The distinction between thoughts and beliefs is like the one between utterances and beliefs. An utterance may express a belief, but it is a mistake to identify the utterance with the belief. Similarly, a thought may express a belief, but it is a mistake to identify the thought with the belief. The mistake becomes manifest when we notice that the occurrences of utterances and thoughts are explained by the beliefs they express. Thoughts like utterances occur to us as expressions of beliefs. Thoughts occur. Beliefs do not. Occurrent beliefs are a fiction of philosophies that equate mental states with conscious occurrences. Occurrent beliefs do not exist.[3]

The fact that beliefs are functional states renders the problem of distinguishing them from acceptances more perplexing, not less. In earlier work, I was inclined to identify acceptances with certain performatives. If I say, "I accept what you say," then I appear to have accepted what you said. Such an account would have the advantage of making acceptance into a voluntary state and thereby distinguish it from belief which is not. I now think that such a representation of the matter is too simple. When I say, "I accept what you say," I have *committed* myself to accepting what you say, but whether I actually do so remains open. If my next assertion contradicts what you said, then I have not accepted what you said, as you will soon say. It is, I think, a mistake, one I made, to identify the verbal commitment to accept something with the acceptance of it. In fact, verbal commitments like episodes of judging may ordinarily result in the state of acceptance, but there is a logical gap between saying that one accepts something or even judging that it is true, and accepting it. The reason is that episodes of saying and judging are, being episodic, evanescent while acceptances are not. Judging that something is the case on the basis of background information in light of reason will ordinarily yield acceptance, but the activity of judging and the state of belief are not identical. My acceptance does not consist of the episode of judging, however considered and reflective, any more than it consists of the episode of saying I accept, however considered and sincere, though both yield acceptance in the paradigm case.

If both belief and acceptance are functional states, how are they to be distinguished? The preliminary reply is that belief is functionally related to belief, inference and desire, while acceptance is functionally related to acceptance, reasoning and preference. However, that would assume that the difference in functional role between the first-level states and the metalevel states is antecedently understood, which, though it may have some intuitive clarity, requires philosophical elucidation.   Let us focus on the functional role of acceptance. Acceptance is based on rational evaluation.   Acceptance that **H** introduces a kind of rational equilibrium over rational reflection at a point in time in the sense that rational reflection on the present evidence will not change my acceptance of **H** or the degree of probability of **H** which is a factor in the acceptance of **H** at the present time. Thus, if **R** is the rational consideration of the evidence for **H** at *t* and I accept that **H**, then the antecedent probability of **H** is stable at that time over conditionalization on **R**, that is, $p_t(\mathbf{H}) = p_t(\mathbf{H/R})$.   This distinguishes the acceptance that **H** from belief that **H**. Belief that **H** does not stabilize the probability of **H** over conditionalization on rational consideration of the evidence because belief may arise without evaluation of the evidence.

A similar point can be made about the relationship between preference and utility.   Preference represents a kind of rational equilibrium over rational reflection concerning utility in the sense that rational reflection on the present evidence will not change my preference or the degree of utility I assign to the thing preferred at the present time. So if **R** is the rational consideration of the evidence concerning the merits of alternative **A** at *t* and I prefer that **A**, then the antecedent utility of **A** is stable over conditionalization on **R**, that is, $u_t(\mathbf{A}) = u_t(\mathbf{A/R})$.   This distinguishes the preference that **A** from the desire that **A**. Desire that **A** does not stabilize the utility of **A** over conditionalization of rational consideration of the evidence because desire may arise without evaluation of the evidence.

Finally, a related point can be made about the relationship between inference and reasoning. Though we do not have any standard measure of the cogency of a sequence of statements, **S**, if we imagine such a measure, *c*, the same observations can be made about *c* as about *p* and *u*. Reasoning represents a kind of rational equilibrium in the sense that rational reflection on the present evidence will not change the degree of cogency I assign to **S**. If **R** is the rational consideration of the evidence concerning validity of **S** at t and I reason that **S**, then the antecedent cogency of **S** is stable over conditionalization on **R**, that is, $c_t(S) = c_t(S/R)$. This also distinguishes inference that **S** from reasoning that **S**. Inference that **S** does not stabilize the cogency of **S** over conditionalization on rational consideration of the evidence because inference may arise without evaluation of the evidence.

The notion of probability I take to be defined in the standard way as well as the notion of utility; though conditionalization, like the notion of cogency, I have left undefined. The conditional measures of utility and cogency are the measures of utility and cogency on the assumption that **R** has a probability of 1. The measure of cogency is a probability that **S** is valid. On some measures of probability, the probability that a sequence is valid is either 1 if the sequence is valid or 0 if the sequence is not valid, but this does not capture our degree of uncertainty about probability which may have any value in the interval of 1 and 0. I am assuming that the functor c can take any value in the interval of 1 and 0. I assume that measures of probability, utility and cogency are metamental notions because of the ratiocination required to obtain coherent assignments, and at the same time, I assume that they have a functional role in decision making.

The synchronic equilibrium or stability of the metamental states of acceptance, preference and reasoning over reflective rational consideration of the present evidence is what distinguishes them from the first-order states of belief, desire and inference. It is important, however, to distinguish this synchronic stability over rational reflection on the present evidence from diachronic stability over time in the light of changing evidence. Dynamic responsiveness to changing evidence is a feature of the metamental states of acceptance, preference and reasoning. These states are necessarily subject to continuing revision in the light of new evidence. Belief, desire and inference may prove unresponsive. Our beliefs, desires and inferences often remain unchanged in the light of evidence that they are unreasonable. If someone I regard as impeccably trustworthy informs me of news I accept, the news may, nevertheless, not have any immediate impact on my belief, desire and inference. I may reason that it would be reasonable to change my beliefs, desires and inferences on the basis of the news I accept, but my beliefs, desires and inferences may be unresponsive to my ratiocination. I do not mean to suggest that the first-order states are inflexibly unresponsive to new evidence. Often such evidence causes change in these first-order states. I only suggest that it need not, and experimental study suggests we are less responsive than we might suppose. The metamental states of acceptance, preference and reasoning are, by contrast, responsive to new evidence because they are states resulting from evaluation in terms of evidence and, consequently, they are responsive to changes in evidence. New evidence calls for new evaluation, and, consequently, acceptance, preference and reasoning must be continually responsive to the changing background of evidence.

Thus, the picture I offer of the first-order states is that they arise in us automatically and unbidden, sometimes against our will and judgment. We may prefer to have different beliefs, desires and inferences because rational reflection leads to a negative evaluation of them in the light of new evidence. Such evaluation leads to a shift in assignment of degrees of probability, utility or cogency and to a shift in acceptance, preference and reasoning. The latter states are by their nature responsive to new evidence and the re-evaluation it requires so that they produce a rational equilibrium or stability in relation to rational reflection on the evidence. This equilibrium should not be taken to presuppose actual reflection, however. The metamind must operate according to heuristic rules, "rules of thumb," for adjusting acceptance, preference and reasoning to new evidence in a way that corresponds to the results of reflection without actually reflecting. The burden of reflective reconsideration of every acceptance, preference and reasoning in the light of new evidence would be beyond our capacity.

It should be noted here that I am not assuming a computational model of responsiveness to new evidence. Others have argued that a shift in probabilities would require computations beyond our capacity in simple cases. However, there is no reason to assume that measures of probability, utility and cogency are computed by a computational program rather than resulting from other principles. The argument against measures of probability, utility and cogency based on noncomputability is as fallacious as an argument that the law of gravity cannot hold because bodies cannot compute gravitational forces. Neither the mind nor the metamind are limited by a theory of computability. Stochastic principles can account for the shifts without the assumption that they are computed.

Moreover, in many cases of acceptance and preference, rational reflection would be irrational because otiose. As I see my fingers move and believe that they do, I accept what I believe without reflection. As I desire to save the file I have been creating, I prefer to satisfy that desire without reflection. Nevertheless, what I thus accept and prefer is stable over rational reflection on the evidence, for, in these cases, the heuristic principles that tell me to immediately accept and prefer these things without reflection function to produce a state that is in equilibrium or is stable over such reflection. These principled responses may conceal the distinction between belief and acceptance, between desire and preference, when belief is immediately accepted and satisfaction of a desire is immediately preferred, but the distinction remains. Heuristic principles are no more than that and will be overridden when the situation calls for reflection. We may, in fact, think of the heuristic principles as being flagged by special situations, and in those situations the formation of the higher-order state is suspended for rational reflection.

Thus, though there is some similarity between the functional role of belief, desire and inference at the first level and the role of acceptance, preference and reasoning at the metalevel in that each will influence what thoughts occur to us, what decisions we make and what conclusions we reach, there will also be a critical difference. The difference is that acceptance, preference and reasoning represent the evaluations of reason at a given point in time. We may, therefore, think of those states as not calling for further rational consideration, deliberation and reflection on present evidence. They represent synchronic equilibrium of reason, and their functional role is to influence how we think, what we decide and what we conclude without need for further rational consideration of present evidence.

Another way of representing the functional role is in terms of what we consider reasonable. I have emphasized elsewhere that these mental states are ones we may consider worthy of our trust and, therefore, trustworthy and reasonable for us. To put the matter in the first person, I am worthy of my trust in what I now accept, what I prefer and how I reason because these are states of synchronic equilibrium over rational consideration. Consequently, I am trustworthy and, finally, reasonable in what I now accept, what I prefer and how I reason. However, my synchronic reasonableness depends on diachronic reasonableness, for I am aware of my fallibility and vulnerability to correction on the basis of new evidence. I am worthy of my trust at the present moment because of my readiness to change, correct and improve in terms of subsequent evaluations. My synchronic reasonableness at the metamental level is a function of my diachronic reasonableness at that level. The reasonableness of my metamental states at any one time is a function of the reasonableness of the way in which I change those states over time. Moreover, my reasonableness is not only a matter of what methods or principles I now use to change acceptances, preferences and reasonings, for I must change those in a reasonable way as well. The reasonableness of my acceptances, preferences and reasonings at any time is, therefore, a matter of my reasonableness in how I change. I must be worthy of my trust and trustworthy in how I change in response to new evidence. The functional role of my trustworthiness and reasonableness at the metamental level is the freedom to be guided by my acceptances, preferences and reasonings without further reflective rational consideration because of my trustworthiness and reasonableness in how I change my acceptances, preferences and reasonings. The metamind allows me to proceed reasonably on the basis of my acceptances, preferences and reasonings at a point in time without requiring unending reflection on the reasonablenes of them. The dynamic responsiveness of the metamind to the demands of reason makes it worthy of our trust and permits us to trust our metamental states of acceptance, preference and reasoning without further consideration of the rationality of it. That trust defines the functional role of metamind in the life of reason.

NOTES

[1] My earlier views are to be found in Keith Lehrer, "Knowledge, Truth and Ontology," in *Language and Ontology*, 1982, pp. 201-11, "Belief, Acceptance and Cognition," in *On Believing*, edited by H. Parret, 1983, pp. 172-183, "Metaknowledge: Undefeated Justified Belief," *Synthese*, 74, 1988, pp. 329-347, "Metamental Ascent: Beyond Belief and Desire," (Presidential Address), in *Proceedings and Addresses of the American Philosophical Association*, 63:3, 1990, and *Metamind*, Introduction, Clarendon Press, Oxford University, 1990.

[2] Cf. Tyler Burge, "Our Entitlement to Self-Knowledge," *Proceedings of the Aristotelian Society*, *New Series*, Vol. XCVI, pp. 91-116, esp. "Briefly drawn, my line of thought will be this. To be capable of critical reasoning, and to be subject to certain rational norms necessarily associated with such reasoning, some mental states must be *knowledgeably* reviewable. ... Critical reasoning is reasoning that involves an ability to recognize and effectively employ reasonable criticism or support for reasons and reasoning. It is reasoning guided by an appreciation, use, and assessment of reasons and reasoning as such. As a critical reasoner, one not only reasons. One recognizes reasons as reasons. One evaluates, checks, weights, criticizes, supplements one's reasons and reasoning. Clearly, this requires a second-order ability to think about thought contents or propositions, and rational relations among them." p. 98.

[3] I am indebted to an unpublished paper by Scott Hendricks for this observation.

COMMITMENTS DEFINED WITH THE HELP OF PUBLIC CONCEPTS

Andrew Woodfield
University of Bristol

I. AN ASSUMPTION ABOUT ACCEPTANCE

In the first chapter of *An Essay on Belief and Acceptance* (1992), Jonathan Cohen sets out various distinguishing features (see diagram 1).

Diagram 1

FEATURES	BELIEF	ACCEPTANCE
EPISTEMIC COMMITMENT	+	+
ACTIVE	--	+
VOLUNTARY	--	+
FEELING	+	--
HAS INFERENTIAL ROLE	+	+
DEDUCTIVE CLOSURE	--	+
SYSTEMIC CONSISTENCY	--	+
NECESSARILY LANGUAGE-LINKED	--	+

The last entry on the list encapsulates Cohen's observation that believers are not necessarily language-users, whereas acts of acceptance are necessarily connected with language. A dog can believe the proposition that the cupboard door is closed, but he cannot be credited with accepting this (or any other) proposition, because the concept of acceptance requires that 'what is under consideration is tied to some type of linguistic formulation even if this formulation is never uttered aloud' (Cohen *ibid* p12).

In this paper, I make the working assumption that Cohen is right to say that acts of acceptance are language-linked[1]. Having assumed that it is so, I inquire why it is so. The reason, I discover, is that this concept *accepting* is the concept of a type of act whose paradigmatic instances are elements in speech-transactions.

The paper also has a wider aim, namely, to investigate how it is *possible* that some mental acts are inextricably connected to language-processing. My speculations are tentative, and, like all first stabs, they leave plenty of loose ends. But the problem is worth addressing, for if it is true that language impregnates a certain subclass of acts of propositional thinking, this would *seem* to contradict a currently orthodox position in cognitive psychology. The Fodor/MIT view is that there is a language module which resides *outside* the 'thinking faculty' or 'central processor' such that the outputs of the former are inputs to the latter and certain outputs of the latter are inputs to the former, but the internal workings of the two systems are autonomous of one another.

II. TAXONOMIC ISSUES

Beliefs and acceptances have quite a few features in common. As diagram 1 indicates, they both have *inferential roles*. Cohen thinks that the *type of content* they have is the same, because 'it is possible to move from one to the other without change of content. People often accept just what they believe, and believe just what they accept' (*ibid* p39). To understand the difference between the two attitudes, he says, you need not enter into debates about the nature of content or the semantics of content-clauses. Also, the range of propositions available to a language-user as candidates for belief or disbelief *coincides* pretty much with the range of propositions that the person would be able to accept or reject.

Yet believing is psychologically different from accepting. Diagram 1 listed some of the respects in which they differ, but these differentiae do not seem to flow from a single source. The diagram does not help us much if we are looking to locate the two attitudes in a general classification-scheme. *Is* there a single scheme into which they both fit? If there is, what taxonomic relationship do they have to each other within the scheme?

As far as I am aware, there is no classification-scheme which makes belief and acceptance two species of a single psychological genus. Cohen writes as if they do belong to the same genus when he asks (in section 14), 'Do the concepts of belief and acceptance exhaust their genus?'. But Cohen's generic category comprises all cognitive attitudes 'which may be implied by the utterance of indicative sentences with an affirmative intonation' (*ibid* p73). This is a gerrymandered grouping, not a specification of a taxon in a psychological classification-scheme.

I favour the idea—which Cohen airs—that whereas the concept of belief is the concept of a *mental* state, the concept of acceptance finds its natural home in a system for classifying *speech-transactions*. If this is true, it explains why non-linguistic animals cannot be credited with accepting p, even when they believe p. This idea needs to be developed carefully, however, because a person may accept something mentally and privately *without* performing any speech-act.

Suppose that it is a conceptual truth that no proposition can be *accepted by S* unless S comes into contact with a linguistic formulation of that proposition. Why should there be such a conceptual truth? How can a concept that is defined in this way be useful and have empirical application? From a cognitivist perspective it is puzzling that the subject's ability or inability to verbalize should make a difference to which mental attitudes he has. The natural ordering of the matter is as follows. First the Subject has certain mental attitudes, a subset of those of which he is capable. Second, the question may be raised, with respect to each of these mental attitudes, whether the Subject can or cannot express it verbally. If accepting were just another cognitive mode in the same family as believing, disbelieving, wishing, hoping, expecting, fearing etc, it would be problematic that a content which *is* available to an animal in these other modes should be in principle unavailable in accepting mode. Agreed, dogs cannot believe that 12 +23=35, that tomorrow is Tuesday, or that light travels in straight lines. But dogs—we are told—cannot accept any contents at all, not even ones that they understand.

To explain this peculiarity, one might refer to the channel by which the content enters the mind. Suppose that Fido has a mental representation of food being served on to a plate. Call this MR. Provided MR is inside Fido's central processor, it can be entertained in various attitudinal modes (Fido can hope it, wish it, believe it, etc). But MR cannot enter Fido's central processor as a consequence of linguistic communication, because Fido has no language module. One possible hypothesis, then, is that in order for a content to be *accepted*, the representational vehicle of that content has to enter a certain part of the mind, or be activated in the mind, as a consequence of activity in the language module.

Another possible hypothesis might be that acceptance-content is really different in kind from primitive belief-content. Suppose someone tells you there is food on a plate, and you accept what they say. Although you and Fido represent the same state of affairs, Fido represents it in a different way from you. Relative to a fine-grained method of individuating contents, there is a difference in content. If a speaker ascribed the belief to Fido and the acceptance to you, the speaker would utter the same that-clause in both ascriptions. But sameness in the reports is certainly no proof that the psychological states are the same or that they have the same kind of content.

Perhaps the 'different content' hypothesis could be combined with the 'different channel' hypothesis. This would give a stronger account of the contrast between believing and accepting. The wider implications do seem rather radical, though. If mental contents that come in via the language channel are different in kind from the primitive contents that arise from sense-perception, one is led to wonder how the two kinds of contents interact and become integrated.

A further point to consider. Cohen makes the intriguing suggestion that mental acts of acceptance are *interiorizations* of speech-acts. He says (on p79), 'It is reasonable...to view any kind of acceptance as an interiorization of the corresponding speech-act'. The Interiorization Hypothesis stands in need of elaboration. It isn't easy to find a viable interpretation of it. Care must be taken to avoid interpretations which would render it circular and impossible.

Interiorizing a speech-act is presumably a *process* of reproducing something linguistic within oneself. What exactly occurs during the process, and when—in relation to other processes—does it occur? Is it a medium-term Vygotskian developmental process, or a short-term on-line process carried out during every particular act of acceptance?

Circularity problems loom. Here is one circular hypothesis: 'In order to perform action B at time t, the agent must go through process A, and process A consists in an operation *performed upon that very action B*'. It is logically impossible for a particular act B to satisfy this condition. B would have to have occurred before it could be performed.

Here is another useless hypothesis: 'In order for S to do B at t, S must go through process A, and process A is an operation upon a *prior* B-type action authored by S'. This would imply that it was impossible for S to do B *for the first time*. To be viable, the Interiorization Hypothesis must be co-tenable with all logical principles, conceptual truths and empirical laws. In the next section I argue that a satisfactory interpretation of the Interiorization Hypothesis is indeed possible.

III. BREAKING DOWN ACTS OF ACCEPTING

A thorny question about terminology needs to be confronted at this stage. Are there two *senses* of the verb 'accept', two distinct *concepts* of acceptance? I say not.

The concept *mentally accepting,* which refers to a psychological operation, is distinct from the concept *verbally accepting,* which refers to a public speech-act. Each of these is a *complex* concept constructed by qualifying a single root concept, *accepting.*

A similar point applies to the counting of word-senses. Parsimony is achieved if the verb 'accept' has one meaning. When this verb occurs in the two adverbially qualified verb phrases 'mentally accept' and 'verbally accept', it contributes the same meaning to both. The semantic difference between the two phrases is due entirely to the different adverbs.

There are the three linguistic expressions ('accept', 'mentally accept' and 'verbally accept'), and there are three concepts expressed by them. The term 'accept' on its own does not express *two* of the three concepts. We shall take it, then, that the second-order term, 'the concept *accepting*', is a genuine definite description which uniquely specifies one concept[2].

Although there is only one taxonomic concept of acceptance and accepting is a single type of act, particular acts of that type may take a variety of *forms* and may be performed in various *ways*. The concepts corresponding to the various ways (e.g. concepts specified with the help of adverbs) are not concepts of distinct act-types. They are not taxonomic. For instance, the concept *mental acceptance*, when applied to a particular act, classifies the token as being of the accepting type, and additionally presents the token as having been performed mentally. That it was performed mentally is not type-identifying information.

We are now ready to make a first shot at decomposing the sequence of events that make up a certain conversational transaction. It is a transaction in which one party performs a dateable act of acceptance. Two parties are involved. The Subject S occupies the role of *Accepter*; an Other person O plays the part of *Proposer*. We need to mention a proposer, for as Cohen rightly says, 'Fundamentally, the term 'acceptance' suggests a (posited) giver of premises or rules of inference as well as a (positing) receiver' (*ibid* p13).

The transaction begins when O offers a proposal to S by causing S to hear an indicative sentence Z uttered with assertoric intonation. After a short interval S replies to O by saying 'Yes', or 'Right', or by producing some other sound, gesture or mark of assent. (I shall assume that S uses a sound-signal.) What went on during that short interval? S was not merely verbally active at the *end* of the interval but was also cognitively active *during* the interval. Events inside S's head played a crucial part in determining that S performed an act of acceptance. Thus we *start off* from a position that opposes Quine's behaviourism. Quine thinks that the mentalistic implications of the ordinary notion of assent are inadmissible, so he replaces assenting with *surface assenting*—an entirely meaningless act[3].

I propose to segment the cognitive activity into phases, and I shall hypothesize that inside S's head is a system of interconnected functional units. These will be represented as boxes on a 'black box' diagram. Each unit or 'homunculus' carries out some of the operations that occur during the different phases. Functional decomposition is a well-known technique in cognitive psychology; I shall not attempt to justify it but I simply use it in the hope that it will provide illumination in this case. In our first shot at decomposition, the model of cognitive architecture that we employ is quite standard. It posits that the language module is separate from the reasoning system. Later we may have cause to feel unsatisfied with this model, but it seems a promising place to start.

Each box is supposed to perform a part of the task that S achieves. It is important that no box be endowed with the capacity to achieve the whole task. Only the whole person can fulfill the role of Accepter. The point is to explain in more basic box terms *how* that task is done. To minimize the risk of committing 'homunculus fallacies', I shall describe the subpersonal units and their operations without using the word 'accept' or its synonyms.

Diagram 2

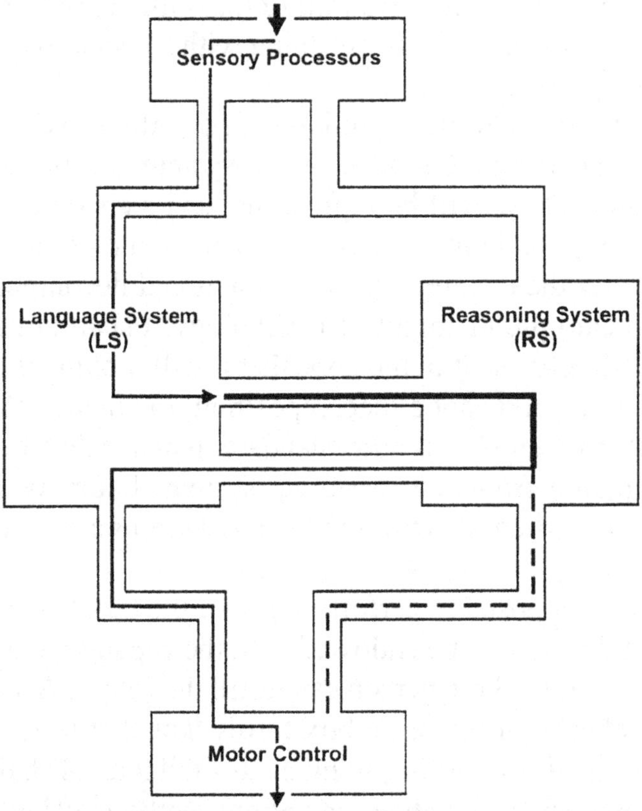

Phase One (thin line):   Interpretation of input-sentence.
Phase Two (thick line): Evaluation of proposition. (Interrupted thick line
                         indicates potential continuation leading to non-
                         linguitic action.)
Phase Three (thin line): Preparation of appropriate verbal signal.

Diagram 2 shows a part of S's cognitive architecture. It includes her
sensory processors, her motor control system, plus the two most
important units for our purposes, her Language System LS and her
Reasoning System RS.

I segment S's activity into phases One, Two and Three. Phase One:
Upon receiving the auditory stimulus produced by O, LS interprets it
as a linguistic object having phonetic, phonological, syntactic and

semantic structure. Phase One is complete when LS has identified the propositional content of Z as uttered by O.

Phase Two begins with LS presenting that proposition to RS. RS evaluates it and decides to add it to the set of propositions which it stores for potential use as premisses in practical and theoretical reasoning. Once p is assimilated into the stock of premisses, S may draw upon p at any time.

Phase Three is initiated when RS sends back to LS the information that it has added the proposition to the premiss-store and instructs LS to prepare a verbal response of assent. This is not sufficient to release an overt response. In general, whether S actually will produce an utterance depends upon S's motivation and her perception of the ongoing conversation. The production of verbal output is contingent upon operations performed by other black boxes inside S's head which we are relegating to the background. In our paradigm case, however, S overtly signals her sincere assent to O's proposal.

In diagram 2, the different thicknesses shown in the line are an expository device intended to distinguish three channels through which information is carried. The activation of these three channels correspond to the three Phases of the process.

Can we describe what goes on in more detail? It is tempting to open the two important black boxes. The danger is, of course, that the deeper we decompose, the more speculative our account becomes. But I think we can go a little further without straying from a common sense view of how the mind works.

In Diagram 3, LS and RS are each depicted as having a tripartite structure. Certain operations are assigned more specifically to subsystems within each system. Let us run through the functional competence possessed by the Evaluator, for example. Upon receipt of a presented proposition, the Evaluator is capable of either *sending* or *withholding* the instruction 'Add p to the premiss-store', and also capable of sending the instruction 'Don't let p into the premiss-store'. The Evaluator also has it in its power to send back three types of message to the Sentence Synthesizer. Each message is an instruction to prepare to produce a sign of assent, or a sign of refraining from assent, or a sign of dissent. The diagram models a person who is able to verbally accept what O says, or verbally signal the reserving of judgement, or verbally reject what O says.

Diagram 3

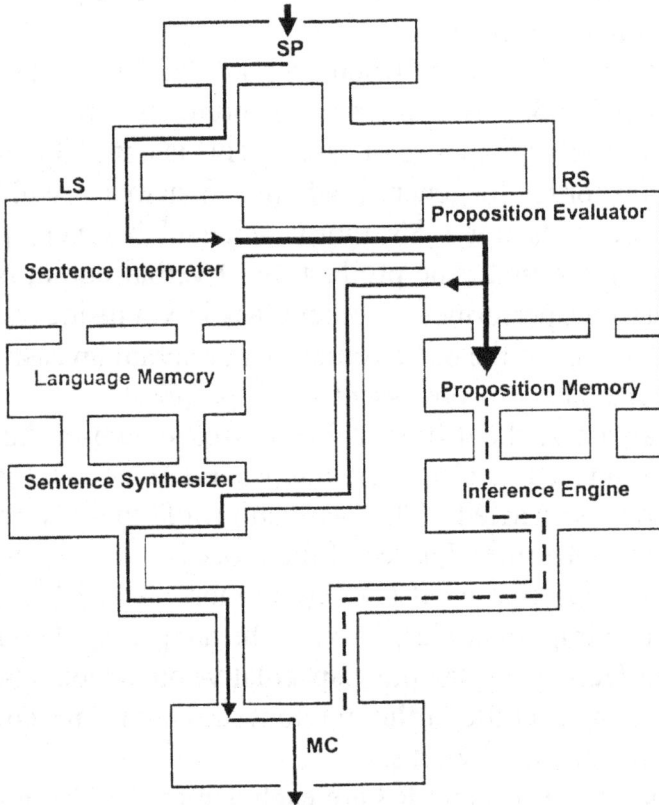

Black box diagrams depict structures and competences; they are not primarily designed to illustrate the flow of information during any *particular* performance. They accommodate a range of alternative processes. But the continuous line shows the channels that would be *activated* in paradigm cases of acceptance. The 'thin' channel is active during Phase One, the 'thick' middle channel during Phase Two, and the 'thin' channel during Phase Three.

In the paradigm case, all three channels are activated. Signals are passed through them at the time of performance. I now want to suggest that activation of the Phase One channel through LS and the Phase Two channel through RS is more important than activation of the Phase Three channel through LS.

Consider the following non-paradigmatic case. The two participants in the conversational transaction go through the same routine as before, except that S produces no verbal response. The channels mediating Phases One and Two are active in just the same way as before. O's uttered sentence is interpreted by LS. LS presents a proposition to RS for consideration. The Evaluator instructs the Proposition Memory to add p to the premiss-store. But suppose the Sentence Synthesizer receives no instruction to respond, because the Phase Three channel is not activated. It is true, nevertheless, that S accepted what O said. This is a clear case of *tacit* acceptance by S of an explicit proposal by O, a dateable occurrence in the course of a two-party conversation. S's resulting attitudinal state possesses the same forward-looking inferential potential that S's attitudinal state had in the paradigm case.

Moreover, there might well be a satisfactory explanation of *why* RS sent no instruction to the Sentence Synthesizer. Perhaps there was no need to do so! In many situations a listener is able to communicate acceptance of the interlocutor's proposal by doing nothing. In normal conversation, silence indicates acceptance. People *presume* that listeners will accept what they are told by an interlocutor who is patently serious and sincere. It is a convention amongst language-users that when the listener accepts what she is told, she need do nothing positive to signal that she has accepted. Acceptance is the default option, and both parties know this.

Channel Three activation is not so important, then, because there are speech-situations in which verbal signaling is optional. The very same token act of accepting p at time t may occur either with or without the expressive mark or 'handshake' which publicly signals that Phases One and Two have been satisfactorily completed. For this reason I submit that appropriate information flowing through channels One and Two constitutes the *cognitive core* that underlies the act of accepting what someone else says. Channel Three has the secondary job of *publicizing* the events in channels One and Two. Tacit acceptance of someone's proposal, where channel Three is dormant, is a *variant* of the paradigm of explicit acceptance.

In cases of tacit acceptance, S still performs a communicational act, for the following reasons: (a) S's cognitive processing through channels One and Two is stimulated by S's perception of O's speech-act; (b) at the time of acting, S is playing a role in an ongoing speech transaction, and S's act will normally affect the subsequent course of the conversation.

We now turn to the question of what happens inside S when S accepts a proposition in a *purely mental* way. I mean an act that S performs privately, and not in the context of a conversation with another party. As we have seen, the role of Accepter is complementary to the role of Proposer. In a conversation, an interlocutor outside S *supplies* a linguistic input to LS. This drives LS, causing it to *present* a proposition for consideration which RS *receives*. When S accepts that p in the purely mental way, there is no external Proposer. Some substitute must stand in for the external proposing agency, because there can be no accepting where nothing is proposed, nor can receiving take place unless something is given.

My suggestion is that in an act of purely mental acceptance LS *internally supplies* the sentence which generates the proposition that is presented to RS for consideration. The input to the acceptance-process is endogenous. But the cognitive mechanism that carries through the process once it has been initiated is the same as the mechanism that mediates S's tacit acceptance of things that other people say. Or, more accurately, the *core* of it is the same.

In diagram 4 there is an additional (thickly marked) channel connecting the Sentence Synthesizer to the Sentence Interpreter. Call this the 'endogenous input channel'. SS draws upon information stored in Language Memory. It can construct new sentences out of remembered words and phrases in accordance with syntactic rules, and it can also retrieve from memory whole sentences that were once heard and which at the time of hearing were perhaps not wholly understood. SS stimulates Sentence Interpreter with these representations of sentences. The diagram is deliberately fuzzy about the location at which these representations are inserted into Sentence Interpreter;

perhaps there are several locations, one at the place charged with low-level phonological processing of input, another at a place where it does some semantic interpretation, and one at a point close to the final propositional identification stage. Perhaps the insertion-point depends on the amount of interpretation that has already been done on the sentence when SS delivers it. These are details that we need not settle for present purposes. Let us simply assume that at whatever point the representation of the sentence penetrates Sentence Interpreter, once it gets inside that sub-system it gets forward-processed in the same way that an ordinary heard utterance would have been processed. As far as Sentence Interpreter is concerned, it does not matter where the linguistic object came from.

Diagram 4

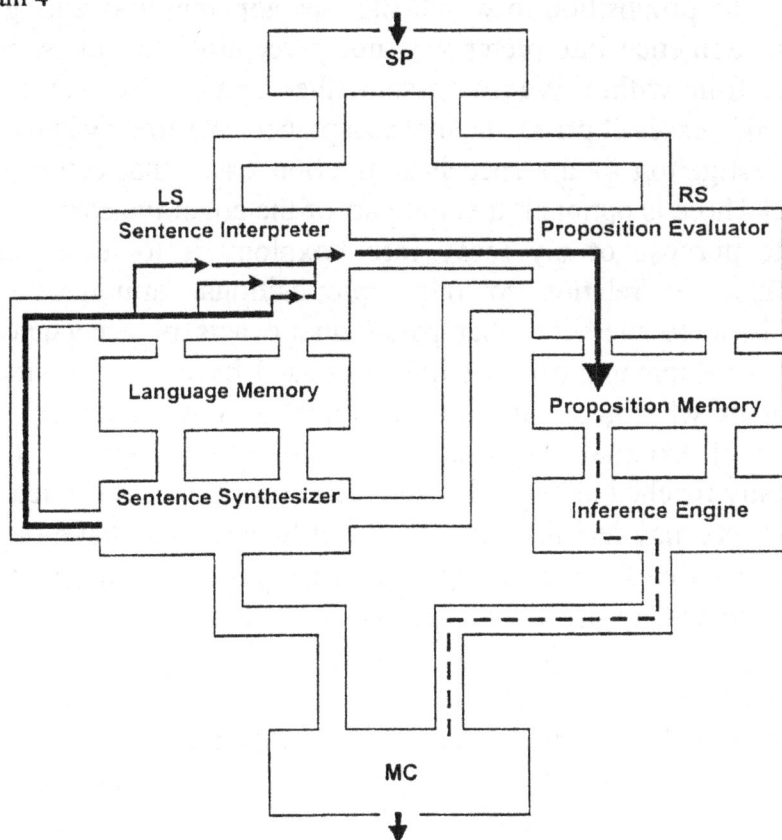

The line in diagram 4 is supposed to illustrate the flow of information inside S during a bout of private thinking. Signals travel from the endogenous input channel through a section of channel One and on through channel Two. The phenomenology associated with this process may vary from case to case. Sometimes it seems to S that a thought just pops into mind. Or maybe S remembers an occasion when she heard someone utter sentence Z. Perhaps S did not understand Z at the time of first hearing, and she now attempts to interpret it. In one way or another S is brought to consider a proposition, and she decides to add it to her store of premises.

In the private case, S produces no verbal utterance. She is not motivated to publicize what is going in channels One and Two, because no other person is around. If she had produced a verbal sign of assent, and if other people had been present, they would have been unable to identify the proposition to which she was apparently assenting. The input to Sentence Interpreter was not perceptible to others, it was initiated from within. We may assume then that channel Three is not activated in cases of private mental acceptance. We already know from our investigation of the speech-transaction cases that activation of channel Three is optional. It is not part of the cognitive core.

The purpose of my foray into boxology is to locate mental acceptance in relation to other propositional attitudes. I was sympathetic to the view that paradigmatic acts of acceptance are elements in communicational transactions. I have now provided an account of what goes on when a subject accepts privately, in the absence of external input, and with no external output. I have practically reached my goal, but one extra refinement is needed.

Readers may feel that any act of tacitly accepting that p ought to count as a case of mental acceptance. It has just as much right to that title as the case of private acceptance. In neither case is there is any overt response. This leads to a possible objection to my way of classifying the cases. 'Surely,' says the objector, 'in both of the so-called 'non-paradigm' cases, what goes on is all inside S's head. If private acceptance is a purely mental act, then so is tacit acceptance!'

Not so. There are two adverbially modified predicates that must be carefully distinguished. One is 'accepted purely mentally'. The other is 'accepted mentally'. The former covers the private cases where the linguistic stimulus is self-generated. The endogenous input channel must be active. There must be no distal stimulus from the senses. Of course, channel Three is not active either—but that is not the important distinguishing mark.

In contrast, the locution 'accepted mentally' has a much less definite meaning. It covers a variety of cases, in some of which the input originates outside S, in others of which the input originates inside S. In using this locution to describe a particular act, you do not specify which agency did the corresponding proposing, although in calling it 'accepting' you envisage some correlative proposing as having been done by some agency or other. The locution 'mentally accept' is semantically indeterminate in this respect. Any case will be covered by it, provided the cognitive core of the process is there. This means that even the paradigm of overt acceptance is covered by the term. When S verbally accepts (and the act is felicitous and sincere), she mentally accepts too.

It is interesting that 'mental' and 'mentally' are semantically unmarked with respect to the question whether acts of a certain kind that fall within their extension are done as purely private internal transactions or as moves in a social transaction. For it means that some mental act-types *are* speech act-types. The two realms are not mutually exclusive.

The account has many advantages. It can, I submit, provide plausible descriptions of the variant modes of accepting and rejecting, and informative explanations of each of the ways of *failing* to accept and *failing* to reject—through mistakes, insincerity, and so on.

It also furnishes a construal of Cohen's problematic remark about interiorization. Remember his actual words: 'It is reasonable...to view any kind of acceptance as an interiorization of the corresponding speech-act' (*ibid* p79). When I first read the book, I was puzzled by this. I took the term 'corresponding speech-act' to mean *speech-act of accepting* the relevant proposition. But I now think that the relevant speech-act is, or ought to be, that of *proposing* the proposition. It 'corresponds' to any act of acceptance in the sense that it is the necessary complement of any act of acceptance. Without it, no act would count as an act of acceptance.

So construed, I think that Cohen's statement is almost correct. I say 'almost', because S internally reproduces a token of a *type* of thing which is *normally* the product of a speech-act of proposing. The linguistic object supplied to LS is the product of SS's 'simulating', standing in for, a possible act of proposing. With this modification, the Interiorization Hypothesis is true. *Every* act of acceptance involves an internalized representation of something linguistic.

Furthermore, this model suggests an interesting developmental hypothesis. The developmental hypothesis is that children acquire the capacity to perform acts of purely mental acceptance as a result of learning to accept propositions put to them by other people. This looks like an interesting claim to test.

IV. FINAL OBSERVATIONS

The wider aim of this paper was investigate how it is *possible* for certain mental acts to involve language. I have shown that the cognitive processing that underlies mental tokens, even purely mental tokens, of the type *accepting* does indeed incorporate a language-processing element. This will be so, not just for the type *accepting*, but for any act-type that is defined in terms of a communicational transaction. Such acts are communicational in type and also mental in type. Many types of act fall into this category (e.g. proposing, agreeing, questioning, rebutting, refuting, etc.). Felicitous performance of any of these acts requires that the agent should *understand* something that is said. So *linguistic understanding* is perhaps the most general and most basic kind of act that is both mental and communicational.

My model of cognitive architecture assumed that the language-processor was independent of the central processor. The assumption of separateness implies that all linguistically infected mental acts are *hybrids*. They are acts which folk-psychology treats as mental acts, but which are not realizable by the central processor alone. They all have a component which is realized by the language module. Proper achievement of acts of these types necessitates the cooperation of two subsystems, one of which lies outside the centre responsible for conceptual thinking and reasoning. Let us say that the representational format proper to the central processor, the format which encodes S's conceptual representations of propositions, is an inner language called 'Mentalese'. Then acceptance is hybrid in the sense that a part of the process that realizes the act uses internal representations that are not in Mentalese. The language module does not 'understand' Mentalese; the job of LS is to *construct* and then *output* Mentalese sentences when it is stimulated by sentences of English or some other public language.

A great deal more could and should be said about this conception of how the mind works. This is not the place to launch into a detailed investigation, but there are a couple of final remarks that I want to make.

First, the illustrative model, because of its crudeness, falsifies the picture in several ways. For instance, instead of saying that the central processor takes propositions as inputs and operates upon propositions, I ought to have employed vocabulary appropriate to the subpersonal level. Propositions are the contents of propositional attitudes. Such attitudes are held by the whole person. What RS really takes in and computes over are its internal representations of propositions (i.e. sentences of Mentalese).

Another obvious defect of the model is its apparent assumption that the only tasks that need to be carried out, when a hearer tries to identify a speaker's message or proposition, are: (i) to identify which sentence was uttered in which language, and (ii) to retrieve the meaning of that sentence. This assumption is false. The interpretation of what someone said in a particular context demands a great deal of central processor activity. The hearer usually needs to draw upon background beliefs, knowledge of the context, and beliefs about the speaker's specific intentions. The hearer sometimes has to carry out reasoning, has to judge which of two alternative interpretations is the more likely, and so on. In many cases the sentence underdetermines the proposition expressed. Thus *identifying what O said* is itself a hybrid mental act, and the role of LS is to carry out just one component of the processing that underlies this act.

I fully recognize that communication relies upon pragmatic factors as well as knowledge of the language. The model needs to be modified to take account of this. But I do not think that it affects the main point. It is still the case that a *part* of the underlying process consists in operating upon an internal representation of a public language sentence.

My second remark relates to the doctrine of *social externalism* concerning the contents of thoughts. In section II, I mentioned two hypotheses that might explain why not all believers are capable of being accepters. The second of these was the 'different contents' hypothesis. I should like to elaborate briefly on this option.

According to the account given, the proposition which is accepted by S is always something said or sayable in a language that S knows. It is a message that S identifies partly on the basis of a sentence. The sentence is either supplied from outside by O, or supplied endogenously and treated as something that a possible interlocutor might have uttered. Even when the sentence is supplied endogenously by SS, it is a sentence of a *public* language, because it must be of a type that a possible O could have uttered, and it must be such that, if it had been uttered, S would have been competent to interpret it. An act of acceptance is felicitous and successful only if S understands the relevant sentence.

Social externalism is the doctrine that the contents of some of S's thoughts are partially individuated by reference to the meaning-rules that govern the public language that S uses. Burge (1979) pointed out that in situations where a generally competent English-speaking S has expressed a belief sincerely, we are happy to say 'S believes that such and such', filling in the content-clause with the same words that S used, even in cases where S incompletely understands the meaning of one of the words. Burge then argued that S's belief-content is partly constituted by the socially agreed meanings of the English words. The sort of Subject to whom Burge's argument applies is a trained, competent language-user, a person who acquires beliefs through linguistic communication, who habitually defers to authoritative experts about the meanings of words, and who happily agrees that public word-meanings are *his* meanings. Provided S 'more or less' understands the sentence he uses and does not misunderstand it, his mental content matches his utterance-content. They both have 'social content' (see Loar 1987).

Burge claims that 'to a fair degree, mentalistic attribution rests not on the subject's having mastered the contents of the attribution, and not on his having behavioral dispositions peculiarly relevant to those contents, but on his having a certain responsibility to communal conventions governing, and conceptions associated with, symbols that he is disposed to use. It is this feature that must be incorporated into an improved model of the mental'. (Burge 1979, p115). Not all philosophers agree with Burge. But let us suppose for the sake of argument that he is right. How would this bear upon the nature of *acceptance?*.

The first point to stress is that *if* the argument works for belief, it works even better for acceptance. Burge's thought-experiment requires an S who can express his beliefs linguistically. You cannot begin to set up the thought-experiment in relation to animal beliefs. For the same reason, you cannot apply Kripke's disquotation principle to animal beliefs. The principle says "If a normal English speaker, on reflection, sincerely assents to 'p', then he believes that p" (Kripke 1979, pp248-9). The antecedent of the disquotation principle concerns an act of sincerely assenting to a *sentence*. Animals cannot satisfy this condition. So the question does not arise whether non-language-users conform to the disquotation principle, nor does the question arise whether animal beliefs have social contents.

In contrast, whenever S *accepts* a proposition, there is guaranteed to be a sentence in the offing which S would be prepared to utter assertorically, if S felt it appropriate and desirable to do so. It is rare for an Accepter actually to do this. But uttering 'Yes' to someone else's utterance is tantamount to uttering the sentence oneself. That sentence (or a suitably tailored variant, to account for indexical elements) is the one that S would utter if S wished to assert the proposition that she accepts. So every case of accepting satisfies this pre-condition of Burge's thought-experiment. The content that S mentally accepts is the same as the partly socially fixed content of an actual or potential speech-act. The argument applies with equal force to the contents of all propositional acts that are tied to language.

The Burgean considerations lend support to the following hypothesis: acts of accepting have a different kind of content from primitive (animal) beliefs, though it is the same kind of content as that which characterizes the beliefs of competent language-users.

If the hypothesis is correct, a further modification needs to be added to diagrams 2, 3 and 4. I noted that, strictly, the diagrams should not show LS feeding *propositions* as inputs into RS. The proper thing to say is that RS receives and then manipulates Mentalese representations of propositions. Now we have to add that, for a large number of the thoughts that S entertains, the corresponding Mentalese representations inside S's head do not fully determine the contents of the thoughts. The social and linguistic community to which S is attached also help to determine the contents of those thoughts, and therefore help to determine what it is that S accepts. An individual's act of acceptance is not wholly realized by the processes that go on inside the individual's head[4].

NOTES

[1]The claim that only language-users can accept propositions is not patently obvious. It needs to be defended, as Cohen indeed does. The best defence will not consist in an appeal to ordinary usage. A person might say, for example, 'Look at Rover lying down, resignedly, after his attempt to steal that food from the cupboard. He accepts now that the cupboard door is closed'. This is perfectly normal usage. Secondly, the more fine-grained claim–which I am assuming to be true–is that every act of accepting a proposition is tied to some linguistic formulation. Plenty of people would be unhappy with this. In his commentary, Richard Bradley presented the following apparent counter-example. A motorist carelessly drives his car into a tree. He gets out of the car and surveys the wreckage. He accepts that he is responsible for the damage. No sentence that expresses the proposition that he is responsible for the damage is spoken, or even imagined.

My immediate response to the dog example is that, although people say such things, it is not literally true that Rover *accepted the proposition*. Rover was not aware of that proposition, and moreover he would not have recognised the proposition if it had been put to him (which it was not). Regarding the second type of case, I say that many ascriptions of acceptance do not claim that the agent performed a dateable mental act, but rather they claim that the agent was already in, or entered, a dispositional state of acceptance. That is the natural interpretation of Bradley's example. The motorist was so disposed that, if the proposition had been put to him, he would have performed the mental act of accepting it. Actually performing the mental act *does* require the agent to process a linguistic formulation of the proposition.

Admittedly, I do not mount a detailed defence. I just take Cohen's position as my working assumption. My main interest is to explain how a language-link of this sort could possibly obtain and what its implications might be.

[2]This is not Cohen's position. He says (p12) 'The word "accept" is often used to signify the speech-act of assent whereby a person may orally (or in writing) agree to the truth of a proposition whether or not this oral (or written) agreement accords with his actual state of mind. But the sense with which I am primarily concerned is the one in which this word signifies a mental act, or a pattern, system, or policy of mental action, rather than a speech-act'. Thus he holds that the verb itself is ambiguous, it expresses two different concepts, one being a concept that covers cases of verbally assenting, the other being a concept that covers mental acts of a special sort. He immediately goes on to make the point that we already mentioned, that such mental acts are 'linguistically infected'. Indeed the mentalistic concept of acceptance is such that it is true *a priori* that every act which satisfies this concept is a mental act in which the agent carries out an operation upon a linguistic entity.

[3]Quine's aim is to reduce understanding to verbal disposition. The method of query and assent, query and dissent plays a big role in his account. Here is a passage explaining the move to surface assent (from Quine 1975, p91).

'It has been objected that when I talk of query and assent I am not really escaping mentalism after all, because assent itself has a mental component. It is objected that assent is no mere mindless parroting of an arbitrary syllable; utterance of the syllable counts as assent only if there is the appropriate mental act behind it. Ver well, let us adopt the term *surface assent* for the utterance or gesture itself. My behavioural approach does indeed permit me, then, only to appeal to surface assent; assent as I talk of it must be understood as surface assent. This behavioural notion has its powers, however, and must not be underrated.....One partial criterion of what to count as a sign of assent is that a speaker is disposed to produce that sign whenever a sentence is queried in circumstances in which he would be disposed to volunteer the sentence himself. Even surface assent, thus, is not just the parroting of any arbitrary syllable.'

[4]This is a revised draft of the paper delivered to the Colloque 'Croire et Accepter' held in Caen in April 1995. The participants made many helpful comments which I have taken into account. I am particularly indebted to Richard Bradley, to Dan Sperber, and to Pascal Engel the organiser.

REFERENCES

Burge, T. (1979) 'Individualism and the Mental', in *Midwest Studies in Philosophy vol IV* (ed) P. French et al. Minneapolis, University of Minnesota Press.

Cohen, L.J. (1992) *An Essay on Belief and Acceptance*. Oxford, Clarendon Press.

Kripke, S. (1979) 'A Puzzle About Belief', in *Meaning and Use* (ed) A. Margalit. Dordrecht, D. Reidel.

Loar, B. (1987) 'Social Content and Psychological Content' in *Contents of Thought* (eds) D. Merrill and R. Grimm. Tucson, University of Arizona Press.

Quine, W.V. (1975) 'Mind and Verbal Dispositions', in *Mind and Language* (ed) S. Guttenplan, Oxford. Clarendon Press.

INTUITIVE AND REFLECTIVE BELIEFS

Dan Sperber
CREA, Ecole Polytechnique

I used to be a full-time anthropologist. Anthropologists often make statements of the form: The So-and-so believe that... Few of them have bothered to discuss what they mean by belief (the most notable exception being Rodney Needham, 1972). Over the years, I raised several objections against these attributions of beliefs and I have tried to outline a more fine-grained account of the cognitive attitudes involved (Sperber 1975, 1982/1985, 1990, 1994b, 1996). Just as the common term jade corresponds to two substances, jadeite and nephrite, with similar phenomenal properties but quite different chemical structures, the folk-psychological term belief, I have argued, corresponds to two psychological categories, similar in some behavioural and epistemological respects, but different in cognitive organisation and role. I call these two psychological categories intuitive beliefs and reflective beliefs. In this paper, I would like to develop the argument in a manner that addresses questions and objections that I have received from psychologists and philosophers of mind.

I. INTUITIVE BELIEFS

When we claim of an organism that it possesses a cognitive system, we attribute to it at least two kinds of representations. The overall function of a cognitive system is to allow the organism to adjust its behaviour to a changing environment. For this, a cognitive system must contain representations of actual states of affairs, a data-base, so to speak. It must also contain representations of behaviours to be engaged in by the organism, representations capable of guiding these behaviours, in other terms, plans. The simplest link between data and plans consists in having the triggering of every plan-guided behaviour conditional on the addition to the data-base of a specific datum. For instance, if a representation of a cat approaching is added to the data-base of a mouse, this activates a flight plan.

Simple cognitive systems have a data-base, i.e. a place in their functional architecture where representations can be stored, and such that any representation stored in this place is, without restrictions, acted upon as if it were a representation of an actual state of affairs. It is a moot point whether such representations should be called beliefs when they occur in the data-base of organisms that lack a public language and the very concept of a belief. Humans, on the other hand, think and talk of some of their mental states as beliefs . Unlike eliminativists who deny that the category of belief is instantiated at all, I will argue that it is instantiated by objects belonging to different natural types.

Does the human cognitive system contain a data-base too, where beliefs are stored, or are a person s beliefs beliefs merely in virtue of being conceptualised as such by the believer? Suppose that a person s belief that P was so identified by, say, a prefix representing the person s own attitude of belief such as (1):

(1) Bel (P)

Would it be enough that Mary entertained (1) for her to believe that P? Surely not. She could entertain (1) as an object of doubt, desire, fantasy, etc. For her entertaining [Bel (P)] to amount to her believing that P, she would have to treat [Bel (P)] as factual, to believe it too. Needless to say, embedding it under the same prefix Bel , as in [Bel (Bel (P))], would start an infinite regress. So, in the functional architecture of human minds too, there has to be a data-base such that any representation stored in that data-base is treated as a representation of an actual state of affairs, i.e. as a belief.

What makes the data-base a *data*-base, or a *belief box*, to use Stephen Schiffer s phrase, is that the representations it contains, by the very fact of being so located, are freely used as premises in practical and epistemic inferences. Data-base beliefs are intuitive in the sense that, in order to hold them as beliefs, we need not reflect and not even be capable of reflecting on the way we arrived at them, or on the specific justification we may have for holding them. The presence of a representation in our data-base causes us to treat it as data. Moreover, if we trust our cognitive mechanisms, then the very fact that a representation has been inscribed by these mechanisms in our data-base is *good reason* to treat it as data.

Every representation stored in Mary s data-base is a belief of Mary, but the converse is not true, and this for two reasons, one generally acknowledged, the other generally ignored. We may be justified in attributing to Mary the belief that there are no kangaroos on Jupiter, and indefinitely many other comparable beliefs, even though they are not represented at all in her mind. For Mary herself, these tacit or virtual beliefs follow straightaway from the beliefs that are actually and explicitly represented in her mind. Thus, she would immediately agree and hence she believes, at least in a dispositional sense that there are no kangaroos on Jupiter. This observation is compatible with the view, generally taken for granted, that every belief of Mary that *is* represented in her mind is represented *in her data base*, and is a belief of hers in virtue of being so represented. I want to to argue against this view. There are not one but two ways in which propositional attitudes in general, and beliefs in particular, can be inscribed in the mind.

The very fact that humans can entertain desires, suppositions, or fictional representations, which are not freely used as premises in inference, shows that not all their mental representations are stored in the same way and in the same place. One possibility is that there are other bases or boxes in the functional architecture of the mind. (such permanent boxes, which define each a basic type of mental representation, should not be confused with the temporary buffers of inference engines, where a number of premises with different cognitive statuses may be brought together for joint processing.) The existence of a desire box is a quite plausible. One might also, in principle, but much less plausibly, have a box for suppositions, a box for guesses, a box for deemings, etc. Multiplying hypothetical boxes is not, however, the only way to account for the mutiplicity of propositional attitudes.

II. REFLECTIVE ATTITUDES

Humans have the ability to represent representations. I would argue (see Sperber & Wilson 1986/1995; Sperber 1994a ,1994b) that this meta-representational ability is as distinctive of humans, and as important in understanding their behaviour, as is echolocation for bats. Humans have the ability to represent three types of representations: mental representations, public (e.g. linguistic) representations, and abstract representation. Mary might thus have the following three meta-representations in her data-base:

(2) Peter believes that the Earth is flat
(3) John said that the Earth is flat
(4) The hypothesis that the Earth is flat is absurd

Representations embedded in meta-representations which are themselves stored in the data-base are, in a sense, present in the data-base, but they are insulated from other representations in the base by the meta-representational context in which they occur embedded. They are not automatically treated as data. Mary, for instance, has the proposition that the Earth is flat represented at least three times in her mind, but not as a belief of hers. She cannot detach it from any of the contexts in which it occurs and store it directly in her data-base. This embedded representation may play a role in a number of inferences. Mary is in a position to infer for instance that:

(5) John said something that Peter believes
(6) What Peter believes is absurd
(7) Peter believes that the Earth is not spherical

Drawing inferences about a meta-represented representation may involve detaching it provisionally and copying it in the temporary buffer of some inferential device where it will processed together with other premises. However the output of such a process must be re-embedded in an appropriate context in order to arrive at a warranted conclusion. For instance, deriving (7) from (2) might be done by provisionally disembedding (8) from (2), processing it together with some premise such as (9), inferring (10), and re-embedding (10) in the context (11):

(8) The Earth is flat
(9) For all x, if x is flat, then x is not spherical
(10) The Earth is not spherical
(11) Peter believes that...

Having certain meta-representations in one's data-base amounts to having a propositional attitude to the representation meta-represented. Consider, for instance:

(12) It is dubious that the devil exists
(13) The claim that the Earth is flat has been refuted
(14) Everybody knows that real truffles are expensive

Believing (12) amounts to doubting that the devil exists. Believing (13) amounts to disbelieving that the Earth is flat. Believing (14) amounts to being of the opinion that real truffles are expensive. Amounts to in what sense? In the sense that an individual understanding and believing (12), (13), or (14) will, ipso facto, have the corresponding attitudes to the embedded propositions.

Via the meta-representational route, an indefinite variety of different propositional attitudes may be taken to the meta-represented representation. I will call such attitudes reflective attitudes. I doubt that reflective attitudes fall into sharply bounded, mutually exclusive, well-defined categories. There is, for instance, a continuum of reflective attitudes between absolute conviction and radical disbelief, with all shades of doubt in between.

REFLECTIVE BELIEFS

Among reflective attitudes, a great many are, more or less prototypically, credal attitudes, that is, attitudes of belief in the ordinary, somewhat loose sense of the term. (14) provides an illustration, and so do (15)-(20) :

(15) Peter is sincere when he says that he is in pain.
(16) I remember that, the day we first met, it was raining.
(17) There are indubitable signs that someone has been searching the house.
(18) It is a scientific fact that a glass of wine a day is good for the heart
(19) It has been proven that communism does not work.
(20) That the Father, the Son and the holy Ghost are one is a Holy Mystery.

A person in good faith believing (14)-(20) should be disposed to assert in each case the embedded representation, or to assent to its assertion by others, and this whether or not the embedded representation happens to occur unembedded in her data-base, i.e. whether or not that representation is a data-base, intuitive belief. The observation of such a person's behaviour would, then, warrant attributing to her the corresponding beliefs, but not necessarily the corresponding intuitive beliefs.

Two rather uncontroversial assumptions about human cognition should lead one to recognise that humans must be capable of holding credal attitudes in at least two ways. The two assumptions are:

· The human mind has an ability to hold representations as beliefs
· The human mind has a meta-representational ability

From these two assumptions, it follows[1] that humans are capable of having beliefs about representations. Such meta-representational beliefs may imply (demonstratively or non-demonstratively) that the representation meta-represented is true. In other terms, a belief of meta-representational content may provide a *validating context* for the embedded representation. When this occurs, the individual has, ipso facto, a credal attitude to the representation embedded in the meta-representational belief. In other terms, the individual has two credal attitudes: one of content V(R) where V is a validating context, and R is a representation; the other of content R. The credal attitude of content V(R) is a data-base belief. The credal attitude towards the embedded representation R is not a data-base belief. I will call such credal attitudes toward representations embedded in a validating context of the form V(R), reflective beliefs . There is an indefinite variety of possible validating contexts: reference to authority, to divine revelation, explicit argument or proof, etc. Hence, just as reflective attitudes in general, reflective beliefs are best seen as a fuzzy and internally diversified category.

III. DISQUOTATIONAL INCONTINENCE

Probably the most common way in which we acquire reflective beliefs is through communication. You ask the railway employee when is the latest Sunday train to Oxford. At 11:45, he answers. You are then likely to form an data-base belief of roughly the following tenor:

(21)   The railway employee (who is to be trusted on such matters) said that the latest Sunday train to Oxford is at 11:45.

If you hold (21) as a data-base belief, then, by this very fact, you hold (22) as a reflective belief:

(22)   The latest Sunday train to Oxford is at 11:45.

Such a description raises an obvious objection. If you believe what the railway employee told you, then, surely, you immediately disembed or "disquote"[2] what he said, extract the information from its validating context, and add it to your data-base, where it becomes a regular intuitive belief, which you might keep holding even if you forget how you have arrived at it. In contrasting intuitive beliefs and reflective beliefs, then, I am, it could be objected, contrasting a basic category of genuine beliefs with a mere step in the derivation of some of these beliefs, a step at which their content occurs embedded in a validating context.

Let us call disquotational incontinence the thesis that whenever a conceptual representation occurs in a validating context, it is ipso facto disembedded from this context and dropped into the data base. If humans suffer from disquotational incontinence, then, indeed, it is plausible that all their beliefs are data-base beliefs. However, I want to argue that the disquotational incontinence thesis is false, and that reflective beliefs are a genuine psychological category.

I am not denying, of course, that many of our data-base beliefs have been extracted from validating contexts. For instance, in the (21)-(22) example, you may well have disquoted *the latest Sunday train to Oxford is at 11:45* and have stored it in your data-base. Defenders of disquotational incontinence, on their part, would not deny that we can have, in the data-base, beliefs of the form V(R). They would grant, for instance, that you may believe (21), but they would argue that, if you do, this leads you to believe (22), in the same basic sense of believe, a claim which, in this particular instance, is plausible.

There are two points of disagreement, however:

- Disquotational incontinence means that whenever you hold an intuitive belief of content V(R), you also hold an intuitive belief of content R.
- In order to derive from disquotational incontinence an argument against reflective beliefs, it must be further assumed that when you believe both V(R) and R (as in the case of (21)-(22)), behaviour expressing your belief R is always directly based on your disquoted data-base belief R,

and never on a reflective belief R embedded in your data-base belief V(R).

I will argue against these two claims. But before this, let me raise an onus of proof issue.

At first blush, it might seem that the onus of proof is on whoever proposes the existence of a new psychological type, in this case reflective beliefs. However, if you grant me trivially that data-base beliefs and a meta-representational ability are part of the basic human psychological equipment, then the possibility of a wide range of propositional attitude of a reflective kind follows. For instance, if you *believe* that it is dubious that that the devil exists, then you *doubt* that the devil exist. Doubting is a reflective attitude; it is about representations (e.g. claims, hypotheses), not directly about states of affairs. Most reflective attitudes (e.g. doubting, pondering, disbelieving, accepting as a working hypothesis, granting for the sake of argument, etc.) do not warrant disquotation anyhow. Reflective belief is just one of the many reflective attitudes made possible by the joint existence of data-base beliefs and meta-representations. In order to cast doubt on the existence of reflective beliefs, one must assume a mechanism which systematically disquotes them. To assume disquotational incontinence and deny the actual existence of reflective beliefs is, then, to make an extra hypothesis, and, therefore, to bear the onus of proof.

Defenders of disquotational incontinence might accept the onus of proof and argue that the proof requested is ridiculously easy. I will make it even easier by granting that if you have some intuitive belief P, and if you are disposed to infer spontaneously Q from P, then it is reasonable to attribute to you the intuitive belief Q. Well, then: If you have a belief of the form V(R), where V is a context that you understand as validating, then, surely, you are disposed to infer spontaneously R from V(R) or else, what does it mean to understand that V is validating? Disquotational incontinence follows from trivial assumptions about spontaneous inferribility. Right? Wrong!

In earlier papers (Sperber 1982/85, 1990), I presented an argument against disquotational incontinence based on considerations of rationality and good cognitive design. Half-understood representations such as the dogma of the Holy Trinity can be objects of belief. However, disquoting such half-understood representations and using them unrestrictedly as premises in inference, on par with well-understood representations, would be, I argued, epistemically hazardous. For instance, contradictions could arise undetected. Half-understood information may be epistemically useful, but only if it is treated with cognitive caution. This argument, which I still find reasonable, is not quite compelling. It could be, for instance, that our cognitive system is not well-designed in this respect, and indulges in disquotational incontinence in spite of the cost. In this paper, I present a new and I believe stronger argument against disquotational incontinence.

IV. REPRESENTATIONAL CAPACITY

To accept the existence of a data-base is to assume some representational capacity by means of which data are represented in the data-base. I will, for expository purpose, describe this capacity as a language of thought, a mentalese, and I will focus on the conceptual repertoire, the lexicon of this mentalese, but the argument should go through, mutatis mutandis, with any kind of account, e.g. connectionist, of the conceptual capacity involved. For the argument to go through, all that is needed is that the representational capacity should have limits, at any given time in the cognitive life of the individual, and surely, that must be true. In a nutshell, I will argue that it is possible to meta-represent representations which are not directly expressible within the conceptual repertoire of the data-base. Such representations can be embedded in a validating context, and yet cannot be disquoted.

Any language, public or mental, has a finite lexicon. In public languages, it is possible to supplement this lexicon with an indefinite range of expressions of the form "α", where α may be any symbol, for instance an onomatopoeia, a foreign word, or a word or phrase from the language itself but with a sense different from the one assigned to it by the grammar. Such symbols may be indicated, in writing, by quotation marks, or, in speech, by intonational patterns. However, both in writing and in speech, expressions may be logically quoted without this being explicitly indicated at all. In particular, an expression α should be considered quoted at the logical form level if the grammar of the language does not assign it a semantic interpretation, or assigns it an interpretation quite different from the one with which it occurs in the utterance. Knowledge of the foreign language from which such an expression might be borrowed, or knowledge of special codes, or pragmatic inference, may make it possible to paraphrase the intended meaning, but it may also occur that the intended meaning of the expression mentioned remains more or less obscure.

Mentalese also must allow for a device like quotation marks, and for the use of this device to supplement its lexicon with expressions in quotes. In thinking, we may experience the need for a concept unavailable in our mental lexicon, and which we don't yet grasp well enough to add it to the lexicon. We may meta-represent the yet-to-be-developed concept by means of a mental place-holder. A good place-holder may be a phrase of mentalese in quotes, the meaning of which is evocative of the concept we are seeking.

The need for a quotational device in mentalese is particularly evident in the case comprehension, and this in more ways than I need to go into here (See Sperber & Wilson 1986/1995). We understand public utterances by associating with them representations in mentalese. An utterance may contain an expression we do not fully comprehend, either because it does not belong to the public language being used and occurs in quotes in the utterance itself, or because our knowledge of the public language is faulty and does not provide us with a meaning for the expression. In such a case, we must be capable of entertaining thoughts containing expressions such as "'α', whatever it may mean" where "α" is a meta-representation of a not fully understood concept.

Imagine young Lisa hears her science teacher say:

(23) There are millions of suns in the universe.

Lisa trusts her teacher, and is willing to believe what he says. However, until that moment, she understood "Sun" as a proper name referring to a single object. She does not know what sun might mean as a common noun. She can guess that suns must be things like *the* Sun, and also that the teacher means something more specific than this, and that therefore she does not comprehend the teacher s full meaning. We may therefore attribute to her the following intuitive beliefs:

(24) The teacher (who is to be trusted on such matters) said that there are millions of "suns" in the universe.
(25) There are millions of Sun-like things in the universe
(26) There are millions of "suns", whatever the teacher means by sun, in the universe.

However we should not attribute to Lisa an *intuitive* belief of content (23), because she does not have the conceptual means of representing it in her data-base. On the other hand, we should not hesitate to attribute to Lisa the belief, in the ordinary folkpsychological sense of "belief", that there are millions of suns in the universe. After all, she is now willing to say (23) herself, and to assent to its expression by others. In so doing, she is not repeating words of which she has no understanding, as she might a Latin formula. She has partial understanding of what she says, as shown by the fact that she is disposed to draw some consequences from it, e.g. that there are many suns.

Young Bob hears his Sunday School teacher say:

(27) The Father, the Son, and the Holy Ghost are one.

Bob trusts his teacher, and is willing to believe what she says. Let us suppose that Bob understands every individual word in this statement. Still, he has only very partial understanding of the statement as a whole. He has only the vaguest and most insecure idea of what the Father, the Son, and the Holy Ghost *being one* might mean. We may, nevertheless, attribute to Bob intuitive beliefs such as the following:

(28)   The teacher (who is to be trusted on such matters) said
         that the Father, the Son, and the Holy Ghost are one.
(29)   It must be true that the Father, the Son, and the Holy
         Ghost are one, whatever this means

We cannot attribute to Bob an intuitive belief of content (27), since he does not have the conceptual means to represent such a content. The problem here is not that Bob is lacking any concept in particular; it is that his concepts, arranged in such a syntactic structure, don't provide a full-fledged meaning, suggesting that at least one of the concepts expressed by his teacher's utterance is not the one standardly encoded by the words used. On the other hand, Bob is, now, a true believer. He does believe, and will tell you so himself, that the Father, the Son, and the Holy Ghost are one.

Lisa is exhibiting belief-behaviour vis-à-vis (23), and Bob vis-à-vis (27). By folkpsychological standards of belief attribution, they believe what their respective teachers told them. They could not hold (23) or (27) as intuitive beliefs, but they can, and, I submit, do, hold them as reflective beliefs.

At this point, defenders of disquotational incontinence may want to deny that our folkpsychological standards of belief attribution are strict enough, and demand, for instance, that a belief that P should not be attributed to an individual who does not properly understand P. One problem with such a stricter criterion is that a great many of the beliefs that anthropologists and historians of ideas study would not count as beliefs anymore (but, maybe, as quasi-beliefs, as Recanati 1997 envisages, before dismissing himself the notion). Beliefs in Holy Mysteries such as the Trinity, which are defined as truths beyond the pale of human understanding, would, by definition, not be beliefs at all. Such a terminological move would have obvious costs and no clear benefit (in particular, no explanatory purchase). Anyhow, if there were some smart positive terminological proposal with clear benefits, I would not particularly want to resist it. My point is not terminological; it is that there are at least two cognitively distinct manners of holding true, i.e. of believing as commonly understood.

My argument so far has been that that we can meta-represent more representations than we can construct, and that, therefore we can believe reflectively contents that we cannot hold as intuitively given data. I have focused on half-understood concepts and representations, because they provide the strongest kind of evidence for my case. Whatever view you take of our conceptual repertoire, given our meta-representational ability, there must be concepts and representations our grasp of which is such that we can *think about them* without being able to *think with them*. In other terms, there must be concepts that we can meta-represent, without being able to deploy them to represent the object or properties they are the concepts of. Similarly, there must be representations that we can meta-represent, without being able to deploy them to represent the states of affairs that would make them true. Such concepts and representations may occur in a meta-representation embedded in a validating context, yielding an undisquotable reflective belief. Ergo reflective beliefs are a stable ingredient of our mental life.

Once you have had to accept the existence of reflective beliefs in order to handle the problem raised by partially understood beliefs, you might as well see what further light this might throw on human cognition. I want to suggest that reflective beliefs do, in fact, play a major role in human cognition, and that not just partially understood beliefs, but also many well understood beliefs are reflective beliefs, paradigmatic examples of the latter being provided by scientific beliefs. Some of the concepts that are used in scientific claims are well-understood by scientists, but they may remain out of the reach of their intuitions. These are concepts that scientists can indeed *think with*, but, in most cases, only *by thinking about them*, that is, only reflectively. Typically, the validating contexts of beliefs containing such scientific concepts are not (for competent scientists) in the form of a reference to an authority, but in the form of an argument or a demonstration. Such arguments and demonstrations are not of a kind delivered by spontaneous inference, and must be reflected upon in order to see their force.

Of some concepts, we have an intuitive grasp. We can use them unreflectively, and without normally running into paradoxes—unless a philosopher is intent on pushing us where we would not spontaneously go. Of other concepts, we may have only a limited grasp. Of yet other concepts, we may have a full grasp, but a grasp of a kind that can only be deployed reflectively. Not every kind of concept can enter in every kind of belief.

V. INTUITIVE AND REFLECTIVE CONCEPTS

Many of our beliefs are grounded in perception and in spontaneous and unconscious inference from perception. You see autumn leaves under a bare tree, and you spontaneously form the beliefs:

(30) There are leaves under this tree.
(31) This tree has lost its leaves

You hear the doorbell ringing, and you spontaneously form the beliefs:

(32) The doorbell is ringing.
(33) There is someone at the door.

You see your friend Martha frowning, and you spontaneously form the beliefs:

(34) Martha is frowning
(35) Martha is worried about something

When a child, you were shown a bird and told: this is a sparrow . You spontaneously formed the beliefs:

(36) This is a bird
(37) Sparrows are birds

In all four cases, the first belief is based on perception, the second on inference. If challenged, you might be able to produce, ex post facto, a missing premise which, together with the perceptual belief, warrants the inferential belief. However, the fact is that you arrived at the inferential belief without engaging into deliberate or conscious inference. All beliefs that are the output of perceptual processes are intuitive in a standard psychological sense, and so are all beliefs that are the output of spontaneous and unconscious inferential processes taking intuitive beliefs as premises. Intuitive beliefs can be activated in our mental life without activating or even remembering the premises from which they were derived. You probably do believe, for instance, that sparrows are birds, but do you remember whether you formed this belief by generalising from an instance shown to you, or by being told about sparrows?

What is the conceptual repertoire on which intuitive beliefs draw? Perceptual devices take sensory data as input and deliver as output conceptual identifications of the distal stimuli having caused the sensation. Perceptual devices must draw, for this, on a conceptual repertoire which contains all the concepts of the things that can be perceptually identified. Spontaneous inferential processes derive intuitive beliefs from perceptual beliefs and from other inferentially derived intuitive beliefs. Some inferentially intuitive beliefs are about things that cannot be directly perceived. These inferential processes must therefore be able to draw on a conceptual repertoire that goes beyond that of the perceptual processes. If we take together the conceptual repertoires of perceptual processes and of spontaneous inferential processes, we get the conceptual repertoire of intuitive beliefs, or, other terms, a repertoire of intuitive concepts.

Rather than arriving at intuitive beliefs such as (30)-(37) by means of your own perceptions and inferences, you might have arrived at them via communication. Someone you trust might tell you any of (30)-(37). You would then disquote the content of the communication from the belief that it has been communicated and believe this content directly. Communication plays here, to some extent, the role of experience by proxy. You might yourself have formed such beliefs via perception and spontaneous inference, had you been placed in a position to experience their perceptual basis. Whether acquired directly or by proxy, intuitive beliefs must be exclusively represented by means of the intuitive repertoire.

Not all our beliefs are intuitive in the sense of being derived from perception plus spontaneous inference, either directly or by proxy. Consider (38)-(42):

(38) The prime factors of 9139 are 13, 19, and 37.
(39) Water is H_2O.
(40) A king and two knights are not enough to force a checkmate.
(41) Where the judiciary is not independent, there can be no true democracy.

(38)-(41) are examples of propositions that may be understood and believed. In ordinary circumstances and for most people at least I am hedging in order to avoid orthogonal issues to which I will soon revert, the states of affairs that make these propositions true cannot be perceived, but only inferred, and, moreover, inferring them requires some conscious and deliberate thinking. Often, such beliefs are acquired not via ratiocination, but via communication. But communication in this case does not provide one with experience by proxy. No experience could have triggered the spontaneous formation of these beliefs anyhow. These beliefs, then, are not, at least for most of us, intuitive beliefs in the intended sense. Moreover, in most cases, when such non-intuitive beliefs serve as premises in the derivation of further beliefs, the inferential processes in which they are involved are conscious and deliberate ones. Non-intuitive beliefs typically beget further non-intuitive beliefs.

The conceptual repertoire of non-intuitive beliefs is richer than the intuitive repertoire. You may learn a new concept, say in mathematics, chemistry, philosophy, or chess, understand it properly, be able to make it work for you in constructing hypotheses or arguments, but not be able to draw spontaneous inferences on the basis of its occurrence in a conceptual representation. The inferences in which such concepts are involved are performed by invoking explicit schemas or procedures. Some mathematical geniuses may "see" prime numbers as primes, and infer intuitively the prime factors of many numbers. Most of us may know quite well what a prime factor is, but be able to discover the prime factors of 9139 only by painstaking calculations. A chess expert may "see" all checkmate positions, intuit all the possible outcomes of endgames, and therefore believe (40) intuitively. A chess beginner, on the other hand, may have properly understood the concept of a checkmate, but have to verify every instance; for such a beginner, concluding that a king and two knights are not enough to force a checkmate involves testing, one by one, alternative moves.

Of some concepts, we have a reflective mastery, but no intuitive grasp. We understand them because we have beliefs about them. These reflective concepts, as I will call them, are introduced by explicit theories which specify their meaning and the inferences that can be drawn on their basis. The possibility of such reflective concepts follows from the existence of the human meta-representational ability.

Of course, a concept may start its life in the mind of an individual as a reflective concept and later become an intuitive one, that is, come to determine spontaneous rather than deliberate and conscious inferences. For instance, when you were first taught, as a child, the difference between odd and even numbers, "odd" and "even" were probably reflective concepts for you: you had to think hard in order to decide whether a given number was odd or even, or what followed from a number being such. By now, I assume that these two concepts have become quite intuitive to you. Incidentally, the reverse movement from intuitive to reflective is also possible: for instance, you may have had an intuitive grasp of the concept of weight, which was at least temporarily lost when you became aware of the necessity to distinguish weight and mass. You may then have deployed the concept of weight reflectively, at least in classroom contexts. Such movement from intuitive to reflective status and back may be involved in concept revision (in which case, it is not a simple matter to decide whether, strictly speaking, the *same* concept is involved throughout).

How easily, in the cognitive life of the individual, may reflective concepts become intuitive concepts? We may characterise the range of possible answers by sketching two extreme ones, a radically empiricist one and a radically nativist one. According to a radically empiricist answer, all concepts are acquired by learning the words that encode them. No concept is immediately intuitive, but all concepts may become intuitive, provided they are used often enough (just like shoe-lacing is not immediately intuitive but becomes so with practice). According to a radically nativist answer, there is an innate range of intuitive concepts, a subset of which becomes actualised in the actual intuitive repertoire of any given individual. An individual's intuitive repertoire does not contain all the concepts in this innate range, but it cannot contain concepts outside that range. Therefore, reflective concepts that fall outside the innate range can never become intuitive concepts. I assume that these two extreme views are wrong and that truth lies somewhere in between. Susan Carey (1985, 1991), for instance, has developed a view more on the empiricist side. I have explored a view more on the nativist side (Sperber 1994b, 1996). All this remains, for the time being, quite speculative.

The question of the relative fluidity, viscosity, or rigidity of the intuitive and reflective repertoires is a fascinating one, but it is orthogonal to the argument of the present paper. Even if the extreme empiricist view were correct, and all reflective concepts were capable of becoming intuitive ones, it would still be the case that, at any given time in the cognitive life of an individual, some concepts are mastered only in a reflective way, and therefore the beliefs into which these concepts enter cannot be intuitive beliefs. Assuming that there there are only two categories of beliefs, intuitive and reflective, then intuitive concepts can occur both in intuitive and reflective beliefs, and reflective concepts can occur only in reflective beliefs.

VI. BELIEVING THE SAME THING TWICE

The difference between intuitive and reflective beliefs is one of mental inscription, and not necessarily of content. A representation involving only intuitive concepts may be believed intuitively or reflectively. It might even be possible that some contents be believed both intuitively and reflectively by the same individual at the same time, each belief playing a different role in the believer's thinking and behaviour.

One may come to hold a belief both intuitively and reflectively by adding in the data-base a copy of a reflective belief disembedded from its validating context. Consider again the railway example (21)-(22). You went to the railway employee and, on the basis of what he told you, you formed two intuitive beliefs, the second being disembedded from the first:

(21) The railway employee (who is to be trusted on such matters) said that the latest Sunday train to Oxford is at 11:45.
(22) The latest Sunday train to Oxford is at 11:45.

If you kept the meta-representational belief (21) in memory, you thereby kept a reflective belief of content (22), that is, you were in a position to assert (22) or use it in your thinking not only as a plain data-base belief but also as a reflective belief, at least implicitly connected to its validating context. Suppose that after coming back from the information desk, your had the following dialogue with your travelling companion:

(42) *She*: So, when is the latest Sunday train to Oxford?
     You: It is at 11:45.

In answering, you were doing two things. You were reporting what the employee told you, and you were expressing your belief that the latest Sunday train to Oxford is at 11:45. You were expressing your belief *by* reporting the employee s utterance: your echoing his utterance without any reservation amounted to endorsing what you were echoing.[1] In this case, your utterance is best seen as an expression not of your intuitive belief, but of your reflective belief: you were speaking under the authority of your informant. Months later, you may well have remembered only that the latest Sunday train to Oxford is at 11:45, without any memory or interest of the way in which you formed this belief.

One may also take a reflective stance to a belief that, initially, was purely intuitive, and come to believe it reflectively too. The belief that the Earth is flat has been, no doubt, a widespread intuitive belief in human history. In fact, the intuitive pull of this belief is such that, for most people who know it to be false, it still takes a moment reflection to understand that an aeroplane could not cross the Atlantic in a straight line. In the sixth century, the monk Cosmas, author of a *Christian Topography*, believed that the Earth was flat (see Wilford 1981, chapter 4). I assume that he believed it intuitively. Before becoming a monk, he had been a great traveller and must have drawn on this intuitive belief when thinking about his past and future journeys. It is clear from his writings that Cosmas came to believe in the flatness of the Earth, not just intuitively, but also reflectively. He provided several validating contexts for this belief, some based on the authority of the Scriptures, others based on rational arguments, such as the absurdity of the very idea of antipodes. Cosmas used his reflective belief that the Earth was flat to construct his *Topography*, and to argue against those who, following the Greeks, believed that the Earth was spherical.

Reflective beliefs being a broad and loose categories of subtly different credal attitudes, the same content may come to be reflectively believed in different ways. A student may believe a mathematical theorem in a validating context consisting in an acknowledgment of the authority of her teacher. She may later understand the proof and use it as a validating context for the same content.

Mathematicians themselves may come to believe the same proposition in a different but still reflective way. Consider, for instance, Fermat's conjecture, which was firmly believed to be true more firmly than most empirical beliefs—before it was actually proven in 1994.[4] Still, the belief has changed, not in its content, but in its validating context. It used to be something like (40), and now it is something like (41):

(40) It is a very-well supported conjecture that, for $n>2$, $x^n+y^n = z^n$ cannot be solved in integers x, y, z, with $xyz \neq 0$.

(41) It is a theorem that, for $n>2$, $x^n+y^n = z^n$ cannot be solved in integers x, y, z, with $xyz \neq 0$.

This change in validating context goes together with a profound change in the epistemic role that this reflective belief may play in mathematical reasoning. Fermat's conjecture was something to be proven; it can now be used as a premise in deriving new theorems (and, for all consequences of Fermat's conjecture that were already known, the proof changes them into absolute theorems).

***

To wrap it up:

We have two kinds of beliefs. We have intuitive data-base beliefs, which are inscribed in our mind in a manner such that they are automatically treated as data. They are expressed in an intuitive mental lexicon that allows spontaneous inference. Intuitive beliefs are a most fundamental category of cognition. Given the fact that we have intuitive beliefs and a meta-representational ability, we also capable of having reflective beliefs and reflective concepts, or to take a reflective stance towards intuitive concepts and beliefs. Reflective beliefs are a loose family of derived attitudes that are continuous with other reflective attitudes of a non-credal kind.

While reflective beliefs, unlike intuitive beliefs, are not a basic category of cognitive architecture, they play a major role in the development and transmission of cultural representations, allowing concepts and ideas that are only half-understood, or that are well understood but only within the context of explicit theories, to stabilise in a human population and to expand the range of thoughts that can be entertained, way beyond what would be possible on a strict intuitive basis. It is arguable (see Sperber 1996) that much of culture, from religion to science, is made of reflective concepts and beliefs.

NOTES

[1]Non-demonstratively: one could block the inference by making the further assumptions that beliefs cannot be about representations. However such an assumption is blatantly false.

[2]I will be using "disquote" in a loose sense, where detaching from propositional attitude context counts as disquoting.

[3]For a detailed discussion of echoic utterances, see Sperber & Wilson 1981, Wilson & Sperber 1992, where we use the notion to reanalyse irony.

[4]I am grateful to Martin Andler for comments on this example.

REFERENCES

Carey, Susan (1985). *Conceptual change in childhood*. Cambridge, Mass: MIT Press.

Carey, Susan (1991). Knowledge acquisition: Enrichment of conceptual change? In S. Carey and R. Gelman (eds.) *Epigenesis of mind: Studies in biology and cognition*. Hillsdale: Erlbaum.

Needham, Rodney (1972). *Belief, language and experience*. Oxford: Blackwell.

Sperber, Dan (1975). *Rethinking symbolism*. Cambridge: Cambridge University Press.

Sperber, Dan (1982/1985) Apparently irrational beliefs, In S. Lukes & M. Hollis (eds.), *Rationality and relativism* (Oxford, Blackwell, 1982). Revised version in D. Sperber (1985). *On anthropological knowledge*. Cambridge: Cambridge University (1985).

Sperber, Dan (1990). The epidemiology of beliefs. In Colin Fraser & George Gaskell (eds.) *The social psychological study of widespread beliefs*. Oxford: Clarendon Press.

Sperber, Dan (1994a). Understanding verbal understanding. In Jean Khalfa (ed.) *What is Intelligence?* Cambridge University Press.

Sperber, Dan (1994b). The modularity of thought and the epidemiology of representations. In L. A. Hirschfeld & S. A. Gelman (eds), *Mapping the Mind: Domain specificity in cognition and culture*, New York: Cambridge University Press, 39-67.

Sperber, Dan (1996). *Explaining culture: A naturalistic approach*. Oxford: Blackwell.

Sperber, Dan & Deirdre Wilson (1981). Irony and the use-mention distinction. In P. Cole (ed.) *Radical pragmatics* (New-York, Academic Press, 1981) 295-318.

Sperber, Dan & Deirdre Wilson (1986/1995). *Relevance: Communication and cognition*. Oxford: Blackwell, 1986. *Second Edition*, Oxford: Blackwell 1995.

Wilford, John N. (1981). *The mapmakers*. New York: Alfred Knopf.

Wilson, Deirdre & Dan Sperber (1992) On verbal irony. *Lingua* 87, 53-76.

THE SIMULATION OF BELIEF

François Recanati
CREA

I. QUASI-BELIEF

1.1 Sperber on quasi-belief

The hermeneutic mode

In his book on Symbolism (Sperber 1974) Sperber distinguished between two modes of evaluation for sentences. In the normal, descriptive mode we first determine which proposition the sentence expresses; then we evaluate the resulting proposition as true or false. Interpretation precedes truth-evaluation. In the symbolic or hermeneutic mode, truth-evaluation takes place first. The sentence is assigned the value 'true' before interpretation, and it is the knowledge of the sentence's truth which guides interpretation. (In current philosophical terminology, we know that the sentence is true, but we don't know which truth it expresses.)

Sperber gave the following example. Lacanians believe that "the unconscious is structured like a language". They are not sure what this means, but they trust Lacan, who said so. The Lacanian dictum can be interpreted in an indefinite number of ways, as there is an indefinite number of dimensions of similarity between any two things. The process of interpretation exploits the interpreter's belief that the proposition expressed by the sentence is true. The sentence is believed to be true because it has been uttered by Lacan, who is believed to be a truth-teller. The interpreter (the Lacanian) therefore eliminates all interpretations incompatible with the presumed truth of the sentence, and explores the remaining possibilities, without necessarily choosing among them.[1]

When Sperber published his book Lacan was upset by what he thought was an attack. I myself was a Lacanian at the time, and I knew Lacan. Seeing him upset prompted me to look at Sperber's book. The description of the hermeneutic mode seemed to me to capture the Lacanian mind rather adequately. Among Lacanians, I had noticed that which interpretation was offered of a Lacanian dictum (such as 'The unconscious is structured like a language') did not really matter. The diversity of interpretations was admitted. What really mattered was the perpetuation of the Lacanian faith, i.e. the maintenance of the universally admitted claim that *what Lacan says is true*.[2]

Meta-representations and the belief box

In Sperber's work, the distinction between the two modes of interpretation is closely related to a distinction between two ways of being stored in the mind. A representation can be directly fed into the 'belief box', or it can be embedded within a meta-representation which itself figures in the belief box. In the first case the representation interacts with other representations in the mind and this interaction yields action: mental action (inference) or bodily action caused by beliefs in conjunction with desires. In the meta-representational case the representation is *insulated from* other representations. I can believe that John said that p, without believing that p. The proposition that p is represented, but it is not directly in the belief box. It is there only indirectly, via the meta-representation of which the proposition is a part. This meta-representation is what interacts with other representations in practical and theoretical reasoning. In contrast, the proposition that p which occurs in the meta-representation 'John said that p' is insulated and does not interact with other propositions in the belief box.

An insulated proposition can be emancipated, however, if the meta-representational frame within which it is embedded is a *validating frame*: a frame such as 'It is true that....' If we believe that it is true that *p*, we are licensed to believe that *p*; we are free to 'disquote'. Once emancipated, the embedded proposition can interact with the other propositions in the belief box and the rest of the system.[3]

According to Sperber, the Lacanians who 'believe' that the unconscious is structured like a language in effect believe a validating metaproposition to the effect that *Lacan says that*, hence *it is true that*, the unconscious is structured like a language. Normally, when a validating meta-representation is accepted, the object-representation is emancipated and transferred into the belief box. Validating meta-belief normally leads to belief. But there are exceptions, according to Sperber: sometimes emancipation is blocked. When that is so, the validated representation cannot go into the belief box; it can only give rise to a 'quasi-belief'. That is what happens in the Lacanian case.

Semi-propositional representations

Sperber speculates that representations stored directly in the belief box must have a certain cognitive format, while representations stored only indirectly, via meta-representations, are not similarly constrained. For example there are 'semi-propositional representations' which are not fully determinate but contain something like 'parameters' in the manner of Barwise and Perry (1983). They are useful to cognitive processing, but, according to Sperber, they are insulated from the belief box by being confined to the meta-representational format.

Consider the representation that Cicero's prose is full of synecdoches, entertained by someone who has only a vague idea of what synecdoches are, but who trusts the teacher. The representation is semi-propositional: it includes a partly unanalysed symbol. This can be indicated by putting quotation marks around the relevant constituent:

(1) Cicero's prose is full of 'synecdoches'

Its including a partly unanalysed symbol prevents (1) from being fed into the belief box. Such a representation can only be entertained meta-representationally. One can have beliefs *about* a representation which one does not fully understand (e.g. one can believe that it is true), but that is all one can do with such a representation, according to Sperber. In order to give rise to a genuine belief, a representation must be fully understood. I will call this 'Sperber's constraint'.[4]

Why should semi-propositional representations be prevented from going into the belief box? Sperber's response is that there would be too great a risk of inconsistency if they were included (Sperber 1985: 54-5). Semi-propositional representations are not fully understood, hence we are unable to determine whether or not they are compatible with other representations in the belief box. To avoid contradictions, it is better to store in the belief box only representations which we fully understand, i.e. representations such that we can, in principle, check whether or not they contradict other representations in the belief box.

Summing up

Quasi-belief involves two components, in Sperber's framework:

    (i) the quasi-believer has a validating meta-belief, to the effect
       that a certain representation is true; yet
    (ii) that representation cannot be emancipated and give rise to
       a genuine belief, because it is semi-propositional.

In what follows I will discuss three aspects of this treatment of quasi-belief. I will first consider the relation between quasi-belief and the validating meta-belief mentioned in (i). Is the quasi-belief identical to the meta-belief, or is it distinct from it and caused by it? Sperber does not directly address this issue. He sometimes suggests that quasi-belief is reducible to meta-belief. On the other hand, he generally talks of quasi-belief as if it were a distinct and genuine attitude, on a par with belief (cf his distinction between 'representational belief' and 'factual belief'). In §1.2 I will argue in favour of the view that quasi-belief cannot be reduced to meta-belief.

The second aspect I want to discuss concerns the content of the quasi-belief (§§1.3-4). Sperber says that the primary object of quasi-belief (the representation which the quasi-believer accepts) is semantically indeterminate. I will argue that it need not be. Except in rather special cases, 'deferential' representations have both a determinate character and a determinate content. They are not semantically but epistemically indeterminate.

The third issue to be dealt with concerns Sperber's constraint. Is it true that the representations which are the object of quasi-belief are prevented from going into the belief box? Is quasi-belief an attitude distinct from belief, or is it merely a species of belief? I will not provide a definitive answer to that question in what follows, but I will point out that Sperber's argument for his constraint rests on an individualistic prejudice.

1.2 Is quasi-belief reducible to meta-belief?

The representational theory of the mind

Many philosophers think that the proper objects of propositional attitudes such as belief are 'propositions', construed either as sequences of semantic values or as sets of possible worlds. If we take this line, we are almost irresistibly led to the view that quasi-belief is reducible to meta-belief, because of the following argument.

Genuine attitudes, on the propositionalist view, take propositions as contents. The object-representation (i.e., the representation the meta-belief is about) does not uniquely determine such a content, because it is semi-propositional. Hence there is no attitude whose content corresponds to the object-representation. The only genuine attitude involved in quasi-belief is the attitude whose content corresponds to the *meta*-representation; for the latter is fully propositional, in contrast to the object-representation. Now this attitude is, simply, belief: the quasi-believer *believes* the validating meta-representation. It follows that 'quasi-belief' is nothing other than a certain type of meta-belief.[5]

Another position is available, however. A growing number of philosophers think that the object of the attitudes—and the attitudes themselves—can be split in two. According to the representational theory of the mind, put forward in the seventies (e.g. Harman 1973, Fodor 1975, Field 1978), to believe that p is to accept a representation r which means that p. This suggests there are two distinct relations at work: a primary relation (acceptance) between a cognitive agent and a representation, and a secondary relation (belief) between the agent and the proposition which the representation expresses. That theory, which takes representations to be the primary objects of the attitudes, has received considerable support from more recent studies concerning indexical belief and the puzzles of cognitive significance. As Perry has shown, the puzzles evaporate as soon as we draw a principled distinction between the accepted representation and the proposition thereby believed (Perry 1980). Thus a rational subject may believe and disbelieve the same thing, provided she does so under different 'modes of presentation', i.e. by accepting different representations.

Once we take the representationalist line and grant the dual aspect of the attitudes, it becomes very natural to treat quasi-belief as a genuine attitude. What, according to Sperber, characterizes quasi-belief is the fact that the accepted representation does not uniquely determine a proposition (Sperber 1985: 51). This is compatible with there being a genuine attitude toward that representation. Belief and quasi-belief can be construed as *two attitudes towards representations—two varieties of 'acceptance'*:

- one believes that p iff one accepts a representation which means that p;
- one quasi-believes that p iff one accepts a representation whose meaning is partly indeterminate.

The argument from learning

Among the data to be explained is the continuity between quasi-belief and belief. This continuity manifests itself in learning. In learning, quasi-belief gradually turns into belief (Sperber 1985: 53). We start by quasi-believing something which the teacher tells us, but which we do not fully understand. Still, we have partial understanding, and this enables us to use the representation in reasoning and to establish connections between the semi-propositional representation which we accept and other things which we believe. Exploring those connections sometimes leads us to genuine understanding, hence to belief.

Consider the synecdoche example. In the representation (1), repeated here,

(1) Cicero's prose is full of 'synecdoches'

only one symbol is partly 'unanalysed' (as Sperber puts it). We understand the representation, except for one particular constituent. Even that constituent we partly understand, however. For example we know that a 'synecdoche' is a trope, distinct from metaphor, irony, litote, and hyperbole. But we do not know exactly which trope it is. We may also be aware of a few examples of synecdoches which the teacher gave. From the general definition of a trope, plus the semi-propositional knowledge about 'synecdoches' (including the fact that such and such examples are examples of 'synecdoche'), plus propositional knowledge about other tropes, we may sometimes gather what a synecdoche is. As a result, the semi-propositional knowledge that a 'synecdoche' is a trope, and that Cicero's prose is full of 'synecdoches', becomes fully propositional: quasi-belief gives way to belief.

I do not see how we can account for this continuity without acknowledging a genuine attitude of 'acceptance without understanding' (quasi-belief). In the situation I have described, learning consists in manipulating a representation which one does not fully understand, up to the point where one understands it. We start by accepting a representation without understanding it; this attitude of acceptance leads us to use the representation in a certain way; and by so using the representation we end up understanding it. What makes learning possible is the use to which the representation is put, and that use itself depends on the initial attitude of acceptance which motivates it.

Could we say that what motivates our use of the representation in learning is 'nothing other than' the validating meta-belief? No: without an appropriate attitude *toward the object-representation* (rather than merely an attitude toward the meta-representation), there would not be the appropriate use of it which eventually makes understanding possible. This attitude is *caused by* the meta-belief, but it is distinct from it. When emancipation is possible the validating meta-belief δ*p* causes the belief that *p*. When emancipation is not possible, the validating meta-belief does not lose all causal power; it still causes *acceptance* of the half-understood representation. Acceptance, under such conditions, is what I call 'quasi-belief'.

§1.3 Semantic indeterminacy

Two forms of semantic indeterminacy

In §1.2 I stressed the dual nature of objects of thought. A primary attitude of acceptance, directed toward representations, is involved both in belief and in quasi-belief. According to Sperber, the difference between belief and quasi-belief lies in the semantic status of the accepted representation. To believe that *p* is to accept a representation *r* which is semantically determinate and expresses the proposition that *p*. In quasi-belief, according to Sperber, the accepted representation does not uniquely determine a proposition. The representation is partly uninterpreted.

In what sense is the representation supposed to be partly uninterpreted? At least in the sense that it does not possess a determinate 'content'. But a question arises, concerning the 'character' of the accepted representation. As we shall see, there are two possible interpretations of Sperber's claim that the accepted representation is semantically indeterminate. It can be indeterminate at the content level or, more radically, at the character level.

When we accept a representation which expresses the proposition that *p*, that proposition is the 'content' of the representation. As Perry repeatedly stressed, the accepted representation also possesses a 'character' over and above its propositional content. The 'character' of a representation is that aspect of it which contextually determines its truth-conditional 'content' (Kaplan 1989); it functions as a mode of presentation for the proposition which the representation contextually expresses.

It is well-known that the character of a representation may fail to determine a content, in certain contexts. That is, it is possible for a representation to be endowed with a character but no content, if the context is inappropriate. If I say 'He is tall,' but the man I take myself to be demonstrating does not exist, no proposition is expressed, even though the uttered sentence has a definite character. Here a particular sentential constituent (the pronoun) is responsible for the defectiveness of the utterance at the content level. Another example is Austin's (1975: 96-7):

(2) He said I was to go to 'the minister', but he did not say which minister.

The speech act which (2) reports is 'rhetically' defective (i.e. defective at the content level)[6] because a particular constituent (viz. the definite description) is contextually uninterpretable. The quotation marks, here as in the synecdoche example, indicate that a constituent of the representation remains uninterpreted.

There is a clear difference between the Austinian example and the synecdoche example, however. In the Austinian example the relevant constituent remains 'uninterpreted' at the *content* level; the representation possesses a (phatic) meaning, but part of its (rhetic) content cannot be computed for lack of contextual information (viz. which minister the speaker is referring to). In the synecdoche case, it is less obvious that the representation possesses a determinate meaning. Compare (2) with (3):

(3) He said that Cicero's prose is full of 'synecdoches', but he did not say what a synecdoche is.

In (2), the meaning of 'the minister' is clear, but its contextual application is unclear. As a result, there is an indeterminacy at the content level. In (3) it is the meaning itself which is unclear: the hearer does not know what 'synecdoche' means.

What I have just said suggests a radical interpretation of Sperber's claim concerning the semantic indeterminacy of the accepted representation, in quasi-belief. According to that interpretation, the representation includes a symbol which is not even interpreted at the character level.

Is quasi-belief semantically indeterminate?

I find the more radical version of Sperber's claim unpalatable. It entails that a constituent of the accepted representation, hence that representation itself, is uninterpreted in the most radical sense. My first objection to this view is that the accepted representation is supposed to be *mentally entertained*; but it is hard to think of a symbol being mentally entertained without being 'interpreted' in some fashion or other. There is a sense in which all mental entertaining *is* 'interpretation'; hence it is not obvious that we can talk of mentally entertaining uninterpreted symbols. In contrast to what happens in external language, if a mental sentence is well-formed, it *must* possess a definite meaning.

A second difficulty I have concerns the possibility for a meta-representation to be fully interpreted when the object-representation itself is partly uninterpreted. Sperber seems to accept Semantic Innocence. The meta-representation (for example, 'Lacan believes that the unconscious is structured like a language') literally *contains* the mentioned representation ('the unconscious is structured like a language'), in Sperber's framework (Sperber 1985: 54). Yet Sperber thinks that prefixing 'It is true that' (or 'Lacan believes that') to a semantically indeterminate representation can yield a semantically determinate meta-representation. It is hard to see how this view can be compatible with Semantic Innocence. If Semantic Innocence holds, the semantic incompleteness of the object-representation can hardly fail to entail the semantic incompleteness of the meta-representation (see e.g. Prior 1976: 153-54).[7]

Sperber could reply that Semantic Innocence applies to 'oblique' constructions such as 'It is true that ...' or 'Lacan says that...', but not to *direct quotation.* Thus, if 'glive' is a non-word and 'John kept gliving' is ill-formed, 'It is true that John kept gliving' (or 'Lacan said that John kept gliving') is bound to be ill-formed too; but the direct quotation 'Lacan said: "John kept gliving"' is well-formed.[8] Since quotation marks can turn non-words into words in this manner, why not accept that there are mental quotation marks? That is, in effect, Sperber's suggestion. That suggestion is quite compatible with the analysis of quasi-belief I am about to provide. On that analysis, however, the representation accepted by the quasi-believer need not be construed as semantically indeterminate, at whatever level of interpretation.

1.4 The deferential operator

Deferential representations

We can maintain that the representations accepted by the quasi-believer are endowed with a character—indeed we can even maintain that they have a definite 'content'—if those representations are allowed to include a specific constituent which I call the deferential operator. Deferential representations (i.e. representations including the deferential operator) are an alternative to Sperber's semi-propositional representations.

   The deferential operator $R_x(\ )$ applies to a symbol σ and yields a complex expression $R_x(\sigma)$ whose character is distinct from that of σ. The character of $R_x(\sigma)$ takes us from a context in which the speaker tacitly refers to a certain cognitive agent x, to a certain content, namely the content which σ has for x, given the character which x attaches to σ. The complex symbol $R_x(\sigma)$ therefore has both a character and a content. It is endowed with a complete, two-tiered interpretation (in an appropriate context). What is special with the expression $R_x(\sigma)$ is that its content is determined 'deferentially', via the content which another cognitive agent, contextually referred to, attaches or would attach to σ in the context of utterance.

   In (1)

(1) Cicero's prose is full of 'synecdoches'

the last constituent is a deferential symbol whose character is a function from contexts in which users of the symbol 'synecdoche' are being referred to, to the contents which the symbol 'synecdoche' has for those users. In the particular context in which we imagine this representation to be tokened, the relevant user (the x who is being tacitly referred to) is the teacher; hence the symbol's content, in this context, is the content which the symbol 'synecdoche' has for the teacher. Which content it is, the student does not know; but he trusts the teacher and therefore quasi-believes the proposition, whatever it is, which the accepted sentence expresses.

Epistemic vs. semantic indeterminacy

A representation including the deferential operator expresses a proposition of which the quasi-believer is unaware: this is the feature which Burge stressed in his articles on externalism, which bear directly (and explicitly) on the issue of quasi-belief (Burge 1979, 1982, etc.).

Burge's view contrasts with Sperber's. Sperber thinks the representation accepted in quasi-belief does not have a determinate content. Rather, it is semantically indeterminate (semi-propositional). On the view I have sketched, following Burge, there is a determinate content, even if it is unknown to the quasi-believer. Thus the speaker who utters

(4) I have 'arthritis' in the thigh

expresses the proposition that she has arthritis in the thigh, even if she does not know what arthritis is. Her use is deferential. In the same way, the student accepts a representation, viz. (1), which by virtue of the semantics of the deferential operator, expresses the proposition that Cicero's prose is full of synecoches. On this view, the object of acceptance in quasi-belief is not a semi-propositional representation (i.e. a representation incompletely interpreted) but a deferential representation (i.e. a representation including the deferential operator).

Deferential representations can be semantically indeterminate in some cases: this will be so, in particular, when a deferential use turns out to be *ungrounded* because no user x has the cognitive resources for determining the content of the term to which the deferential operator applies. For example there are cases in which a certain term is used deferentially by everybody; everybody defers to the others, in such a way that no determinate proposition is ever expressed. In more standard cases, however, we need not deny that the sentence expresses a definite proposition.[9]

Sperber's intuition of indeterminacy can still be captured. Deferential representations, though semantically determinate, are *epistemically* indeterminate: the quasi-believer does not know which proposition the deferential representation she accepts expresses. (This is what makes ungroundedness possible). Sperber's claim concerning semi-propositionality can therefore be construed as a claim concerning the epistemical state of the user, rather than a claim about semantic content.

Deferential representations and the belief box

Beside the question, whether a determinate proposition is expressed, there is a further question: whether that proposition can be believed. Here we need not depart from Sperber's treatment, according to which quasi-beliefs are not genuine beliefs. We can side with Burge and argue (*pace* Sperber) that a definite proposition is expressed, while simultaneously holding, with Sperber, that that proposition, being deferentially expressed, cannot be 'believed' in the full sense of the term (*pace* Burge).

Sperber's evolutionary argument to the effect that belief requires understanding is still in force. Deferential representations are highly risky: the believer has no control over which proposition is expressed, and inconsistencies can proliferate. Hence the policy of banning deferential representations from the belief box can only be profitable to the cognitive system. Sperber's constraint, according to which whatever is believed must be understood, can thus tentatively be maintained. In virtue of that constraint, accepting a deferential representation does *not* amount to believing the proposition which it (deferentially) expresses, but merely to quasi-believing that proposition.

Sperber's argument is far from decisive, however. There is a prima facie objection to the claim that deferential representations are banned from the belief box. In §1.2 I stressed the continuity between quasi-belief and belief. This continuity shows that deferentiality is a matter of degree. Now there is but a short step from acknowledging that continuity to acknowledging the pervasiveness of deferentiality, i.e. the fact that *most concepts are deferential to some degree* (especially in childhood). In view of that fact, Sperber's conception of belief appears much too narrow.

There is another objection. Sperber's position rests on cognitive individualism: it is assumed that cognitive agents have their beliefs under control, in the sense that they know what they believe. But there is a clear sense in which cognitive agents do not know the propositional contents of their beliefs: that is the lesson of externalism. There is nothing exceptional about deferential representations, in that respect. In many circumstances cognitive agents entertain or accept representations the propositional content of which is uncertain to them.

As I will suggest below (§2.3), the correct position is intermediate between Sperber's and that of his externalist opponents: there *is* a tension between deferentiality and beliefhood, even if it is implausible to draw a sharp boundary between beliefs and quasi-beliefs. In other words, whether quasi-belief is construed as a species of belief (as the externalists would have it), or as an attitude distinct from belief (as Sperber suggests), there is a contrast between quasi-beliefs and what we may call *core* beliefs. That contrast is more dramatic if we accept Sperber's constraint, but it does not vanish if we reject it.

Be that as it may, I will not try to settle the issue over Sperber's constraint in this paper. In part 2 I will be primarily interested in the category of 'acceptance without belief'. Quasi-belief is an instance of that only if Sperber is right, that is, only if belief requires understanding. If Sperber is wrong, and quasi-belief is a species of *belief*, what I will say about acceptance without belief will not be much affected, for quasi-belief is only one putative instance of that attitude. Beside quasi-belief there is another instance, namely 'assumption'. And I take it to be uncontroversial that 'assumption' is an attitude distinct from belief.

II. ACCEPTANCE

2.1. Belief and acceptance

The belief faculty

The belief faculty can be seen as a mental 'module' consisting of two things: the mental encyclopedia or belief box (a set of representations), and an inferential device (Sperber 1985: 54). The function of the belief box is to store true representations of the world, which can then be used to guide action. The function of the inferential device is to *exploit* the representations in the belief box, that is, to derive consequences from them—to use them as premisses in theoretical and practical reasoning.

In order to ensure that representations stored in the belief box are true, there are input conditions, i.e. conditions which a representation must satisfy before it can enter the belief box. The main condition is *validation*: in order to go into the belief box, a representation must be validated, i.e. its tokenings must result from a reliable cognitive mechanism—a mechanism which normally delivers true representations as outputs. Among the mechanisms in question we find perception and communication. Inference is also a validating mechanism: by feeding a representation from the belief box to the inferential device, we obtain further representations which are (inferentially) validated and can therefore go into the belief box.

If Sperber is right, there is another input constraint beside validation: to go into the belief box the representation must be fully understood. That constraint is what bars deferential representations from entering the belief box (§1.4). (As we have seen, the rationale for

Sperber's constraint is that the thinker is not in a position to check whether a deferential representation is consistent with other representations in the belief box).

Through exploitation, the belief box can be enlarged, because representations which are inferred from representations already in the belief box are themselves 'validated'. Exploitation is also what enables us to check whether a candidate for the belief box (i.e. a representation delivered by a reliable mechanism) is OK and yields no contradiction with representations already in stock.[10]

As I have just described it, the belief faculty is a natural system with two components whose functions are determined within the system: the function of the belief box is to store the sort of representation (viz. true representations) which it is the function of the inferential device to exploit. In this framework, quasi-belief understood à la Sperber can be characterized as involving a divergence between the natural function of the inferential component (to exploit representations in the belief box) and the way it is actually used (to exploit representations which do *not* satisfy the input constraints and therefore are not in the belief box).

Acceptance defined

Acceptance can be defined as *the disposition to exploit a representation*, i.e. to feed it to the inferential device. We find this disposition both in belief and in quasi-belief. It is in virtue of this disposition that representations in the belief box freely interact with other representations. In quasi-belief also representations are exploited, even though they are not fully understood. As we saw in §1.2, learning is possible because the deferential character of the representation does not prevent it from being exploited. The student can draw a number of consequences from the quasi-belief that Cicero's prose is full of 'synecdoches' (e.g. she can infer that Cicero was a sophisticated writer). Similarly, the Lacanian can base his decision to purchase linguistics books on his deferential quasi-belief that the unconscious is structured like a language. Practical reasoning often takes deferential premisses.

What is the relation between belief and acceptance? Belief entails acceptance. Representations in the belief box are ipso facto accepted (i.e. when a representation is in the belief box, the cognitive agent is automatically disposed to exploit it). But there are cases of acceptance which are not cases of belief. That a representation is in the belief box means not only that the cognitive agent is disposed to exploit it, but that she is disposed to exploit it *because the representation satisfies the input constraints*. Every case of belief is therefore a case of acceptance, but not conversely. In 'acceptance without belief', the cognitive agent is disposed to exploit a representation which does *not* satisfy the input constraints and therefore does not belong to the belief box.

As there are two putative input constraints (the validation constraint and Sperber's constraint), there are two putative forms of acceptance-without-belief. Quasi-belief is the disposition to exploit a representation which is prevented from going into the belief box because it is not fully understood. The other form of acceptance-without-belief, which I call 'assumption', is the disposition to accept a representation which is prevented from going into the belief box because it is not validated. The relations between the five types of attitude I have distinguished—belief, quasi-belief, acceptance, acceptance-without-belief, and assumption—are displayed in Table 1.

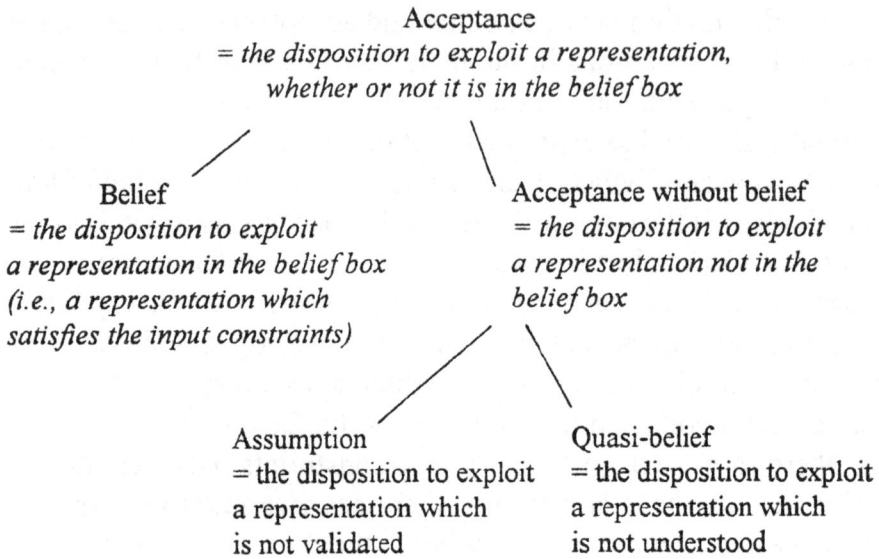

Acceptance
= *the disposition to exploit a representation,*
whether or not it is in the belief box

Belief
= *the disposition to exploit*
a representation in the belief box
(i.e., a representation which
satisfies the input constraints)

Acceptance without belief
= *the disposition to exploit*
a representation not in the
belief box

Assumption
= the disposition to exploit
a representation which
is not validated

Quasi-belief
= the disposition to exploit
a representation which
is not understood

Table 1

Table 1 presupposes that Sperber's constraint applies to representations in the belief box. If Sperber is wrong and there is no such constraint, then quasi-belief is a species of belief (Table 2).

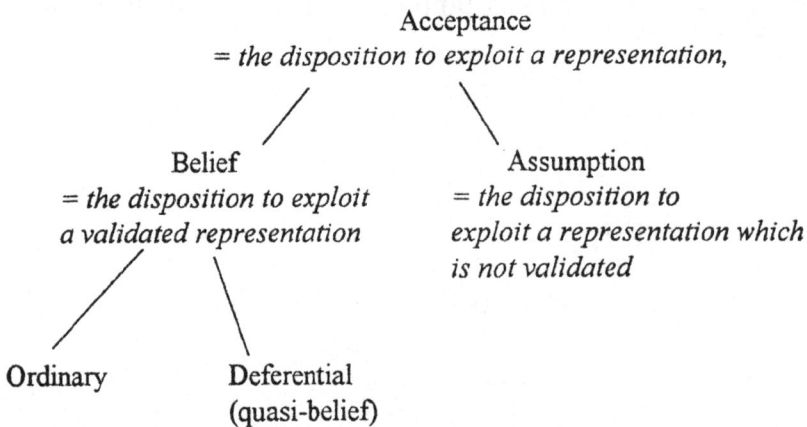

Acceptance
= *the disposition to exploit a representation,*

Belief
= *the disposition to exploit*
a validated representation

Assumption
= *the disposition to*
exploit a representation which
is not validated

Ordinary

Deferential
(quasi-belief)

Table 2

The primacy of belief

Whatever we think of the relation between belief and quasi-belief, the relation between belief and acceptance is clear. Acceptance is the most general notion, but the notion of belief is primary. We need the notion of acceptance, broader than that of belief, only because *within the belief module* there is a sub-system (the inferential device) which can be used to do something other than fulfill its function within the module (exploit representations in the belief box). The sub-system is individuated in part by its function within the belief system, hence the notion of acceptance, *qua* disposition to run the sub-system in question, presupposes the notion of a complete belief system.[11]

In acceptance-without-belief, the inferential mechanism is fed an input distinct from its normal input. This makes acceptance-without-belief a case of *simulation*, in the technical sense. There is simulation whenever a mechanism M which has a function within a system S, and exists only because of that function, is used 'off-line' (Nichols et al. 1996; Currie 1995), 'outside' the system. Such a use is parasitic on the normal use (as the mechanism exists only in virtue of its normal use). As we shall see in the next section, acceptance-without-belief is the simulation of belief not only in this technical sense but also in a more phenomenological sense.

2.2 Pretending to believe

The simulative component

I gave two examples of quasi-believer: the student, who quasi-believes that Cicero's prose is full of 'synecdoches', and the Lacanian, who quasi-believes that the unconscious is structured like a language. Both examples support the claim that quasi-believing involves pretending.

In the foreword to Pinker's *Learnability and Cognition*, we find the following sentence:

> In developing the ideas presented in this book, I was lucky to have encountered audiences who refused to believe them, students who refused to pretend to understand them, and children who refused to behave in accordance with them. [Pinker 1989]

In that passage Pinker clearly implies that an element of pretense is involved in normal student behaviour. Phenomenologically, this seems to be right. Students often pretend to understand what they do not understand. The student who has only a vague idea what a synecdoche is can assert that Cicero's prose is full of synecdoches or assent to that assertion; in so doing the student does more than mimick the teacher: she simulatively anticipates the state of knowledge she will be in when appropriately trained. As I insisted in §1.2, such simulative anticipations form an integral part of the learning process.

The Lacanian also pretends to believe. Here I speak from my own experience. Having been a Lacanian myself, I can testify that Lacanianism (and a good deal of what is known as 'Continental philosophy') rests on something like a game of make-believe. To be a Lacanian is to use a certain language (Lacanian language) *as if* one understood it. The Lacanians assert things which they do not understand, and which they are unable to interpret except in a very vague and hesitating manner. Still, they believe that Lacan himself understands those things, and speaks truly. To belong to the Lacanian community, there are two individually necessary and jointly sufficient conditions: (i) to hold the meta-belief concerning Lacan qua truth-teller, and (ii) to engage into a simulation of Lacan's speech, i.e. to use his words while pretending to understand them. I insist that those conditions are sufficient. No real understanding of Lacanian langage is required to belong to the Lacanian community. It is enough if one pretends to understand. In contrast, one must really believe that Lacan speaks truly. Someone who only pretends to believe this would not be accepted as a member of the community.

Note that this phenomenological quality of pretense that we find in quasi-belief does not by itself entail that quasi-belief is the simulation of belief, hence something distinct from belief. If we reject Sperber's constraint, we can still account for that phenomenological quality, by pointing out that the quasi-believer *pretends to understand*. This is compatible with his having a genuine (deferential) belief.

In contrast to quasi-belief, assumption can only be construed as the simulation of belief. When someone assumes that *p*, he or she behaves *as if* the representation that *p* was validated, while in fact it is not. Here the agent unmistakeably *pretends to believe*: Assumption, from the very beginning, emerges as something distinct from belief.

Assumption

A classical example of assumption is the lawyer who believes her client guilty but assumes his innocence while defending his cause. For the lawyer to assume this is for her to *pretend to believe* that her client is innocent. Another well-known example is hypothetical reasoning. In hypothetical reasoning, we pretend that something is the case, and we reason from that assumption. The representation assumed is fed to the inferential mechanism, and consequences are derived. This is like running a simulation.

Reasoning from assumptions is at the heart of the natural deduction approach to logic. In natural deduction, the act of 'assuming' is the act of *simulating assertion*. Propositions assumed are propositions which are fictively asserted. From those propositions consequences are derived, which inherit the fictitious character of the assumptions from which they are derived: they are not actually asserted, because they are derived from propositions which themselves are not asserted, but assumed (simulated). In other words the consequences are derived only 'under assumption', that is, simulatively. Yet the simulation establishes that such and such consequences 'follow from' such and such assumptions; and this fact concerning the implication relations between propositions can be genuinely asserted.

The following inference from P → Q to ¬ Q → ¬ P illustrates the role of assumptions in natural deduction:

[1] P → Q   (premiss)
[2]   ¬Q   (assumption)
[3]   ¬P   (1, 2, Modus Tollens)
[4] ¬Q → ¬P   (2, 3, Conditionalization)

We start from a certain premiss, viz. the conditional proposition P → Q (step [1]). From that premiss we want to infer the proposition ¬Q → ¬ P (step [4]). We do that by first 'assuming' the antecedent ¬Q of the conditional we want to infer (step [2]); this means that we pretend to assert ¬Q. (That the antecedent ¬Q is not really asserted, but only assumed is shown by the indentation of the line where it occurs.) From ¬Q and [1] we infer ¬P, by Modus Tollens (step [3]). As ¬Q was not really asserted, the consequence ¬P is not asserted either; being derived 'under assumption', the consequence ¬P is no less fictitious than the assumption ¬Q from which it is derived. This is why ¬P also occurs on an indented line. But the inference rule of Conditionalization (or Conditional Proof) enables us to infer the conditional in [4] from the fact that, under assumption [2], the proposition [3] can be derived.

Assumption as pretense

It is sometimes claimed that the form of simulation involved in reasoning from assumptions is a sub-personal procedure much like the building of a mental model in carrying out an inference; the point being that a sub-personal procedure of that sort has nothing to do with the personal process of 'pretending' (Sperber, in conversation). But there is an obvious continuum between that form of simulation and other forms which clearly engage the subject: imagination and phantasies, games of make believe, fiction, empathy. It is hard to deny that those activities are conducted at the 'personal' (rather than sub-personal) level. Yet the continuity with reasoning from assumptions is manifest. Given this continuity, the burden of proof lies on the side of those who want to posit a sharp division between the two sorts of case.

Consider children's games of make believe. Two children pretend, say, that a certain stick is a sword. If this is not pretense in the personal sense, what is? What the children do is create a common disposition to exploit a representation which is not validated. They pretend in the sense that they do as if the representation was validated, and act accordingly. They assume that the stick is a sword.

From children's games of make believe to fiction there is but a short step, as Walton and others have shown (Walton 1990; Currie 1990). The consumers of a fiction assume the 'truths' of the fiction, i.e. exploit them as if they were validated. More precisely, the participants in the fictional game (the producer and the consumer) pretend that the representations of the fiction are *communicationally validated*: they pretend that the author is telling known facts. As Lewis says, 'the storytellers pretend to pass on historical information to their audience; the audience pretends to learn from their words, and to respond accordingly' (Lewis 1983: 276). That the pretense in question takes place at the personal level is shown, inter alia, by the well-known fact that fiction involves the affects of the audience.

One might argue that the activity of 'pretense' exemplified by children's games and by fiction involves communication (between the person who pretends and her audience) and cannot be used to analyse *attitudes* like acceptance-without-belief; for attitudes are intra-individual, while communicational activities are interpersonal. But I think it is not quite right that pretense *in general* implies communication. There are various forms of pretense, some which involve communication, some which do not. Children's pretend play themselves are not necessarily interpersonal and cooperative. A solitary child can pretend that a certain stick is a sword, and play with the stick accordingly. This is a standard case of assumption.

Among the forms of pretense which are not intrinsically communicational we find imaginative or counterfactual phantasies, to which fiction is obviously related. Kahneman and Tversky have studied those phantasies which they construe as 'the running of a simulation model' (1982: 201).[12] They claim that there are 'rules of mental simulation', which must be experimentally investigated and which govern counterfactual thinking. The mental simulation they talk about is responsible for the emotions which we associate with imagined situations: 'counterfactual emotions', as Kahneman and Tversky call them (1982: 206). Here as in earlier cases (fiction, games of make believe) we can conclude from the involvement of affects that the mental simulation at issue is not sub-personal.

Another important family of cases, some of which are also affect-involving, concerns the simulation of the psychological states of other persons. There are two sub-cases. In *empathy*, knowing the situation of another person, we simulate and predict that person's emotional attitudes and reactions. In the other, more intellectual type of case we simulate and predict the *propositional* attitudes of a person x, by assuming the representations which (we know) x accepts and feeding them to the inferential mechanism. This is the process of *simulative belief ascription*, which has been the focus of much research in recent years.

Pretending to quasi-believe

I have mentioned two putative cases of acceptance-without-belief. In one type of case (quasi-belief) a representation is validated but it is not fully understood. In the other type of case (assumption) the representation is not validated; we only pretend that it is. An interesting example, involving both types of case at once, is discussed by Sperber in his paper on quasi-belief.

Sperber describes the case of old Filate, a Dorze villager, who once asked him (the anthropologist Sperber, doing fieldwork in Southern Ethiopia) to go and kill a dragon. Filate obviously accepted the representation 'there is a dragon nearby'. To that request anthropologist Sperber replied that he 'would not know how to find the dragon'. Sperber therefore also accepted the representation that there was a certain dragon nearby. Though both Sperber and his informant Filate accepted the representation that there was a dragon, their mode of acceptance was, to some extent, different.

Sperber insists that Filate's attitude was toward a deferential representation:

What if I <Sperber> had expressed doubts that such an animal exists? He <Filate> would have told me what he knew: they were golden all over; whether it was real gold or just the way they looked, he didn't know. Yes, their heart was of gold, real gold. *How should he know* if a heart of gold could beat? *He was merely quoting* what people who had killed these animals were reported to have said, and they know better than any of us. (Sperber 1985: 61; my emphasis)

Two things clearly emerge from this passage. First, the representation 'There is a dragon nearby' is *communicationally validated* for Filate. He believes this representation to be true because it has been transmitted to him by someone trustworthy. Second, the representation is deferential; it includes a constituent, viz. the concept 'dragon', which Filate only partly understands. Filate therefore *quasi-believes* that there is a dragon nearby.

What about Sperber himself? Sperber also may be said to have accepted a deferential representation (during his exchange with Filate); for the concept of a 'dragon' is cultural, and cultural concepts are deferential. But it cannot be said that Sperber quasi-believed that there was a dragon nearby. For he did not take this representation to be validated, communicationally or otherwise. Rather, he assumed that representation, for the sake of his communicational exchange with Filate.

Sperber says: 'Being asked to slay a dragon is a rare experience. It nevertheless evokes many childhood memories, fears and dreams' (Sperber 1985: 62). Western children are used to listening to tales involving dragons, to playing games of make-believe involving dragons, etc. They are expert in fictional dragon-talk. As a former westerner child, Sperber knew the game, and could play it with Filate. That is what he did (somewhat reluctantly). Sperber's acceptance is therefore a case of assumption, while Filate's is more on the side of quasi-belief.

The fact that the representation at issue is no less deferential for Sperber than it is for Filate has an interesting consequence. In assuming that there is a dragon nearby, Sperber does not simulate a *belief* (in

Sperber's strong sense). Since the representation is deferential, it can only give rise to a quasi-belief, hence Sperber simulates a *quasi-belief*. In contrast to Sperber, Filate does not simulate that quasi-belief: he actually has it. We see that assumption *qua* simulation can operate either on (non-deferential) belief or on quasi-belief. At this point it is very tempting to opt for the picture suggested by Table 2: as there is a general category of assumption with covers both the simulation of quasi-belief and the simulation of (non-deferential) belief, there is a broad category of 'belief' which includes both deferential belief (quasi-belief) and non-deferential belief (belief in Sperber's strong sense).

2.3 Conclusion: Beyond belief

Core beliefs

Assumption is the simulation of belief. As for quasi-belief, it is debatable whether it is a species of belief or another form of belief simulation. Whichever option we choose, however, there is a deep similarity between assumption and quasi-belief. They both result from a cognitive mechanism which cannot be considered as part and parcel of the 'belief faculty' understood in a restricted sense.

Remember what I said of the belief faculty (§2.1). It consists of a belief box and an inferential mechanism. To go into the belief box, a representation must be validated. At this point it is useful to draw a distinction between two sorts of validation processes. Inference is a *secondary* validation process: whatever is inferred is validated, but inference itself takes validated representations as inputs. (Only if that is so will inference count as a validating process.) Memory also is a secondary validation process; for whatever is in memory must have been validated: we cannot remember something which has not already entered the belief box.[13] Perception, on the other hand, is the prototype of a *primary* validation process, that is, of a validation process which does not take already validated representations as inputs.

Beside perception, there is another primary validation process: communication[14]. Communication tends to be less reliable than perception, but the main difference between perception and communication is this. Whenever a representation is perceptually validated, it is 'understood', that is, appropriately connected to experience. But representations which are communicationally validated can be very poorly understood, and connected only to the communicative experience itself. Those 'deferential' representations give rise to what I called 'quasi-belief'.

Is quasi-belief a species of belief or not? Two conflicting types of consideration make it difficult to answer that question. On the one hand, deferential representations play a central role in our mental lives. If they were banned from the belief box, in conformity to Sperber's constraint, the resulting conception of belief would be much too narrow; it would no longer correspond to the ordinary, intuitive notion of belief. On the other hand, there is a tension between deferentiality and beliefhood—a tension which seems to justify Sperber's constraint. If deferentiality was fully compatible with beliefhood, we would have no problem imagining a belief system with *generalized* deferentiality. But we do have a problem imagining that. Deferential representations are representations which we can accept without properly understanding them. If no representation was understood, however, the cognitive agent would have no 'beliefs': he would not master a semantic system, but would blindly participate in a practice very similar to that described by Searle in his Chinese Room thought-experiment (Searle 1980). It follows that there must be a core of non-deferential beliefs if there is to be any belief at all. Even if, *pace* Sperber and Donnellan, we accept that quasi-beliefs *are* beliefs, we must acknowledge that they are not *core* beliefs. The more deferential a representation is, the more compelled we feel to distinguish accepting that representation from having a genuine belief.

Let us then characterize the 'core' belief faculty as consisting of an inferential device and a *restricted belief box* governed by a single type of primary validating process: perception. That is in contrast to the *extended belief faculty* which comports another primary validation process, namely communication. The distinguishing characteristic of communicationally validated representations is that they are not necessarily understood; they can be partly understood (quasi-beliefs).

Extending the belief faculty

Even though communication extends the belief faculty and is not part of its 'core', still that extension is of paramount importance. Communication is not merely another source of information which enables us to benefit from the experience of others, rather than being confined to the field of our own experience. Through communication we can acquire new concepts—we can modify our conceptual framework via the kind of epistemic bootstrapping described in §1.2. Thanks to deferential representations, the fact that we don't have a certain concept does not prevent us from accepting what we are told. Not only can we accept what we do not understand, but accepting it makes the acquisition of the missing concept possible. As we keep establishing connections between the deferential representation which we accept and other representations in the belief box, we enrich our conceptual system, up to the point when the original quasi-belief becomes a genuine (non-deferential) belief.

The mechanism of assumption also is an extension of the belief faculty rather than an aspect of its core. At the 'core' level the inference device takes validated representations as inputs and yields validated representations as outputs. That is what the inference device is for: making truths out of truths. In assumption, an extended use is made of the inferential device: it is fed non-validated representations (assumptions) as well as validated representations.

In the case of assumption also the extension of the original system constitutes a significant improvement. The role of the belief system is to guide action. Now planification, which is essential to rational action, typically involves conditional representations. The agent wants something to happen, and realizes that that will happen if p; this leads her to act to make it the case that p. Conditional representations, therefore, are important. Where do they come from? In some instances, observing some recurring correlation, we inductively infer the conditional 'If p then q'. But that is only one source of conditional representations. Another source is *mental simulation*. The simulative generation of new conditionals is the process which Natural Deduction codifies as 'conditionalization' (§2.2). We mentally simulate the belief that p, and subject it to inference. The output (q) is inferred 'under assumption'. Through this simulative process a conditional representation 'If p then q' is generated.

All this suggests the following, overall picture. At bottom there are three distinct faculties: the 'core' belief faculty; the communication faculty; and the mental-simulation faculty. They interact in all manners. In particular, communication and simulation greatly enrich the belief faculty. Communication provides a new variety of representations whose introduction into the belief system enhances conceptual flexibility, while simulation increases the power of the inferential device.

NOTES

[1] A similar mechanism is at work in the interpretation of 'normal' utterances. Thus an act of pointing is multiply ambiguous, but we eliminate irrelevant interpretations: we charitably interpret what we are told, by presuming that our interlocutor respects Grice's maxims. There are two differences between the charitable interpretation of normal utterances and hermeneutic interpretation, however. First, the interpretation of normal utterances is 'definite' while hermeneutic interpretation is essentially open-ended — it consists in exploring the range of possible interpretations. Second, even if the interpreter presumes that Grice's maxims are respected, the normal interpretation of an utterance (based on that presumption) precedes its evaluation as actually true or false. We presume that the speaker respects Grice's maxims, i.e. does his best to speak truly etc., not that he actually speaks the truth.

[2] I shall say more about Lacanian practice in a later section (§2.2).

[3] In the Port Royal Logic we find an interesting analysis of validating meta-representations like 'Aristotle said that the Earth is flat'. Two interpretations are distinguished: the meta-representational interpretation, in which the utterance says something about Aristotle; and another interpretation, in which the utterance says something about the Earth, under the authority of Aristotle (Arnauld & Lancelot 1683: 167-8). A similar analysis has been offered by the French linguist Oswald Ducrot (Ducrot 1980: 44 ff; see also Ducrot 1984: ch. 7-8).

[4] Arguably, that constraint goes back to Russell (1918: 218).

[5] See e.g. Donnellan 1993: 167 for a statement of this view.

[6] Austin's phatic/rhetic distinction corresponds to that between character and content.

[7] The argument from Semantic Innocence works against indeterminacy at the content level as well as against indeterminacy at the character level. If a representation is

'semi-propositional', as Sperber says, and if Semantic Innocence holds, how can the meta-representation including it have a fully propositional content?

[8]The same thing holds for 'Lacan said that John kept "gliving"', which is a mixture of oblique construction and direct quotation.

[9] Sperber himself sometimes talks of the 'proper interpretation' of the semi-propositional representation.

[10] See Fodor 1983 on 'belief fixation'.

[11] As Stalnaker puts it, 'to accept a proposition is to act, in certain respects, as if one believed it' (Stalnaker 1987:80).

[12] This field of study, they say, 'appears exceptionally rich and promising' (Kahneman and Tversky 1982: 204).

[13] There are complications concerning memory which I cannot go into here.

[14] See Reid 1970 (chapter 6) for the analogy between perception and communication.

REFERENCES

Arnauld, A. and P. Nicole (1683), *La Logique ou l'Art de penser*. Paris: Guillaume Desprez.

Austin, J.L. (1975), *How to Do Things with Words*, 2nd ed. Oxford: Clarendon Press.

Barwise J. and Perry, J. (1983), *Situations and Attitudes*. Cambridge Mass: MIT Press.

Burge, T. (1979), Individualism and the Mental. *Midwest Studies in Philosophy* 4:73-121.

Burge, T. (1982), Other Bodies. In A. Woodfield, ed., *Thought and Object*, Oxford: Clarendon Press, p. 97-120

Currie, G. (1990), *The Nature of Fiction*. Cambridge: Cambridge University Press.

Currie, G. (1995), Visual Imagery and the Simulation of Vision. *Mind and Language* 10: 25-44.

Donnellan, K. (1993), There is a word for that kind of thing: an investigation of two thought experiments. *Philosophical Perspectives* 7: 155-71.

Ducrot, O. (1980), Analyse de texte et linguistique de l'énonciation. In O. Ducrot et al., *Les Mots du Discours*, Paris: Minuit, p. 7-56.

Ducrot, O. (1984), *Le Dire et le Dit*. Paris: Minuit.

Field, H. (1978), Mental representation. *Erkenntnis* 13: 9-61.

Fodor, J.A. (1975), *The Language of Thought*. New York: Crowell.

Fodor, J.A. (1983), *The Modularity of Mind*. Cambridge, Mass: MIT Press.

Harman, G. (1973), *Thought*. Princeton: Princeton University Press.

Kahneman, D. and A. Tversky (1982), The Simulation Heuristic. In D. Kahneman, P. Slovic and A. Tversky, eds., *Judgment under uncertainty: Heuristics and biases*, Cambridge: Cambridge University Press, p. 201-7.

Lewis, D. (1983), *Philosophical Papers*, vol. 1. New York: Oxford University Press

Kaplan, D. (1989), Demonstratives. In J. Almog, H. Wettstein and J. Perry (eds.), *Themes from Kaplan*, New York: Oxford University Press, p.481-563.

Nichols, S. et al. (1996), Varieties of Off-Line Simulation. In P. Carruthers and P. Smith, eds., *Theories of Theories of Mind*, Cambridge: Cambridge University Press, p. 39-74.

Perry, J. (1980), Belief and Acceptance. *Midwest Studies in Philosophy* 5:533-42.

Pinker, S. (1989), *Learnability and Cognition*. Cambridge, Mass: MIT Press.

Prior, A. (1976), *Papers in Logic and Ethics*. London: Duckworth.

Reid, T. (1970), *An Inquiry into the Human Mind*, T. Duggan ed. Chicago: University of Chicago Press.

Russell, B. (1918), Knowledge by Acquaintance and Knowledge by Description. In *Mysticism and Logic and Other Essays*, London: Longmans, Green and Co, p. 209-32.

Searle, J. (1980), Minds, Brains and Programs. *Behavioural and Brain Sciences* 3:317-24.

Sperber, D. (1974), *Le Symbolisme en général*. Paris: Hermann. (Engl. trans.: *Rethinking Symbolism*, Cambridge: Cambridge University Press, 1975.)

Sperber, D. (1985), Apparently Irrational Beliefs. Chapter 2 of *On Anthropological Knowledge*, Cambridge: Cambridge University Press.

Stalnaker, R. (1987), *Inquiry*. Cambridge, Mass: MIT Press.

Walton, K. (1990), *Mimesis as Make-Believe*. Cambridge, Mass: Harvard University Press.

PHILOSOPHICAL STUDIES SERIES

1. Jay F. Rosenberg: *Linguistic Representation*. 1974   ISBN 90-277-0533-X
2. Wilfrid Sellars: *Essays in Philosophy and Its History*. 1974   ISBN 90-277-0526-7
3. Dickinson S. Miller: *Philosophical Analysis and Human Welfare*. Selected Essays and Chapters from Six Decades. Edited with an Introduction by Lloyd D. Easton. 1975
          ISBN 90-277-0566-6
4. Keith Lehrer (ed.): *Analysis and Metaphysics*. Essays in Honor of R. M Chisholm. 1975
          ISBN 90-277-0571-2
5. Carl Ginet: *Knowledge, Perception, and Memory*. 1975   ISBN 90-277-0574-7
6. Peter H. Hare and Edward H. Madden: *Causing, Perceiving and Believing*. An Examination of the Philosophy of C. J. Ducasse. 1975   ISBN 90-277-0563-1
7. Hector-Neri Castañeda: *Thinking and Doing*. The Philosophical Foundations of Institutions. 1975   ISBN 90-277-0610-7
8. John L. Pollock: *Subjunctive Reasoning*. 1976   ISBN 90-277-0701-4
9. Bruce Aune: *Reason and Action*. 1977   ISBN 90-277-0805-3
10. George Schlesinger: *Religion and Scientific Method*. 1977   ISBN 90-277-0815-0
11. Yirmiahu Yovel (ed.): *Philosophy of History and Action*. Papers presented at the First Jerusalem Philosophical Encounter (December 1974). 1978   ISBN 90-277-0890-8
12. Joseph C. Pitt (ed.): *The Philosophy of Wilfrid Sellars: Queries and Extensions*. 1978
          ISBN 90-277-0903-3
13. Alvin I. Goldman and Jaegwon Kim (eds.): *Values and Morals*. Essays in Honor of William Frankena, Charles Stevenson, and Richard Brandt. 1978   ISBN 90-277-0914-9
14. Michael J. Loux: *Substance and Attribute*. A Study in Ontology. 1978   ISBN 90-277-0926-2
15. Ernest Sosa (ed.): *The Philosophy of Nicholas Rescher*. Discussion and Replies. 1979
          ISBN 90-277-0962-9
16. Jeffrie G. Murphy: *Retribution, Justice, and Therapy*. Essays in the Philosophy of Law. 1979
          ISBN 90-277-0998-X
17. George S. Pappas (ed.): *Justification and Knowledge*. New Studies in Epistemology. 1979
          ISBN 90-277-1023-6
18. James W. Cornman: *Skepticism, Justification, and Explanation*. With a Bibliographic Essay by Walter N. Gregory. 1980   ISBN 90-277-1041-4
19. Peter van Inwagen (ed.): *Time and Cause*. Essays presented to Richard Taylor. 1980
          ISBN 90-277-1048-1
20. Donald Nute: *Topics in Conditional Logic*. 1980   ISBN 90-277-1049-X
21. Risto Hilpinen (ed.): *Rationality in Science*. Studies in the Foundations of Science and Ethics. 1980   ISBN 90-277-1112-7
22. Georges Dicker: *Perceptual Knowledge*. An Analytical and Historical Study. 1980
          ISBN 90-277-1130-5
23. Jay F. Rosenberg: *One World and Our Knowledge of It*. The Problematic of Realism in Post-Kantian Perspective. 1980   ISBN 90-277-1136-4
24. Keith Lehrer and Carl Wagner: *Rational Consensus in Science and Society*. A Philosophical and Mathematical Study. 1981   ISBN 90-277-1306-5
25. David O'Connor: *The Metaphysics of G. E. Moore*. 1982   ISBN 90-277-1352-9

PHILOSOPHICAL STUDIES SERIES

PHILOSOPHICAL STUDIES SERIES

52. Jesús Ezquerro and Jesús M. Larrazabal (eds.): *Cognition, Semantics and Philosophy*. Proceedings of the First International Colloquium on Cognitive Science. 1992 ISBN 0-7923-1538-3

53. O.H. Green: *The Emotions*. A Philosophical Theory. 1992 ISBN 0-7923-1549-9

54. Jeffrie G. Murphy: *Retribution Reconsidered*. More Essays in the Philosophy of Law. 1992 ISBN 0-7923-1815-3

55. Phillip Montague: *In the Interests of Others*. An Essay in Moral Philosophy. 1992 ISBN 0-7923-1856-0

56. Jacques-Paul Dubucs (ed.): *Philosophy of Probability*. 1993 ISBN 0-7923-2385-8

57. Gary S. Rosenkrantz: *Haecceity*. An Ontological Essay. 1993 ISBN 0-7923-2438-2

58. Charles Landesman: *The Eye and the Mind*. Reflections on Perception and the Problem of Knowledge. 1994 ISBN 0-7923-2586-9

59. Paul Weingartner (ed.): *Scientific and Religious Belief*. 1994 ISBN 0-7923-2595-8

60. Michaelis Michael and John O'Leary-Hawthorne (eds.): *Philosophy in Mind*. The Place of Philosophy in the Study of Mind. 1994 ISBN 0-7923-3143-5

61. William H. Shaw: *Moore on Right and Wrong*. The Normative Ethics of G.E. Moore. 1995 ISBN 0-7923-3223-7

62. T.A. Blackson: *Inquiry, Forms, and Substances*. A Study in Plato's Metaphysics and Epistemology. 1995 ISBN 0-7923-3275-X

63. Debra Nails: *Agora, Academy, and the Conduct of Philosophy*. 1995 ISBN 0-7923-3543-0

64. Warren Shibles: *Emotion in Aesthetics*. 1995 ISBN 0-7923-3618-6

65. John Biro and Petr Kotatko (eds.): *Frege: Sense and Reference One Hundred Years Later*. 1995 ISBN 0-7923-3795-6

66. Mary Gore Forrester: *Persons, Animals, and Fetuses*. An Essay in Practical Ethics. 1996 ISBN 0-7923-3918-5

67. K. Lehrer, B.J. Lum, B.A. Slichta and N.D. Smith (eds.): *Knowledge, Teaching and Wisdom*. 1996 ISBN 0-7923-3980-0

68. Herbert Granger: *Aristotle's Idea of the Soul*. 1996 ISBN 0-7923-4033-7

69. Andy Clark, Jesús Ezquerro and Jesús M. Larrazabal (eds.): *Philosophy and Cognitive Science: Categories, Consciousness, and Reasoning*. Proceedings of the Second International Colloquium on Cogitive Science. 1996 ISBN 0-7923-4068-X

70. J. Mendola: *Human Thought*. 1997 ISBN 0-7923-4401-4

71. J. Wright: *Realism and Explanatory Priority*. 1997 ISBN 0-7923-4484-7

72. X. Arrazola, K. Korta and F.J. Pelletier (eds.): *Discourse, Interaction and Communication*. Proceedings of the Fourth International Colloquium on Cognitive Science. 1998 ISBN 0-7923-4952-0

73. E. Morscher, O. Neumaier and P. Simons (eds.): *Applied Ethics in a Troubled World*. 1998 ISBN 0-7923-4965-2

74. R.O. Savage: *Real Alternatives, Leibniz's Metaphysics of Choice*. 1998 ISBN 0-7923-5057-X

75. Q. Gibson: *The Existence Principle*. 1998 ISBN 0-7923-5188-6

76. F. Orilia and W.J. Rapaport (eds.): *Thought, Language, and Ontology*. 1998 ISBN 0-7923-5197-5

PHILOSOPHICAL STUDIES SERIES

KLUWER ACADEMIC PUBLISHERS – DORDRECHT / BOSTON / LONDON

Made in the USA
Las Vegas, NV
14 November 2024

11636768R00175